THE INFLUENCE OF LAW
ON SEA POWER

THE MELLAND SCHILL LECTURES
*delivered at the University of Manchester
and published by the University Press*

The Law of International Institutions in Europe
by A. H. Robertson, B.C.L., S.J.D., 1961

The Role of International Law in the Elimination of War
by Professor Quincy Wright, 1961

The Acquisition of Territory in International Law
by Professor R. Y. Jennings, 1962

The Sources and Evidences of International Law
by Clive Parry, LL.D., 1965

Rights in Air Space
by D. H. N. Johnson, M.A., LL.B., 1965

International Law and the Practitioner
by Sir Francis A. Vallat, K.C.M.G., Q.C., 1966

The Law of the Sea
by D. W. Bowett, M.A., LL.B., PH.D., 1967

International Law and the Uses of Outer Space
by J. E. S. Fawcett, M.A., 1968

Modern Diplomatic Law
by M. Hardy, M.A., LL.M., 1968

The United Nations in a Changing World
by J. A. C. Gutteridge, M.A., 1970

Economic World Order?
by Professor Georg Schwarzenberger, 1970

*An Introduction to the Law of the European
Economic Community*
edited by B. A. Wortley, O.B.E., Q.C., LL.D., 1972

The Vienna Convention of the Law of Treaties
by I. M. Sinclair, C.M.G., 1973

The Law of the Common Market
edited by B. A. Wortley, O.B.E., Q.C., LL.D., 1974

OTHER BOOKS ON JURISPRUDENCE
AND INTERNATIONAL LAW

W. H. Balekjian
Legal Aspects of Foreign Investment in the European Economic Community

D. W. Bowett
Self-defence in international law

A. O. Cukwurah
The Settlement of Boundary Disputes in International Law

R. P. Dhokalia
The Codification of Public International Law

T. O. Elias
The Nature of African Customary Law

Max Gluckman
*The Judicial Process among the Barotse of Northern Rhodesia
The Ideas in Barotse Jurisprudence*

L. Kos-Rabcewicz-Zubkowski
East European Rules on the Validity of International Commercial Arbitration Agreements

E. I. Nwogugu
The Legal Problems of Foreign Investment in Developing Countries

A. H. Robertson
*Human Rights in Europe
Human Rights in National and International Law (ed.)
Human Rights in the World
Privacy and Human Rights (ed.)*

I. A. Shearer
Extradition in International Law

B. A. Wortley
Jurisprudence

THE INFLUENCE OF LAW
ON SEA POWER

by

D. P. O'CONNELL

R.D., M.A., PH.D., LL.D., D.C.L., F.R.HIST.S.

CHICHELE PROFESSOR IN PUBLIC INTERNATIONAL LAW,
UNIVERSITY OF OXFORD
BARRISTER AT LAW, MIDDLE TEMPLE
FELLOW OF ALL SOULS COLLEGE, OXFORD
COMMANDER, R.N.R.

NAVAL INSTITUTE PRESS

© 1975 Manchester University Press
Library of Congress Catalog Card No. 75 21922
ISBN 0 87021 834 4
Published and distributed in the United States of America by
THE NAVAL INSTITUTE PRESS
Annapolis, Maryland 21402

Printed in Great Britain by
Hazell Watson & Viney Ltd,
Aylesbury, Bucks

CONTENTS

FOREWORD

BY

B. A. WORTLEY, O.B.E., Q.C., LL.D.,

PROFESSOR OF JURISPRUDENCE AND INTERNATIONAL LAW,
UNIVERSITY OF MANCHESTER

By her will the late Miss Olive B. Schill of Prestbury, Cheshire, an old friend of the University, whose portrait is drawn in Lady Katherine Chorley's *Manchester made them*, left the sum of £10,000 to the University in memory of her brother, Melland Schill, who died in the 1914–18 war. The annual income from this sum is to be used to produce and publish a series of public lectures of the highest possible standard, dealing with international law. So far some thirteen sets of lectures have been published during my tenure of the Chair of Jurisprudence and International Law, which expires at the end of September 1975.

In 1974 Professor O'Connell delivered a set of four Schill lectures in the University, based on this book. He has a profound knowledge of the theory and practice of the use of force at sea, and this study can be confidently recommended to students of international law and of international relations, as well as to naval officers and historians. This work is a most up-to-date account of the international law governing the use of force in maritime operations, whether these operations are carried out by States to defend their legitimate interests, or whether by forces operating under the U.N. flag. Captain Mahan wrote his famous works on sea power at the turn of the century; Professor O'Connell now offers a scholarly analysis of the legal problems arising out of the use of sea power today.

The author's careful attention to new and original sources, e.g. British and foreign naval battle signals, has opened up new fields of knowledge, thanks to his intimate knowledge of naval procedures.

Professor O'Connell wishes to make it clear that the views expressed are his own and not of any of the naval or other organisations to which he makes reference or with which he is concerned; he bears the responsibility for his views, which are based on his research into published materials or on sources now available to scholars in general.

Faculty of Law
July 1974

FOREWORD

BY

VICE-ADMIRAL SIR PETER GRETTON

K.C.B., D.S.O., O.B.E., D.S.C.

I take it as a great honour to contribute a foreword to this distinguished book. I cannot pretend to be an international lawyer, and in my day naval officers' education in this field was sadly neglected. But as a sailor I have met some of the practical effects of international law, and as a naval historian I have studied several case histories.

The author is uniquely qualified to write a book of this type. He is an experienced international lawyer, in both the academic and the practical fields, and he is a working historian. In addition, as a reserve officer, he has served in war at sea and fully understands the problems of modern naval operations. As a result of his sea experience his sixth chapter gives a clear look at the weapons and detection systems used in all forms of modern naval warfare. For the non-expert it is indispensable if modern weapon systems are to be understood.

I am particularly impressed by the author's research into more recent events at sea and his clear presentation of the effect of the law on modern weapons. There seems to have been a conspiracy of silence over incidents like the loss of the *Venus Challenger*, which was sunk by guided weapons from an Indian ship during the Indian–Pakistan war of 1971. What would have happened if the ship had been British or American instead of Liberian? Similarly the constraints upon shipping imposed by the French during the Algerian rebellion were hardly reported at the time, and Professor O'Connell gives a well documented account of this unusual episode.

In fact there is no modern naval operation in whatever remote area that has escaped his attention, and the resulting panorama shows what a large number of incidents at sea have taken place since 1945, despite the fact that the great naval Powers have avoided conflict. In many incidents neutral shipping, sometimes British, has been involved, and I would have thought that marine insurers and directors of shipping companies would profit from reading the book.

Whilst emphasising how up-to-date it is, I do not intend to give the impression that the historical past has been neglected. On the contrary, the title of the book is fully justified by its excursions into the past. As a student of the Spanish Civil War I was very interested in the handling of the many naval incidents and arguments of that conflict, which are clearly described, together with the precedents established.

The book comes at a particularly appropriate time, when the law of the sea is under international discussion. Surely some rules for the use of guided missiles at night must emerge. The author brings out the impracticability of using missiles in some circumstances, and the dangers of firing them at night and when they may home on the wrong target. He makes it clear that the gun still has a role to play in certain situations, such as the giving of a clear warning to stop for examination to a merchant ship and in types of low-level confrontation when the use of guided missiles would be wholly inappropriate. Another 'cod war' would be an example. Some of our frigates are being refitted without their 4.5 in. gun, and this I deplore deeply. Even in these modern days a respectably sized gun is still necessary and should be carried in every warship.

The problem of international straits and the disastrous effect on the maritime powers of the more far-reaching claims of the coastal States is fully considered by the author, along with the exploitation of the sea bed, which is of enormous importance these days, though I found the chapter difficult to understand and it is clear that the Law of the Sea conference will be lucky to produce clear rules.

The author's remarks on the rights of neutrals are very timely. In addition, I found his exposition of the rules of engagement most interesting, with examples stretching from the Baltic expeditions of 1918–19 to the Beira patrol and the 'cod war'. The admiral in the Baltic received his orders in three paragraphs. Operations on the Beira patrol required a book!

I hope that members of the naval staff will read this book and ponder on its lessons, which provide strong ammunition for a powerful Royal Navy, able to watch British interests in all kinds of confrontation at sea, whether this country is directly involved or not. A quotation is timely. 'It is no longer sufficient to leave the law to Foreign Ministries. Naval staffs must themselves be equipped to handle the legal aspects of naval planning, whether it be in the matter of drafting rules of engagement or in their interpretation.'

Uninhibited naval warfare between the great Powers seems improbable. Strategic weapons have seen to that. But it is possible to envisage lesser confrontations between, say, NATO and the Soviet Union which could be isolated from land battles. Much thought has been devoted by the author to such a possibility, in which it is probable that international law would have some part to play. Nothing is more certain than that in some part of the world naval conflict, probably between minor Powers, will arise. We must be ready to face the consequences to the free flow of shipping.

This book is mainly for students of international law and for naval officers and historians. But the well informed general public should also greet it with acclaim, for they will enjoy it and learn much.

PREFACE

Much of what still appears in the textbooks of international law on the subject of naval warfare is rooted in the technology, politics, strategy and tactics of the *Dreadnought* era, and is a source of confusion rather than of assistance to naval planning staffs. Yet never before have naval officers felt so acutely the need for professional guidance through the complexities of the rules and notions of international law which impinge upon naval practice and responsibility. Everywhere naval academies, tactical and other specialist schools, war courses and the like are taking an increased interest in the law of the sea, which fascinates as much by reason of its present incoherence and revolutionary propensities as by reason of its traditional concern with the conduct of ships. If international law appears to the naval officer to be a tangle of uncertainties in which he is likely to be ensnared, the technology of naval warfare induces in the legal theorists perplexity and dismay. A dialogue between the two has become an essential component of defence speculation.

Admiral Mahan omitted international law from his catalogue of the factors that made for successful resort to sea power, yet its intrinsic relevance to his thesis is revealed by the fact that, having identified himself as an authority on the intellectual aspects of sea power, he was chosen to be one of the United States delegates to the Hague codification conference of 1899, where his task was to devise laws which would influence the exercise of sea power. Had he written his book after his experience at that conference it is likely that the role of law would have found a place in his exposition of sea power.

Before 1914 the syllabus of the Senior Officers' War Course at Greenwich included a thorough study of international law, and it was probably the diversion of focus from peace-keeping to total war that caused a waning of naval interest in international law until quite recently. In any event, the diet of international law served to naval officers was routine and elementary, and was not intended to stimulate the speculation which is now demanded by the impact of technology upon traditional rules of law.

The Admiralty records reveal that on 9 November 1886 the Commander-in-Chief, Mediterranean, who had not long previously conducted a 'limited war' operation against Egypt in collaboration

xiii

with the French, said that 'a small and handy treatise on International Law would be of great assistance to Naval Officers'. There were, at that time, manuals of international law for naval officers in English and French, by Fergusson and Rosse, and by 1900 there were several English and American textbooks on international law containing the matters with which naval officers were expected to be familiar, by Creasy, Halleck, Wildman, Gardner, Woolsey, Field, Walker, Maine, Hall, Holland, Baden-Powell and Baker. On 2 August 1904 the Admiralty recorded the views of Professor Holland, who said, 'C.O.'s of H.M. Ships are rather overdone with works on International Law and there does not appear to be a call at present for future works.'

This seems to have poured cold water on the idea of a specifically naval treatment of international law, and it was not until twenty years later that the Royal Navy got around to issuing two books to the fleet—the *Naval Prize Manual* of 1923 (O.V. 5316) and *Notes on Maritime International Law* of 1929 (C.B. 3012). Both served H.M. ships through the Second World War, although their sufficiency had been called into question after the experience of the Spanish Civil War by Professor H. A. Smith, a member of the legal sub-committee of the Committee on Imperial Defence. He thought that the Admiralty should consider six questions which would be important in wartime, namely the extent of neutral waters, the arming of merchant ships, *ruses de guerre*, neutral sailing in belligerent convoys, air warfare at sea, and the need for clearer instructions on international law to naval officers. On the first question he pointed out an apparent contradiction between the rule in the *Naval Prize Manual* for determining the neutrality of bays—double the territorial sea, or six miles—and the orders issued to H.M. ships during the Spanish Civil War that bays should be identified by reference to a ten-mile rule.

After four months of study Professor Smith's points were met with the official observation that the two naval books had been in existence for a long time, and the fact that few changes were found necessary in them indicated their 'soundness'.

This is recalled only to show that the debate about how much international law is to be included in the naval officer's diet of digestible facts, and how much effort is to be devoted to the clarification of its rules or of its influence upon policy, is not new; and it may also serve to draw attention to the time it takes to think about these matters, when time in the nuclear age is not a strategic commodity.

The purpose of these lectures is not to furnish the textbook which

Professor Holland in 1904 thought was unnecessary but to try to bring into focus the disparate questions that contemporary international law poses for naval planning. Thereby a structure for future analysis may be devised which may assist naval staff work, and also diplomats and their legal auxiliaries who may have to formulate national attitudes to defence planning in the counsels of nations.

On the day this preface is written the Khmer Rouge government of Cambodia has seized an American merchant ship in the Gulf of Thailand, but possibly within the territorial sea of some rocks, sovereignty over which is disputed, and the Seventh Fleet has been ordered to the area. And so it will go on.

D. P. O'Connell
All Souls College
Oxford
12 May 1975

The first and most obvious light in which the sea presents itself from the political and social point of view is that of a great highway.

Mahan, *The Influence of Sea Power on History*, p. 25

I am master of the earth but the law is the mistress of the sea.

Emperor Antoninus, *Digest,* 14.2, *de lege Rhodia,* 9

CHAPTER I

THE NOTION OF
CONTROLLED SEA POWER

The road from Trafalgar to the Beira patrol may, from one point of view, signify degression from glory to bathos, but it has not ended altogether in an absurdity. For, largely irrelevant though it may be to any sensible naval purpose, and despite its want of cost effectiveness, the Beira patrol has made it clear that sea power can express and sustain legal decisions that could not be represented even remotely credibly in any other way; and it has revealed the peculiar capacity of navies to manifest the concept of law and order among nations. The primary aim of most of the naval Powers in time of peace has traditionally been to reinforce the 'freedom of the seas'—'to protect our ships upon their lawful occasions'. The law-enforcement role of navies is therefore by no means recent; and since navies, alone of the armed services, operate essentially in an international environment their connection with international law has always been obvious. But navies can play the part of the criminals as well as of maritime regional crime squads, and it is sometimes difficult to know which of the two roles they are in fact playing, especially when their missions are invariably veiled in the garb of 'self-defence'. This ambiguity of character is intensifying, and with it the difficulty of legal control of the functions of sea power.

In his analysis of the use to which naval forces have been put in the pursuit of political goals since 1918 James Cable[1] has appended about eighty incidents between the end of the Second World War and 1969 in which naval operations have been mounted. Almost all of them were connected with the law in one way or another, and about a quarter are cases where force has been used ostensibly to uphold the legal *status quo*. About a quarter of them, too, have involved the use of tactical force, including weapon systems. This is an astonishing statistic, which suggests that the naval staff is the international lawyer's most obvious, if it is not his most frequent, client.

[1] *Gunboat Diplomacy*, London, 1970.

But the statistic becomes all the more significant when it is recalled that Mr Cable's list of the occasions of the exercise of naval power has involved no fewer than thirty-seven navies, twenty-four of which have used limited force on at least one occasion. From it he drew the conclusion that naval operations would play at least as great a role in the future as they had in the past, and were not peculiar to an era of imperialism or power politics that belonged to history. This conclusion has been more than vindicated, because since he wrote there have been two naval wars, fought between India and Pakistan and in the Middle East, the transformation of the naval war in Vietnam by the mining of Haiphong, another 'cod war' with Iceland, a fishery dispute between Spain and Morocco involving the use of gunfire, the shelling of the Soviet factory ship *Golfstrim* by the Argentinian navy, the full-scale naval engagement of the Paracels between China and South Vietnam, the Iranian seizure of islands in the Straits of Hormuz, and lesser incidents; so that not only has the rhythm of conflict at sea accelerated but so has the scale of violence and the tendency to progress to higher modes of weaponry, including the use of missiles in three of these incidents.

The graph of resort to coercive sea power is describing an upward curve, and the statistics become ever more portentous: around one hundred instances since 1945 involving just short of fifty navies, and all of them in some degree or other law-based, or at least legally relevant. The gravity of the threat posed to international shipping— to leave aside the question of friendly relations between States—may also be indicated by the fact that since 1970 neutral ships have been diverted, damaged and at least eight of them even sunk, one of them with total loss of life. The fact that the flag States of these ships, the newspapers and world opinion have demonstrated an amazing indifference towards this degree of devastation suggests that violence at sea is more tolerable or less comprehensible than violence on land, and that the ocean could be the scene of a struggle for power among the nations that would be unacceptable on land. If it is possible to envisage a war in Europe between the Great Powers involving the use of conventional weapons, or even tactical nuclear weapons, without necessarily leading to a mutual nuclear holocaust, *a fortiori* it is possible to envisage it at sea, where it can be insulated both physically and psychologically, and where the lethal game of world or local domination can be played to a finish and the fate of nations determined.

The facts may be disillusioning to those who have relied upon international law to secure the end of the use of force, but they are facts and they call for investigation, not only from the point of view of a philosopher of sea power but also from that of the utility and function of law in the exercise of sea power. No presupposition either in favour of international law as an effective element in the harnessing of sea power, or in its disparagement, is warranted for the purposes of this enquiry, because the role that law can play will vary with the levels of political tension and the limited goals to which sea power is in any instance directed. International law may be considered by some to be a simulacrum of law, but it is a phenomenon notwithstanding.

The only prediction that can be made with assurance is that the lower the level of conflict, the more localised the situation and the more restricted the objectives, the more predominant will be the element of law in the governing of naval conduct; and that the law will assume a diminished role—as it did in the Second World War—when the conflict becomes global, when the neutrals have been mostly drawn into it or their sympathies engaged, and when an element of desperation has entered into operational planning. Such conditions as prevailed during the Second World War are unlikely to be repeated, but what is likely is a proliferation of the causes of dispute and of technologically advanced naval methods for dealing with them. When South American navies are equipping themselves with the most modern ships and weapon systems, including the Ikara anti-submarine missile and the Seadart, and Asian navies are following suit, the uses of sea power at an advanced level are not likely to be confined to the traditional naval Powers of the northern hemisphere. There are now thirty-five countries possessing anti-ship missiles.[2]

It is pertinent, therefore, to initiate an enquiry into the impact of law upon the control of conflict situations, and into what it is about naval forces that appears to invest them with a capacity to influence events that air or military forces lack. The answer, in a word, is their ambiguity. Navies alone afford governments the means of exerting pressure more vigorous than diplomacy and less dangerous and unpredictable in its results than other forms of force, because the freedom of the seas makes them locally available while leaving them uncommitted. They have the right to sail the seas and the endurance

[2] In the Third World they include Algeria, Egypt, India, Indonesia, Iraq, Libya, Malaysia, Singapore and Syria. They also include nine Communist countries and five Latin American countries.

to do so for requisite periods, while land-based forces cannot present a credible level of coercion without overstepping the boundaries of national sovereignty. Warships enhance the opportunities of espionage, and make possible the landing and rescue of agents. They carry with them psychological overtones of influence, decision and credibility. Their local availability may encourage governments to resist *coups d'état* by affording the hope of aid or at least the possibilities of retreat. And they are the vehicles most suited to flexibility of pressure according to the exigencies of the moment. In short, navies can introduce into a situation an element of uncertainty that serves the diplomacy of tension by increasing the options of either intimidation or withdrawal. What Lord Grey said is perennially true: 'Diplomacy without force is like an orchestra without instruments'. And as, I recall, the British government statement on defence, 1962, said, 'The ability to assure free movement by sea at the right time and place remains of fundamental importance to these islands; indeed, the sea may in certain circumstances be the one open highway for strategic movement free of international political hindrance'.

But, for naval power to be used effectively for the resolution or promotion of international disputes, the seizure of the advantages afforded by the rules of international law is central to the concept of operations; for the freedom of the seas is not absolute, nor is it coextensive with the areas in which ships can navigate. Questions of the extent of national jurisdiction over the surface of the sea or of the sea bed, protection of ships, rules of the road and rules about installations and pipelines qualify the freedom of naval deployment. In as much as these questions are often controversial in the answers they afford, they offer advantages to those who wish to manipulate them; and in as much as their controversial character can itself be the occasion of dispute or can transform some other issue into a different category or level of dispute, they can become the causes or the objectives of naval power. The law thus plays a central role in clarifying by way of restrictions the goals set for sea power, the range of available options for its exercise and the classification of situations whose indeterminate character could otherwise lead to diffusion of energies and resources. The study of law in relation to sea power is, for this reason, a valid and important aspect of the responsibility of naval planning staffs.

Mr Cable has essayed a division of the principles of resort to limited naval force into four categories. There is, first of all, *definitive force*, where sea power is exercised to produce a *fait accompli*, as when the U.S.S. *Pueblo*, an electronic surveillance ship, was seized in 1968 by North Korea; there is, secondly, *purposeful force*, where naval power is used in the effort to persuade foreign governments to change their policies, as when the Royal Navy attempted the transit of the Corfu Channel or made it possible for British troops to protect the independence of Kuwait; there is, thirdly, *catalytic force*, where sea power is demonstrated with a view to influencing events where instability can lead to a deteriorating situation—and with this use of naval force recent history abounds, from the United States landing in Beirut in 1958 to the appearance of the U.S.S. *Enterprise* in the Gulf of Bengal during the Indo–Pakistan war of December 1971; and finally, there is *expressive force*, where warships are available to emphasise foreign policy objectives without seeking changes in the conduct of other parties.

This classification has marginal utility for a study of law and sea power, because it is obvious that the law enters into the question of naval planning differently in each category. To work backwards: expressive force usually involves legitimate presence, and even though the visible manifestation of power is intended for influence, no disquieting threat is involved, because the law can be relied upon by all parties. Sometimes this type of force is used to demonstrate rights, even when the objective of the demonstration is a territorial right in dispute. For example, the dispute in 1969 over the zone in Algeciras Bay known as the Loop, two miles long and a quarter of a mile broad, results from different views upon how the British and Spanish boundaries in the bay are to be projected. It is not, in itself, a central issue of controversy but an aspect of the overall Gibraltar dispute. It acquires its significance from the fact that intermittent assertions of rights can be made by Spain in the Loop which, if made elsewhere in the port limits of Gibraltar, would strike directly at the disputed question of British sovereignty and not at the ancillary question of its proper limits. So the major dispute can be carried on at an appropriately low level by demonstrations over secondary areas of legitimate dispute, and this has been done by Spanish protests at the anchoring of British warships and merchant ships in the Loop, and at the ostentatious anchoring there of Spanish warships, including a warship of superior level, the carrier *Dedalo*.

Obviously the grip of law tightens upon the other three classifications of sea power in ascending order of tenacity until, at the top, definitive force comes more overtly under the prohibition of the use of force in the United Nations Charter. At this point the political options may prove to be limited by the extent to which the resort to force falls within one or other of the grounds of legality or escapes from the constraints of the law.

It cannot be presumed that definitive force will never be used in violation of international law, for the breach of law is one of the political options always open. But history demonstrates that, except upon the occasions of desperation that developed in the two World Wars, this is an option that is open only upon rare conjunctions of circumstance, and then only where an element of legal ambiguity can be introduced. The *Pueblo* case is the best instance of resort to definitive force since 1945, and it is the contingent situation rather than the gesture of defiance of the law on the part of North Korea that is its most significant aspect. The *Pueblo* was challenged at noon on 23 January 1968 by a North Korean patrol vessel, which was quickly reinforced until the *Pueblo* was surrounded by four patrol craft and covered by two fighter aircraft. She was summoned to heave to, and when she ignored the signal she was fired upon until she yielded and was escorted into Wonsan, where she remained for eleven months. The Secretary of State described the seizure as 'in the category of actions that are to be construed as acts of war'. The United States mounted a naval demonstration on 25 January off the coast of North Korea, including three strike carriers. The Soviet navy conducted counter-manoeuvres with sixteen ships between the coast and the American fleet until on 6 February the latter began to disperse.

The lessons of the incident were hardly learned but they might well have been anticipated. The lack of defence preparation in the *Pueblo* herself, and the fact that she was unescorted while engaged on her electronic surveillance mission, appear to indicate a reliance upon international law for her security and the opportunity to complete her task which was, in the circumstances, unwarranted. Why was it unwarranted? Because, although it seems from North Korean signals which were intercepted by the United States forces that the *Pueblo* was beyond the North Korean territorial sea, this question of fact was easily obscured. North Korea had merely to make the assertion that the *Pueblo* was in her territorial sea but not engaged in innocent passage to introduce a fatal element of inertia and confusion into the situation, especially since the manner of drawing the territorial sea limits across bays allows for a large degree of subjective judgement, as in this case.

The legalities of the seizure may have provided material for stimulating debate at meetings of international lawyers, but they assumed

6

a character of irrelevance once this element of legal doubt had contributed to the subsequent frustration of United States sea power.

Connected with this legal doubt was the error of supposing that, because the Soviet navy also practises seaborne electronic surveillance, the Soviet Union would not permit its clients or its own forces to take any action which might prejudice such activity. This assumption might apply to spying carried out on what are indisputably the high seas, but it is inherently questionable when the allegation is one of spying in the territorial sea; the two activities are politically distinguishable because they are legally distinguishable. Then there was the fact that North Korea's retention of the crew of the *Pueblo* put the onus upon the United States of risking their liberties or of making an act of submission to secure their release. Confronted with North Korea's strictly limited objective of wringing concessions out of the United States in the matter of spying, no act of naval reprisal on the part of the latter was adjudged feasible. The humiliating submission made by the United States forced the abandonment of spying by ship in favour of spying by aircraft, and when one of these was shot down later there was a repetition of the earlier events, and a further American reverse.

The overall lesson of the case is that wherever there can be a legal pretext for the action of an assailant that action is best inhibited or defeated by superior force. The fatal error in the *Pueblo* operation was to allow this superiority to accrue to the party that could veil its aggression behind legal ambiguities. It follows that wherever naval forces are committed to any of Mr Cable's four categories of power, but more especially to the higher of them, for the purpose of asserting or protecting rights in sea areas which are subject to legal dispute, a primary axiom is that the forces used must be superior, or at least capable of the requisite degree of support in the event of challenge. The Royal Navy acted in the Corfu Channel affair,[3] or in the case of the contested passage of H.M.S. *Victorious* through the Indonesia archipelago in 1964, consistently with this axiom. So too did Brazil when she despatched the 6 in. cruiser *Barroso*, five destroyers and two corvettes to overawe the French fishery protection vessel *Tartu* during the 'spiny lobster war' of the same year. Presumably the Brazilian navy did not expect to fight a battle over the incident; the level of force deployed effectively deprived the French of practical means of fishery protection without heavy reinforcement involving a degree of escalation that would ordinarily be politically unacceptable.

[3] I.C.J. Rep. (Merits) 1949, p. 5; see p. 103, chapter VIII, below.

7

Inferior force may be deployed in such areas as the eastern Mediterranean because the law invests the operations with a high degree of predictable immunity from molestation. But to have guided missile destroyers trailing their coats in the Black Sea, in face of the Soviet Union's contention that these are now to be classified by virtue of their firepower as capital ships whose passage is contrary to the Montreux Convention (1936) is not to rely upon the law but to assert a particular and contested interpretation of it. What is relied upon in this case for assurance against assault is the political situation, not the law. Where the law can be used as a political excuse to achieve a *fait accompli* it is fatal to undertake the risk of demonstrating in favour of a particular view of the law if superior force is not available to sustain the option.

The sea, then, is the only area where armed forces can joust with more or less seriousness in order to promote political objectives; the only area where they can be concentrated, ready for intervention but not overtly threatening to intervene. An army that crosses a frontier represents a use of force altogether different from a navy that crosses the seas. The stopping of a merchant ship—as occurred without much newspaper comment on numerous occasions during the Algerian emergency—and, surprisingly, even its destruction with total loss of life—as in the case of the S.S. *Venus Challenger* (1971)[4] during the Indo–Pakistan war, which attracted no newspaper interest at all— does not arouse resentment, apprehension or indignation to the same degree as the landings of the United States marines in the Lebanon (1958), Haiti (1963), or the Dominican Republic (1961) (although it is perhaps more overtly illegal), because on the sea conflict can apparently be insulated and never seems so serious as on land, and because in the nature of things national sovereignty is more jealously defended than international order.

The uses to which sea power which is law-based can be put are infinitely variable. In 1973 the Royal New Zealand Navy despatched two anti-submarine frigates to the French nuclear test zone in the Pacific Ocean in an exercise of purposeful force to deter France from continuing nuclear tests by apparently presenting her with the options of hazarding a frigate, forcing it away from the designated danger zone, or abandoning the tests. The ostensible purpose was not exactly realised, because the frigates took care to make their demonstrations in the danger zone (but outside the territorial sea) in a position and at a time when they were not in fact hazarded, while France confined

4 See p. 87, chapter vii, below, for facts.

herself to the detonation of low-yield devices. As a naval event the exercise was useful mainly in demonstrating that a geographically remote country cannot exercise sea power at all without afloat support (which had to be borrowed from the Royal Australian Navy); as a public relations presentation it was a great success, since the purpose of alerting public opinion all over the world, and especially in France, as to the extent of New Zealand feeling on the matter was achieved. The ultimate objective was to influence the political climate in France so that the French government might be pressed into testing underground, or a future French government into abandoning the tests altogether.

This mild jousting of the French and Royal New Zealand navies occurred in an area delimited by legal controversy and pursuant to political purposes cast in legal form. The New Zealand demonstration was a challenge both to the legality of the testing and to the declaration of a dangerous zone in the high seas. It put squarely in issue, at least as a matter of law, the question whether naval exercises can be conducted to the exclusion of other activities in the high seas. France could, of course, detonate nuclear devices without much naval activity except for the need to ensure minimal risk and to police the part of the high seas designated dangerous. In fact the need to make her view of the law effective required the disposition by tonnage at one time of 40 per cent of the French navy for the purposes of the tests.

The existence of a legal dimension to the exercise of sea power means that it is not only naval staffs or their political masters who are affected. The captain of the ship does not altogether escape the direct constraints of the law, for much of the international law of war enters his own naval disciplinary system by virtue of the internal implementation of treaties. This is notably so with the 1949 Geneva Red Cross Conventions, which, as the Vietnam War illustrated, operate, by medium of military and naval codes, as a system of the rules of warfare, especially in the insulation of civilians from the legitimate objectives of attack. The captain who drives past fishing craft and overturns them in the wash because he believes them to be engaged in infiltration or subversion may, among other things, be in breach of the Convention on Shipwrecked Members of the Armed Forces at Sea, for which he could find himself before a court martial. The instance may be far-fetched (although it came under scrutiny in Vietnam), but it reveals the extent of curbs on individual tactical decisions that derive from the law.

The frequency with which the coercive exercise of sea power has occurred since 1945, and the increasing scale and mode of conflict resulting from it, are related to the accelerating tension among nations respecting their territorial claims. In only a few cases have these claims been of the old-fashioned sort, namely pretensions to additional territory for ethnical, geographical or prestige reasons. In most cases they have been claims to natural resources, and where the traditional territorial element has been present this is because possession of the land is the key to exclusive rights in its marine environment. Looking into the future, one cannot but believe that the occasions for navies to be employed to influence events will be multiplied because the increasing complexities of the law of the sea, with its proliferation of claims and texts and regimes covering resources, pollution, security and navigation are multiplying the opportunities for dispute and the circumstances for the resolution of disputes by the exertion of naval power. New threats will impose on navies new responsibilities, such as preventing the hi-jacking of ships, which may become a variant of the hi-jacking of aircraft, or the protection of the oil pipelines in the North Sea from sabotage, which may become a new focus of terrorism or belligerency.

A struggle for the sources of energy will more likely occur on the sea than on land, because it will appear less threatening to national security, because oil is more readily accessible offshore to external seizure, and because legal disputes over offshore resources can easily be manufactured so as to cover events with the requisite cloud of doubts and ambiguities. Because of the environment, and because of their adaptability to the flexible exertion of force, navies are likely to be used in such situations, and it does not follow that they will be local navies squabbling over neighbouring resources, for the dispute may affect the vital interests of far-away Powers who may be equally disposed to influence events favourably by the despatch of naval forces. Coastal defence navies are the luxuries of countries independent of foreign material resources and of international shipping. Industrial countries may well come to the conclusion that the intensifying instability of contemporary world society magnifies their insecurity and requires them to think of global sea power as a necessary adjunct of self-defence.

The battle of the Paracels of 20 January 1974 is a classical instance of the use of coercive sea power in a territorial dispute connected with control of resources, and it is a portent of the way in which nations will in the future be prepared to resort to superior force in order to vindicate their claims. In this instance South Vietnam and

China both claimed the uninhabited and barren Paracels archipelago sprawling across 136 miles east to west and 93 miles north to south in the South China Sea, no island of which is more than a mile square. South Vietnam claims that in 1802 Emperor Gia Long landed on the islands and set up a company to exploit their resources. In 1932 the French administration and the emperor Bao Baj jointly issued decrees placing them under the administration of Thua Thec Province, and from that date until 1974 Vietnamese troops intermittently garrisoned the islands. During the Second World War they were occupied by Japan for the purpose of controlling sea communications. In 1959 South Vietnam seized forty Chinese trawlers which were fishing in the surrounding waters, and after that date South Vietnamese patrol boats regularly patrolled the area. On the other hand, between 1925 and 1933 Japanese companies worked deposits of phosphate on the islands, and in the 1930s Chinese companies did likewise. The islands are also claimed by the Philippines.

This is precisely the sort of territorial dispute which can be satisfactorily settled only by the classical means of arbitration by reference to the law. But the disposition to use those means is declining in favour of the only alternative, graduated force, and the Chinese manner of going about the matter is a classic use of limited war for proclaimed legal ends.

On 20 January 1974 Chinese troops were landed on Ducan Island in the south-east of the archipelago, forcing the South Vietnamese garrison there to fall back on to Robert Island, with a half-company of sailors holding Money and Patele Islands. At 7.50 a.m. four Chinese Mig 21 and Mig 23 fighter-bombers attacked the three islands while a battalion of Chinese troops attempted landings. The resulting naval action proceeded according to the rules of graduated escalation. When South Vietnamese warships began shelling the invaders, Chinese warships interposed themselves to the point where fending the South Vietnamese away from the islands forced a collision. The South Vietnamese responded by firing into the Chinese ships, one of which was claimed as sunk. The Chinese then deliberately moved to superior force and a higher mode of retaliation. Fourteen Chinese warships moved in upon the South Vietnamese, among them four guided missile destroyers, whose missiles sank an escort ship of 640 tons and damaged four other ships.[5] This was

---

[5] If this information from Vietnamese sources is correct the missiles were probably Styx, fired from a new class of destroyer expected to be operational in 1974 but not as early as the date of the engagement.

checkmate, because the only force available to South Vietnam was land-based aircraft, and it is significant that these were not employed, no doubt because the capability of air-to-surface opposed attack and the requisite training were lacking—an important tactical consideration for the study of limited war.

The aftermath was what was to be expected. China instantly proclaimed that her forces had acted in self-defence; South Vietnam cried 'aggression' and sought the convening of the Security Council. But in the matter of territorial disputes that body has been found to be singularly ill equipped, and the inevitable result was to leave China in possession of the islands and to put yet another premium on the resort to superior force. What is portentous about this case is that the apparent motive for the seizure of the islands was access to a continental shelf that is thought to be oil-bearing, and the fact that China and Japan for like reasons and in exactly the same way dispute the uninhabited Senkaku Islands.

The battle of the Paracels focuses attention on the struggle for marine natural resources, which is likely to be given increased impetus in the near future by the so-called energy crisis. The wide disparity of views among nations respecting the extent to which these resources are to be available for common exploitation or are to be reserved for the exclusive exploitation of coastal States will itself be the occasion of disputes which are likely to lead to conflict. Coastal defence navies will seek to make local claims effective while distant-water navies may challenge them. There will be cases, like that of the Paracels, where one side will be ready for instant force; but the typical case will be like that of the cod war or the Brazilian 'spiny lobster' confrontation, where neither side seeks violence and each wishes to avoid it but is unprepared to yield. In such cases superior force will be resorted to and the law will be an element in the attempt, successful or otherwise, to contain its use.

The fact that already the contested claims to exclusive jurisdiction are so disparate as to be capricious—fifty-four States claiming twelve miles, twenty-six claiming three miles, ten claiming four to six miles, four claiming thirty miles, two claiming eighty miles, eight Latin American and one African claiming 200 miles and single States claiming ten-, eighteen-, 100- and 130-mile limits—is bad enough, but even more dangerous is the unstructured character of the claims themselves. Since the second Law of the Sea conference was mooted many governments have been carried away by euphoria or apprehension into striking attitudes and adopting postures which bear no relationship to the common interests of nations, but are avowedly egocentric, and often not a matter of intrinsic interest to the States which thus behave. Government departments everywhere have produced instant experts on the law of the sea, usually without legal training, whose anxiety appears to be to 'beat the gun' by staking out a claim in advance of the conference so as to present other delegations with a *fait accompli*. No element of *opinio juris* is discernible in this activity; no consideration is given to the elements of effectiveness and consent which are the concomitants of customary law; and, because it becomes impossible to raise the level of analysis above the mere anecdotal, the notion of State practice has become devoid of any significant content.

In this intellectual morass, where opinions and views are a substitute for law, the occasions for controversy, dispute and violence become ever more numerous and frequent. The law of the sea has thus become the stimulus to sea power and not its restraint. None has recognised this more clearly than Admiral of the Fleet of the Soviet Union S. G. Gorshkov. In the eleventh of his series on 'Navies in war and peace', published in *Morskoy sbornik*[6] in 1973 and significantly entitled 'On some problems in mastering the world ocean', he concludes several pages of discussion of the resources of the sea by asserting that the appropriation of these resources is today one of the most important international problems, comparable with the division of the land in the nineteenth century into spheres of influence. He does not confine his criticism to the technologically equipped capitalist States, whom he accuses of usurpation of the seas so as to lead to inevitable contradictions and crises, but castigates also the Afro-Asian and Latin American 'developing countries for their insistence upon revision of all existing norms for the regulation of the use of the world ocean'. This he describes as a 'non-class approach. The simple division of the people into rich and poor was not only unjust but also was deeply in error and insulting to the peoples of socialist countries who have created their own wealth themselves without exploiting anyone, while the imperialist powers have profited from the exploitation of colonial peoples.'

Gorshkov attempts to explain this aspect of contemporary sea power in terms of the dialectical problem posed by these contradictions in the matter of maritime claims. His supposition is that the socialist countries represent the thesis, which is the maximisation of the freedom of the seas so that their resources will not be appro-

[6] Translated in US Naval Institute *Proceedings*, November 1974, p. 55.

priated to bourgeois uses, while the predatory claims to exclusive use represent the antithesis. In the conflict situation that results, naval power is the obvious catalyst. Gorshkov even carries these notions into an assault on the proposals for an international regime to regulate exploitation of the deep sea bed. This he describes as unrealistic, 'since it actually envisions an institution of some sort of international consortium in which, inevitably, due to the objective laws of the capitalist market, the large imperialist monopolies would play the main role'.

Evidently, then, the possibilities of the use of sea power to resolve disputes over natural resources are as familiar to the Soviet naval planning staffs as to any other. Soviet naval thinking as it has evolved during the past ten years has accepted the classical notion of sea power, and along with it the classical view of the way that international law can affect the resort to sea power. In 1963 Admiral Gorshkov said, 'We must be prepared on the whole territory of the world ocean. The Soviet navy is obliged to be prepared at any moment and at any point of the globe to secure the protection of the interests of our State.' Admiral Kasatonov said in 1969, 'Soviet warships entered the Mediterranean to consolidate international peace and security, in conformity with the interests of the Arab States, who are victims of Israeli aggression.' In the same year Rear Admiral Navoitsev said, 'The presence of the Soviet navy in the Mediterranean is a most important factor for stabilisation in that troubled area of the globe.' The contrast between this self-confidence and the impotence of the Red navy during the Spanish Civil War is evident from the complaint of Admiral Kuznetsov, who said, 'At that time it became particularly apparent how important the sea is for us and how we need a strong navy.' The whole world has thus become the forum of the Soviet Union's endeavours to influence events in the interests, as it is presented, of 'law and order'.

The law is thus the point of departure of contemporary theories of sea power, whatever the disposition to ignore it in practice. Countries whose concern is to contain the ambitions of others, or to exert a comparable influence, must have a philosophy of law in relation to sea power; and countries which cannot envisage being involved in the central dramas of maritime disputes (which seem to be as inevitable as were the wars of the past) cannot avoid considering the problem of their neutrality. A naval war between two major Asian States whose warships are denied passage through the straits of south-east Asia for the purpose of confronting one another could erupt in the waters around Australia or Cape Horn, as it did in 1914. Had the Indo–Pakistan war of December 1971 been protracted, and had India effectively implemented her half-promulgated naval blockade of Pakistan by enforced visit and search in the high seas, the possibility of the Powers deciding to convoy their tanker traffic to and from the Persian Gulf would have arisen, and was indeed envisaged. So even the law of neutrality enters into the concept of sea power, and it bears upon the choice of ships and weapon systems.

CHAPTER II

THE HISTORICAL FOCUS OF
LAW AND SEA POWER

The history of sea power in the past 300 years reveals the persistent interaction of law and naval policy, although the emphasis has at different times variously affected the interests to be protected, the areas of sea in which naval power has been deployed, and the weapons to be used. An approach to the subject from the historical point of view makes it possible to envisage a philosophy of law in relation to strategy which can bring some coherence to the analysis of contemporary questions. The law has never been static. Its pliable character has meant that it has been made to serve the purposes of sea power, and so has become a weapon in the naval armoury. Just how it has played this role has depended on the issues that occasioned resort to naval force, but it has always been prominent in giving form and character to the issues as well as in influencing the conduct of those who have sought their resolution.

THE INTERESTS OF LEGAL CONFLICT

The interests upon which maritime policy focused in the early seventeenth century, when the modern law began to take familiar shape, were both economic and ideological. They concerned access to the natural resources of far-off lands which were claimed by Spain and Portugal on ideological grounds to be their commercial monopoly, and they also concerned England's claims to exclusive fisheries in the Channel and the North Sea. The concept of the freedom of the seas was promoted as a means of contesting Venice's claims to sovereignty of the Adriatic or to Gustavus Adolphus's claims to domination of the Baltic, as well as the pretensions of James I of England or of Philip III of Spain. In some of these conflicts, notably in the case of the Anglo-Dutch fishery negotiations in 1610 and 1613, in which Grotius himself played a part, and in which the cannonshot was first adumbrated as the extent of coastal control of natural resources,[1] it was diplomacy that effected the solution, and law that

[1] J. K. Oudendijk, *Status and Extent of Adjacent Waters: an Historical Orientation*, Leyden, 1970, p. 34.

gave formal structure and normative character to the diplomatic achievement. But it must not be overlooked that this high level of resort to law occurred at a time when England lacked the naval forces and therefore the disposition to seek a solution by any other means. It was, in fact, the naval stalemate which issued from the Anglo-Dutch wars in the second half of the seventeenth century that ended the theory of the sovereignty of the seas and established the psychological paramountcy of the freedom of the seas, simply because permanent naval domination of the oceans by one Power was shown to be impracticable.

Whereas in the seventeenth century the struggle had been over economic interests, in the eighteenth it was over strategic interests, and it is at this period that the adroit shaping of the law became a significant adjunct of the effective use of sea power. The basic design was to impose legal impediments to the attempt to gain or to deny access to strategic raw materials, particularly timber for masts and spars which France had to import from Scandinavia or Great Britain from North America; and the legal struggle centred around two institutions, neutral waters and contraband. These two went hand-in-hand in the policies of Great Britain and of France. Their content and their manipulation became themselves subject-matters of dispute, so that the battle for naval supremacy was accompanied by struggles about what rules of law there were and about their observance. Just as strategic objectives influenced what the law had to say, so the law, if it could be made to prevail, influenced the means of attaining those objectives.

The games that were played with the legal rules were strikingly similar then to those that have been played in more recent times.[2] What little research has been done in the diplomatic archives has revealed that in the War of the Spanish Succession and in the Seven Years' War the concept of the cannonshot played a significant part in the effort of the Royal Navy and British privateers to seize enemy shipping and cargoes, and of the French navy and mercantile marine, when inferior in power, to keep its strategic routes open by sailing inshore and sheltering in neutral waters. Initially the question was whether protection was afforded only to ships actually under the guns of a neutral fortress or was extended to ships anywhere along the coast within notional range of artillery which might or might not be there. It is testimony to the force of a legal idea and of the legal

[2] See W. L. Walker, in 22 *B.Y.I.L.* (1945) at p. 210, and H. Kent, 'The historical origins of the three-mile limit', in 28 *A.J.I.L.* (1954).

pen that the latter became the rule by the mid-eighteenth century, although it was a rule that protected the weak and circumscribed the powerful.

The point when the rule that a ship was immune from capture under the guns of a neutral fortress turned into a rule that no ship could be taken within gunshot of a neutral shore may well have been the debate that occurred in the House of Lords on the eve of the War of Jenkins' Ear in 1739, when many of their Lordships expressed indignation at the visit and search of British ships by the *guarda-costas* on the Spanish main, and when Carteret inflamed Parliament with his exclamation 'No search, my Lords, is the cry that runs from the sailor to the merchant, from the merchant to the Parliament!' The cosmopolitan point of view was expressed by the urbane Lord Chesterfield, who said that every nation had dominion over its own coasts, and the only question was how far out to sea those coasts should extend. There can be no doubt that from that date onwards the concept of the territorial sea was established as an area within which neutrality might not be breached.

Again the power of the legal idea is manifest in the manner in which the concept of neutral waters consolidated itself in English prize law from 1750 to the judgements of Lord Stowell in the Admiralty Court during the Napoleonic Wars. This development undoubtedly curbed British sea power, whose exponents were only too eager to engage in cutting-out operations but refrained from doing so in neutral ports and waters because constrained by orders in the case of commissioned ships and by the forfeiture of the prize in the case of letters of marque vessels; and this at a time when British sea power was at its apogee, and the law was an impediment and not an aid to its exercise.

No doubt it was partly the civilising notions of the community of nations and the limitation of war that led to this predominance of law over strategic and tactical interests, but not entirely. Great Britain's dependence upon friendly relations with the neutrals was fundamental and so the overriding policy was to concede the interests of the neutrals, who in the late eighteenth century organised themselves into a formidable bloc to defend those interests. Not only was it prudent to respect their waters and their shipping, but orderly conduct—upon which the Enlightenment put a premium—demanded it. The balance between strategic interest and the maintenance of stable and humane relationships with the neutrals was reflected in the evolution of the law relating to blockade, which, consequent upon the stress of events and the pressures of politics, came to embody the concepts of 'close blockade' and 'contraband'.

The uses to which the law could be put, and how it could engage the favourable interest of the neutrals, are evident from the way in which the rules relating to the seizure of neutral cargoes were manipulated. The old Mediterranean rule was the *Consolato del mare*, according to which neutral goods in captured enemy ships were to be restored to their owners and enemy goods in neutral ships could be seized, although the neutral ships and their neutral cargoes had also to be restored. During the eighteenth century Great Britain adhered to this rule, while the French did not: Louis XIV in the *Ordonnance de la marine* of 1681 substituted for the *Consolato del mare* the rule that neutral goods in enemy ships and neutral ships carrying enemy goods should be appropriated. The opposite policies of the protagonists made the content of the law itself the object of dispute and influenced their relationships with the neutrals. Why did these policies diverge? The answer, on both sides, is one of self-interest wherein the legal rule became an instrument of economic warfare. On the British side the overriding fact was that upon the outbreak of war there was an immediate shortfall in the shipping necessary to sustain the British economy of something like 40 per cent, and the Navigation Acts were customarily suspended to let neutrals into the British trade. Guaranteeing neutral shipping and cargoes from seizure was an encouragement to the neutrals, and the *Consolato del mare* was a supremely useful way of achieving this. The shortfall was mainly due to requisitioning of shipping by the Royal Navy, but it was compounded by slow turn-round in ports when the convoy system was instituted, and by losses to the enemy. In the War of American Independence 2,000 British merchant ships, or a quarter of the total, were taken by the French.

France was not nearly as dependent as Great Britain upon shipping in time of war, and was relatively independent of neutral supplement. It was in her interests to promote a legal rule that would jeopardise neutral sustenance to the British, and hence the rule that neutral ships carrying contraband could be seized. It was also in her interests, as the blockaded Power, to embarrass British relations with the neutrals by promoting a legal rule unfavourable to the Royal Navy's interception of neutral blockade-runners.

The development of the art of blockade during the eighteenth century brought exasperation to the Scandinavian neutrals and led to the declaration of the Armed Neutrality in 1780 that a blockade would be recognised only when it was close and effective—in other words, where it constituted literally a physical barrier to entry into a neutral port. France always took the position that a vessel could not be seized for breach of blockade unless a blockading cruiser gave special warning and notified this in the blockade-runner's log book, while British practice was to assume knowledge of a blockade on the basis of constructive notice. Obviously the different directions in which these countries sought to push the law reflected differences in their habitual strategic situations. There was a similar difference of opinion on the subject of the right to seize a blockade-runner away from the blockading line or beyond the reach of hot pursuit. The Napoleonic War incidents filled the law reports of the British and French Admiralty courts with prize cases in which these issues were canvassed, and there is no doubt that the decisions of those courts had a great influence on the respective naval practices of the two countries.

The Powers at the end of the Crimean War adopted the rule of effective blockade in the Declaration of Paris, but as naval technology evolved, with harbours protected against blockading fleets by batteries of long-range guns, minefields and submarine-launched torpedoes, the law became for a major naval Power like Great Britain an unwelcome encumbrance. In 1909 a conference was called in London to attempt to establish a new legal regime in order to restore equivalence between the law and the exigencies of naval operations, but from the British government's point of view it was disastrous. The new code of blockade adopted there was totally at variance with the interests of a nation that aimed to control the seas as distinct from denying such control to others. The British government did not ratify these rules, but the mere fact that they existed psychologically circumscribed Great Britain's decisions when the First World War broke out and the disparity between these rules and the directions of naval policy became instantly manifest. Great Britain, whose fleet could not remain on station in the Gulf of Heligoland or the Baltic, resorted to the long-distance blockade by means of a cruiser cordon as a reprisal or retaliation for the German proclamation of a war zone around the British Isles. The challenge to this British action from the neutrals, particularly the United States, was so vigorous that for a time it caused Germany to hold her hand in the matter of unrestricted submarine warfare, in the expectation of a confrontation between Washington and Whitehall.

The definition of contraband in the First World War also contributed to a tension between the exigencies of warfare and politics. The Declaration of Paris of 1856 had not defined contraband, but in practice a distinction had been made between absolute and relative contraband, other articles being classified as free. For three years after the outbreak of war in 1914 the British government struggled to maintain the system, until in 1917 the list of articles liable to seizure in neutral ships covered almost anything of strategic value.

The sharp edge of this incision into the traditional liberties of neutral commerce was blunted by devices that have been imitated more recently in the case of the Beira patrol, based upon clearances obtained in advance which make it possible to avoid conflict at sea. In the First and Second World Wars a complex of reprisal orders was evolved, which made use of ship navicerts, cargo navicerts and certificates of origin and interest. In themselves these modalities are of only indirect interest to a study of the way in which law influences naval planning, but they constituted the framework of the exercise of the right of visit and search on the high seas, and so played their role in harmonising the political needs of placating the neutrals with the effective use of sea power in economic warfare.

THE AREAS OF LEGAL CONFLICT

During the Napoleonic Wars, when the neutral status of the territorial sea as an area immune from the exercise of sea power was finally sanctified in the courts, naval interest and the law clashed in an altogether novel respect. The problem concerned the right of the Royal Navy at a time of an acute manning crisis to recover its deserters from the ships, including commissioned vessels, of the United States, both on the high seas and in United States waters. Two issues were involved, one of the right of visit and search, and the other of the extent of the waters within which the right was excluded or qualified, even assuming that it was available on the high seas. In 1807 H.M.S. *Leopard* forced the U.S.S. *Chesapeake* to strike after three broadsides had been fired into her four or five leagues off Cape Henry, Virginia, in an incident arising out of a demand for the surrender of deserters.

The outcome was the closing by President Jefferson of all United States waters to British commissioned ships. The Foreign Secretary, Canning, was prepared to concede that the Royal Navy had no legal right to board neutral warships, but he pointed out that he was un-

able to go too far in making concessions because of the aroused
state of British public opinion, which regarded the Americans as
conniving with the French to defeat the British blockade of France
and the occupied Continental States. The significant point of the
incident is that the law, to be the decisive arbiter of a situation, has
to have the requisite political, and hence psychological, support.
Otherwise the situation will be resolved only by superior force, and
the conflict will be allowed to escalate. The events of 1807 led not
to a resolution of the question but to its prolongation, and eventually
to the unhappy war of 1812.

Throughout the eighteenth century and until the end of the
Napoleonic Wars sea power had been concerned with the elimination
of political rivals and the protection of mercantilist economic policies. The law developed to outwit hovering by smugglers and deny
access to strategic raw materials on the part of enemies, as well as
to preserve good relations, and hence uninterrupted trade, with
neutrals. Following the close of this epoch of imperial struggle, it
returned to its early interest, exclusive control over natural resources,
notably the fisheries of Canada and Newfoundland, and of the
English Channel and North Sea. In the latter areas the problem was
resolved by treaties establishing the three-mile limit and by special
rules for defining that limit in the case of bays. In North America,
however, the Royal Navy found itself for the first time in a fishery
protection role in connection with an attenuated diplomatic controversy with the United States.

This episode is strikingly similar to the fishery struggles such as
the 'cod wars' of the present time, with graduated employment of
force accompanying intermittent negotiations and protest, each side
probing the other's political, psychological, legal and material de-
fences in such a way as to keep political feeling at a low level while
in fact conceding no point of principle. The element of sectional
interest was afforded by the colonial governments of Nova Scotia
and New Brunswick on the one hand and of the American distant-
water fishermen from New Hampshire and Massachusetts on the
other. It was the judicious use of naval power in the 1830s and 1840s
that kept the issues stable and made an eventual solution in 1910
possible.

The other great area of the law of the sea to emerge in the first
half of the nineteenth century was the concept of 'innocent passage'
through the territorial sea. Although the writers of the seventeenth
century referred to *transitus innoxius*, they did so in a philosophical

context quite remote from the notions that generated the modern doctrine of the territorial sea, and until the 1840s the theorists almost universally affirmed the right of the coastal State to close its waters to passing shipping. The imposition of the notion of 'innocent passage' upon the territorial sea was a logical corollary of the coincidence of interests that emerged after the opening up of Latin America to trade, especially to British shipping; the emergence of *laissez-faire* economic policies and the consequent emphasis upon free trade; and the appearance of steam, which meant that expanding merchant fleets would seek the shortest routes without worrying about lee shores and sailing patterns.

The problem of warships in the territorial sea did not arouse any interest until the American Civil War, and then it took the form not of questioning the right of a warship to be there but of the proper extent of neutral waters.

During that conflict the Foreign Office, the Admiralty and the international lawyers were furnished with much food for thought about the rules of naval warfare. In 1864 the United States cruiser *Rhode Island* fired at a Confederate vessel from a point four miles from the coast of the Bahamas while her opponent was within the three-mile limit, and shot fell on the island of Eleuthera. The government of the Bahamas wrote indignantly to the Colonial Office about the matter, demanding that the Royal Navy take a more vigorous attitude towards the protection of British territory. The French government even required the *Alabama* and the *Kearsage* to withdraw well into the high seas before engaging, so that shot would not fall upon French territory; and the British government wrote to the United States, proposing that belligerent action should not take place within range of the territorial sea, so that shot would not fall even with neutral waters. The demonstration during the American Civil War of the increased ballistic capability of ordnance posed for naval consideration the question whether the extent of the territorial sea should remain at three miles or continue to be commensurate with the expanding range of cannon.

It is interesting to recall the different strategic considerations which operated in this period from the period when the three-mile rule was first adumbrated. Ferdinando Galiani, who propagated even if he did not invent the three-mile limit in a work on neutrality written in 1782[3] (when neutrality was a paramount European political issue), saw in this measurement a rule that was admittedly prag-

[3] *Dei doveri dei principi neutrali*, Naples, 1782.

matic but bore some relationship to the scientific measurement of the earth's surface; whereas, as he pointed out, the cannonshot was an imprecise rule of measurement, since it depended upon the calibre of the gun, the smoothness of the bore, the fineness and quantity of the powder, the approximation of the ball to a perfect sphere and its exact relationship to the bore. It has wrongly been supposed that Galiani thought that three miles was an ideal cannonshot limit, and Rear Admiral Mouton[4] has intrigued us with his demonstration from the ballistics manuals that no gun of the Nelson era would fire three miles. In fact no one could have supposed any theoretical limit to artillery before Count Rumford did his experiments on muzzle velocity in Munich in the 1790s, and it was Thomas Jefferson who jumped to the conclusion that Galiani's three-mile limit was the resolution in arithmetical terms of the range of artillery. The point is of no importance except that, as the three-mile limit and the range of cannon began to diverge after 1860, the question was raised whether the one was the genesis of the other so that the three-mile limit had lost its rationale.

Whereas the cannonshot was viewed by naval strategists in the Jeffersonian period as bearing upon the liberty of visit and search and seizure, it was viewed in the 1870s as bearing upon the enforcement of the coastal State's civil and criminal jurisdiction, particularly in the matter of collisions. The Royal Navy had little interest in this question, and in an age of splendid isolation, when naval policy was essentially defensive, it viewed the law as a guarantee of the immunity of neutral waters from the belligerent operations of others, and thought of it as insulating British commerce and communications from the actions of other nations which might be at war. A broad territorial sea might be an advantage to this protective interest, whereas a century earlier it would have been a disadvantage.

So for a time the Royal Navy was inclined to go along with the Board of Trade, which reported that an extension of the territorial sea to the actual range of artillery would probably be a gain for England, considered in relationship to the laws concerning maritime capture, blockade and contraband, and the protection of the coast and coastal shipping from the fall of shot. Palmerston, taking the view that Britain was more likely in fact to be a belligerent than a neutral, opposed any departure from the three-mile limit and carried the Cabinet with him in 1864, but a decade later the Lord Chancellor minuted correspondence with Germany with the remark that Great

[4] *The Continental Shelf*, The Hague, 1952.

Britain had never limited her claim to three miles from the coast, and that the improvements in modern artillery might entitle a country to protect and exercise rights over a larger margin of the high seas.[5]

The argument over the coincidence of the territorial sea and the range of artillery continued until 1914, and the Russian fishery limit of twelve miles, which is the genesis of the present twelve-mile standard, was in fact the supposed resolution into arithmetical terms of the limits of the cannonshot as they were in 1910. Meanwhile the struggle over the law as an instrument of strategy had shifted from one of the areas of operations to one of restraint upon weapons.

THE WEAPONS IN LEGAL CONFLICT

Lord St Vincent, when he heard of Fulton's submarine in 1800, responded to the enthusiasts and the alarmists who urged consideration by the Admiralty of this novel invention with the devastating but sound observation that he saw no reason for Great Britain to acquire a weapon which could not enhance her control of the seas but which, if developed, might deprive her of it.

To a paramount naval Power any new device or weapon which would revolutionise tactics and hence threaten the stately supremacy of a fleet that for two centuries had prevailed with tested means and procedures, this was the observation of a sage. As the nineteenth century progressed, however, such devices and weapons were beginning to appear, and if they were not to disturb the balance of sea power they would have to be outlawed. In other words, the law would have to come to the aid of sea power by trapping technology and harnessing it so as to maintain the *status quo*.

The international community was insufficiently organised at the time of the appearance of the torpedo for any moves to be made to limit or prohibit its use by treaty, but the Hague peace conference of 1899 afforded an opportunity to attempt to outlaw the submarine, and to this end Great Britain, who was represented there by Jackie Fisher (the only tactician of the time who envisaged that the submarine would become a commerce-destroyer by stealth and might escape from the standard rules of war at sea), exerted her energies—in vain, as it happened, because the French, in this, the year following Fashoda, saw in the submarine the only means at their disposal for challenging the Royal Navy.

[5] See H. A. Smith, *Great Britain and the Law of Nations*, London, 1935, vol. II, p. 199.

This was a striking example of the effort to influence sea power by means of law. An equally striking example is the Hague Convention No. XIII of 1907 concerning contact mines ratified by the United Kingdom and the U.S.A. It is evident that the restrictions placed upon the laying of mines in this instrument benefits the superior naval power by confining the enemy's battle fleet while leaving commercial shipping outside the area of danger—so guaranteeing as far as possible the safety of the merchant fleet of the Power that rules the seas.

The fact that these efforts to stamp upon the products of the new naval technology were unsuccessful, either because no agreement was reached or because, when the Powers went to war, the agreement was more honoured in the breach than the observance, is immaterial. What is significant is the realisation that the law could be another weapon in the offensive armament, a weapon which could confine the enemy to his ports, and, by means of blockade and concomitant visit and search over the broad areas of the ocean, deprive him of access to neutral cargoes. The law may not have worked very well in this direction simply because this is a game that two can play, but that it was just as effective as some other weapons in the naval armoury cannot be disputed, as the case studies in the following chapters will show.

CHAPTER III

A CASE STUDY OF
LAW AND SEA POWER:
THE BATTLE OF THE RIVER PLATE[1]

The factor that revolutionised the role of law in sea power after 1899 was the phenomenon of the international conference, which made it possible to bind the Powers, when they could be persuaded, by texts whose expressions, even though open to interpretation, were less capable of manipulation than customary law, and hence less likely to lose rigidity under the pressures of competing behaviour patterns that reflected the actual strategic situation. Where the matter fell within the confines of the Hague Conventions it was possible to reinforce naval power at a belligerent's disposal by mounting concomitant diplomatic operations—as in the case of the River Plate action. And where there was no text on the point and law was called for it was possible to mount a diplomatic conference—like the Nyon conference in 1937—to curb dangerous operations or the use of dangerous weapons. The inter-war period and the early stages of World War II thus afford valuable insight into the relationship of law and naval operations.

On 13 December 1939 the 8 in. cruiser *Exeter* and the 6 in. cruisers *Ajax* and *Achilles* engaged the German pocket battleship *Graf Spee* off the coast of South America. The *Graf Spee* withdrew into Montevideo harbour for repairs to make her seaworthy. *Exeter* was out of action, *Ajax* had a quarter of her main armament out of action, and she and *Achilles*, both heavily outgunned, alone stood between the *Graf Spee* and her escape into the broad spaces of the Atlantic. On 17 December the *Graf Spee* was scuttled off the harbour of Montevideo.

This action affords, perhaps, the best illustration of the fact that battles are not won by the military branch of government in isolation from all other relevant considerations. The Plate was a victory only because professional naval practice was ideally meshed with the political, diplomatic and legal factors that entered into the situation.

Looked at as a whole, the battle of the River Plate was not merely

[1] See bibliography, below, for the sources generally.

an engagement at sea but a complex series of events in which the exchange of fire was only one of the pressures bringing about the destruction of the enemy. In the situation that developed it is possible to find five questions of law, more or less important in both the diplomatic handling of the matter and in the purely tactical decisions that had to be taken, whether in the Admiralty, or on the bridge of the *Ajax* or in the British embassy in Montevideo. Correct judgements respecting these legal elements contributed to a successful outcome, which was the immediate supremacy of British sea power in the south Atlantic, and, in the longer term, the forcing of Germany away from surface operations in order to interrupt British sea routes into unrestricted submarine warfare, which raised another set of legal issues.

It is proposed to analyse briefly each of the five questions of law involved in the River Plate affair with a view to indicating its influence upon the conduct of the operation.

THE SOUTH AMERICAN NEUTRALITY ZONE

The significance of the creation of this zone in the Declaration of Panama on 3 October 1939 will be adverted to in a later chapter.[2] Suffice to say that the British and German governments did not accept the restriction upon their exercise of belligerent operations within 300 miles of the coasts of South America. None the less, the Latin American claim existed, and if it were to be altogether ignored this could damage relations with the republics, whose friendship would be valuable in the economics of the war and, as it turned out in this case, in the strategy of disadvantage to one side and advantage to the other in the matter of facilities.

Hence it was not just a question of ordering Commodore Harwood, in command of the British squadron, to treat the zone as non-existent. At the same time there could be no question of the Royal Navy not patrolling up to the limits of the territorial sea, because the neutrality zone itself was no guarantee that a German attack on British shipping might not occur there. Provided that the matter was handled adroitly, the Declaration of Panama could prove advantageous to Great Britain, because, although respect for it might restrain the Royal Navy from seizing German merchant ships lying in South American ports, these could always be shadowed for the requisite 300 miles; because any attack on British shipping in the

[2] Chapter XII, section 2, below; see also bibliography.

area, which was a matter of greater moment in economic warfare, would thrust upon Germany the opprobrium of defying the American republics and attach them more firmly to the Allied side; and because any resistance made by British warships to such an attack could be represented as self-defence against this breach of law.

Hence it was British policy to allow the Declaration of Panama some tentative legal status, in the expectation that when the collision came it would work to British advantage—as, indeed, it did. That it was desirable to present the case as one wherein Germany was in the wrong, and that this was uppermost in the minds of all concerned, is evident from the fact that Commodore Harwood's first signal concerning the action began by saying that he was in the zone 'chancing encounter' and that 'pocket battleship to westward fired first'; that the tactical précis said 'it has been definitely established that the *Graf Spee* first shot both in first engagement and in subsequent action nearer inshore'; and that the British Minister in Montevideo telegraphed London with evident relief more than once that the *Graf Spee* had opened the engagement.

On this point, then, the British came with clean hands to the diplomatic struggle in Montevideo that followed the arrival there of the *Graf Spee*, while the Germans started with the disadvantage of being, in the eyes of the Uruguayan government, in the wrong.

The British government also had the advantage of knowing that the United States would see that the bias, if there were any, would be against the Germans. On the day after the battle the British ambassador in Washington telegraphed the War Cabinet that President Roosevelt had expressed

great satisfaction at the result of the naval action, and said that the State Department had pressed the Uruguayan Government to intern the *Graf Spee* unless it left within twenty-four hours. He in no way objected to warlike action within patrol zone but said he hoped that we should not take belligerent action against enemy merchant vessels within the zone. I was not very clear about his meaning but I think he meant that we should not fire upon them or sink them until they had left the zone. I said that we could not agree that they should be free to move about so long as they remained in the zone.

The intervention of the United States in Montevideo was decisive in preventing the question of the zone becoming an embarrassing complication. The British Minister reported on 16 December that the Foreign Minister of Uruguay seemed in 'a somewhat different and more friendly mood' after an interview with the United States Minister.

Churchill's view that the neutrality zone was marginally advantageous to the Allies, who should not, therefore, resist it altogether, proved to be correct.

THE ENGAGEMENT IN THE TERRITORIAL SEA

Although Uruguay and Argentina had a theoretical claim to the Plate estuary as inland waters, it was not expected that the existence of this claim would augment in any way the legal issues arising under the Declaration of Panama, and that, provided Germany could be made to appear the aggressor, pursuit of the *Graf Spee* should not stop at the closing line. No question seems to have arisen in Commodore Harwood's mind about chasing the enemy right up the river.

The issue that did emerge was whether in the course of this pursuit passage should be taken through the Uruguayan territorial sea of three miles. The sensitivity of Uruguay on this legal issue was demonstrated both during the chase and in the subsequent diplomatic confrontation.

While the *Graf Spee* was rounding Punta del Este, at the northern closing point of the estuary, the old Uruguayan cruiser *Uruguay* took station symbolically in the territorial sea upon observing the pocket battleship within two miles of Lobos Island. As the captain of the *Uruguay* reported, he 'took this decision in spite of the danger in steering a course between the enemy vessels, and also in spite of the supposed warning of danger given by the German battleship, thus carrying out my duty of enforcing respect for our territorial waters'.

At 19.50 hours *Achilles* was observed by the *Uruguay* to open fire on the retreating *Graf Spee* while *Achilles* was within the three-mile limit. The captain of the *Uruguay* reported that the *Graf Spee* returned the fire, and that 'the whole of the action, with the exception of the first few minutes, took place within territorial waters'.

In the diplomatic manoeuvrings that followed in Montevideo this question of breach of territorial waters became an early issue, so that here again the law became a lever to gain tactical advantage over an enemy. Captain Langsdorff, in his last letter to the German Minister, who referred it to the Uruguayan government just as the *Graf Spee* was leaving harbour to scuttle herself, wrote:

After *Exeter* had been put out of action I decided to make for the port of Montevideo to repair the damage to my vessel. I was aware that the British government recognises only the three-mile zone (even in the waters of the River Plate). As soon as my ship had reached the zone over which the countries contiguous to the Plate claim international condominium (and in spite of the British interpretation of this claim as it was known to me), out of respect for the feelings of the two peace-loving nations I abstained from further part in the action.

I stress particularly the point that in spite of a favourable tactical position and in spite of good visibility I did not open fire on the British cruiser standing off the Isla de Lobos until the enemy had fired on my ship and shot had fallen close.

What Captain Langsdorff was saying was that respect for law required him to yield the tactical advantage he enjoyed at that moment of having the *Achilles* illuminated by the setting sun in a position where visibility and her bearing and distance from the island gave maximum advantage to the *Graf Spee*'s range takers.

The acceptance by the government of Uruguay of the report of its own naval observer that the *Achilles* did fire in the territorial sea proved to be a complicating factor in the negotiations, although, as it happened, it was not a serious one because other considerations came to override it. None the less the point was deemed sufficiently important for strenuous denials to be made by Commodore Harwood. It was pointed out that the cruiser *Uruguay* was beyond the visual horizon of the *Graf Spee* when she saw *Achilles*' guns fire, and hence did not realise that this was return of and not initiation of fire in the territorial sea. It was also argued that passage through the territorial sea is not an infraction of sovereignty, even if it is 'hot pursuit' of an enemy, and not mere transit.

Achilles' track plan has been lost, but the account prepared for the Tactical Division of the Admiralty was based on her firing plot and log. Read with the report made by the *Graf Spee* to the German Admiralty it appears that the battleship, when in the eye of the setting sun, which blinded the cruisers, turned to open the A arcs of both forward and after turrets and opened fire at 20.48, and that *Achilles* replied at 20.54 hours. In fact this was the second time the *Graf Spee* fired in this area. At 19.15 hours she fired a salvo at the *Ajax*, to which no return was made because Uruguayan inhabited areas lay behind the point of aim and shots might have ricocheted ashore. It seems clear that it was the *Graf Spee* that fired first.

A basic misunderstanding appears to underlie this aspect of the diplomatic contretemps. Uruguay claimed a nine-mile territorial sea, and it is certain that the passage past the Isla de Lobos and up the coast was within this limit. But the British government accepted no limit of more than three miles, and it seems that in the discussions at Montevideo the British confused the Uruguayan claim to territorial waters with the claim that the Plate was inland waters. In fact *Achilles* when she returned the fire of the *Graf Spee* was more than three miles from shore.

On the day after the battle the Uruguayan Minister in London called on the Foreign Office to say that his government 'reserved their attitude with regard to the naval action in the vicinity of Montevideo' and 'near the port of Maldonado, and therefore in Uruguayan territorial waters'. The minutes on this Foreign Office docket reveal the confusion between the three-mile, nine-mile and estuary limits.

It will be remembered that the question of the Plate estuary came up recently in connection with English Bank, and we sent instructions to B.A. with the object of safeguarding our position. But it is, I imagine, quite possible that some of the action took place within the Uruguayan three-mile limit; the Admiralty will probably know in due course.

It was decided to take advantage of the disfavour in which the Germans were held and to attempt to put the blame on them.

The Uruguayan government are bound, of course, to make a fuss, just as the Chileans did in the last war over the sinking of the *Dresden*, but the incident comes at, from our point of view, a very opportune moment when the Uruguayans are furious with the Germans over a tactless note from the German Minister.

Although the British found themselves on the defensive on this issue, so, unknown to them, did the Germans. On 15 December the Uruguayan Minister in Berlin saw Baron von Weizsäcker, the head of the Foreign Ministry, and was reported to have protested, 'although not too sharply', at the 'carrying on of the fight' in the sovereign area of Uruguay. Weizsäcker had no information on the point, and said he would ask the Kriegsmarine to look into the matter. As the question of the fate of the *Graf Spee* in Montevideo was at that time a delicate matter, he sought to temporise. Next day State Secretary Baron von Heyden-Rynsch minuted that the navy had reported that it was impossible for the *Graf Spee* to have been in action in the three-mile zone, as the waters were too shallow at that distance in the Plate for her to operate there. There is no record of this being passed on to Uruguay.

As it happened, the diplomatic contretemps over the belligerent actions of both combatants in the territorial sea did not significantly alter the matter, but there were obvious apprehensions that it might have done.

THE HAGUE CONVENTION GAME

The Convention Concerning the Rights and Duties of Neutral Powers in Naval War, No. XIII of those adopted at the second Hague conference of 1907, provides that belligerent warships may not remain in neutral ports for more than twenty-four hours, except that this period may be extended to enable such repairs to be made as are absolutely necessary in order to render a warship seaworthy, provided that no addition is made to its fighting force. Under no circumstances may belligerent warships make use of neutral ports, roadsteads or territorial waters for replenishing or increasing their supplies of war material. They may revictual only to bring their supplies to peacetime standard. A belligerent warship may not leave a neutral port or roadstead until twenty-four hours after the departure of a merchant ship flying the flag of its adversary.

Around this group of provisions a deadly diplomatic game was played for three days after the *Graf Spee*'s arrival in Montevideo. A significant feature of the game is that very little guidance as to the rules or tactics was forthcoming from either London or Berlin. It was local embassy staffs and the naval officers of both sides who sought to exploit the Convention to their respective advantage, and the British, after a false beginning, won the legal battle and therefore put the *Graf Spee* into what her captain at least believed to be an impossible tactical situation.

When the first reports of the *Graf Spee*'s arrival in Montevideo reached Whitehall it took some hours for the War Cabinet to consider the situation and for the despatch of instructions, which went out at 6.35 p.m. on the evening of 14 December. They included directions concerning the Hague Convention. 'Under Article 12 of that Convention the *Graf Spee* should not be allowed to remain in Uruguayan waters for more than twenty-four hours.' The argument was to be that since she had approached Montevideo at high speed she must have been in a seaworthy condition.

The German Minister demanded a period of fifteen days for repairs to make the *Graf Spee* seaworthy. The British Minister demanded that she be expelled in twenty-four hours, as she appeared to be entirely seaworthy and was seeking additional time only to repair her fighting efficiency. The Uruguayan government promptly appointed a technical commission to survey the battle damage, and upon its report issued a presidential decree granting a period of seventy-two hours, which was delivered to the embassies at mid-day on 15 December.

Both Ministers expostulated. To the German Minister the Uruguayan Foreign Minister replied that he based his government's action on the Convention; the German Minister protested that this action was one of sovereign discretion based upon a unilateral interpretation of the relevant articles which Germany could not accept. In his report to Berlin on this exchange he pointed to the 'strong pressure' being exerted by the British Minister.

The latter, on the morning after the *Graf Spee*'s arrival, delivered a note to the Uruguayan government asking for the *Graf Spee*'s expulsion after twenty-four hours. To this the Foreign Minister replied on the sixteenth, pointing out that the Convention had been interpreted during the first world war to the effect that a prolonged stay was permissible in order to repair warships after damage in action, provided that it was to restore their seaworthiness only and not to repair armaments. The technical commission had reported on the repairs necessary to make the *Graf Spee* seaworthy, and Uruguay was adhering strictly to the Convention. In a verbal exchange later that day with the Foreign Minister the British Minister protested that skilled workmen and electrical equipment had been seen to go aboard the *Graf Spee* without being stopped by the Uruguayan authorities. The Foreign Minister riposted with the allegation that the Royal Navy had breached Uruguayan neutrality in the territorial sea. The British Minister reported to London that the Foreign Minister 'appeared much moved' by this matter.

He added with some bitterness that the feelings of the nations of the whole American continent about the whole occurrence, and especially the naval action in the estuary, were causing them to come together for joint action to avoid its repetition.

In this connection I at once said that it was important to note that the *Graf Spee* had fired first both at the very beginning of the whole action and again near the English Bank.

At first the objective of the British embassy was to have the *Graf Spee* expelled before her fighting efficiency was restored so that the sea battle could recommence. But during the course of the day of 14 December a signal was received at the Admiralty from Commodore Harwood asking that everything possible be done to keep *Graf Spee* from sailing, as his cruisers were no match for the battleship alone and awaited reinforcement at the mouth of the Plate. It therefore became necessary for British diplomacy to go into reverse and to aim at keeping the *Graf Spee* in port beyond the granted period of seventy-two hours.

The instructions from the Admiralty went to British intelligence in Montevideo, represented there by an enterprising agent named Miller, who was mainly responsible for the successful outcome of events. He was told to 'raise every possible means to delay Pocket Battleship at Montevideo including sailing of British ships and claim twenty-four hours rule'. Later the Admiralty was to say that the *Graf Spee* should be held until 20 December, by which date the battle-cruiser *Renown* and the aircraft carrier *Ark Royal* would have joined the British squadron.

The reference to the twenty-four-hour rule in the telegram was to the articles of the Convention concerning the obligation of a neutral to delay the sailing of a belligerent warship for twenty-four hours after the sailing of a merchant ship of enemy flag. It was intended to line up the British merchant ships in port and to give notices of sailing to one a day so as to postpone *Graf Spee*'s departure. But when the second note was handed in requesting that the *Graf Spee* be held for twenty-four hours after the sailing of the *Dunster Grange* the Uruguayan government suspended all sailings until the expiry of the seventy-two-hour period already allotted to the *Graf Spee*. So that device failed. This induced a mood of despondency in the British embassy, which was even contemplating sabotage to the *Graf Spee*, and it set in train a scheme to bluff the Germans into believing that capital ships had taken station off the Plate to reinforce the cruisers. The bluff worked, and the *Graf Spee* was scuttled at the expiry of the seventy-two hours.

Captain Langsdorff's last official action in Montevideo on 17 December was to make 'a formal protest against the decision of the Government of Uruguay'.

In accordance with Article 17, Chapter XIII of the Hague Convention, permission for warships of belligerent powers to remain in a neutral port may be granted for a period sufficient to carry out such repairs as are essential for the safe navigation of such vessels. As far back as the year 1914 there was a precedent for this in South America. For several weeks the British cruiser *Glasgow* lay in port carrying out repairs.

He went on to list the damage which, he argued, affected the ship's seaworthiness, including the galleys and bakeries, and concluded:

I hereby declare that the decision of the Government of Uruguay compels me to leave the harbour of Montevideo with a ship which could not be sufficiently repaired to ensure the maximum safety of navigation. To put to sea in such a vessel would be to bring danger upon my crew (over 1,000 men) by negligence.

There is no doubt that Captain Langsdorff believed that he had suffered a legal defeat, and that this circumscribed his tactical options.

THE STATUS OF THE PLATE ESTUARY

When shadowing the *Graf Spee* as she entered the Plate Commodore Harwood did not need to consider the claim that the waters thereof were internal waters because his general instructions, issued to all H.M. ships on the outbreak of war, were to take account only of the three-mile limit, wherever this might exist. But with the possibility of the *Graf Spee* emerging from Montevideo in a bid to escape, the question assumed vital significance. For if the British forces had to remain outside the closing line of the Plate they would be beyond the visual horizon, and would then have to maintain surveillance over both the north and south channels, separated by several hours' sailing time, and this division of their forces, especially when only the two cruisers were available, could have been fatal.

On the other hand, the diplomats put a premium on the suscepti- bilities of the government of Uruguay, and Commodore Harwood was well aware of this. Vice-Admiral Sir Henry McCall, who at the time was naval attaché and who boarded the *Ajax* for talks during the waiting period, has recorded that the commodore's

main concern was the attitude of Uruguay, particularly in regard to her claims to territorial waters. He had that morning received a signal from the Admiralty, telling him that he need only regard the three-mile limit and need pay no attention to the Uruguayan claim to the whole of the River Plate estuary—a claim backed by all other South American repub- lics, with the support of the U.S.A. Realising, however, how much our ships in the South Atlantic depended on the goodwill of those countries, he was hesitant to take advantage of the Admiralty's instruction. When I put these views to our Minister, he too saw the picture in the same light and sent a telegram home to that effect.

The telegram read:

If *Admiral Graf Spee* goes out, I submit that it is politically of the utmost importance that our cruisers should not fire first shot on her within the zone of Argentine–Uruguayan jurisdiction, a claim which I have reason to believe has the support of all the American countries.

He followed this with another telegram four hours later:

I sense that Pan-American solidarity has hardened immensely as a result of the battle and inter-American consultations centred here which have followed. This will emphasise the importance first and foremost of the Argentine–Uruguayan claim to jurisdiction in the whole River Plate estuary.

We are in the fortunate position of claiming that the first shot in this security zone and again in or over River Plate zone was fired by the *Graf Spee* and this was apparently not contested. But in this morning's press I see a German communiqué that the *Graf Spee* ceased fire after entering Argentine–Uruguayan jurisdiction zone except to actually reply to the shots fired on her and thus explaining he did not do greater damage to our cruisers.

The first of these telegrams was sent *en clair* and the second in cipher, the intention being that the Uruguayan government would infer that the initiative in any re-engagement of the forces within the closing line of the Plate would be taken by the *Graf Spee*. There was no time for any reply to be made to these telegrams before the *Graf Spee* sailed and scuttled herself.

The striking feature about this aspect of the situation is that there is no record of Whitehall giving serious attention to the diplomatic and tactical issues raised by the question of the legal status of the Plate estuary. It is clear that Commodore Harwood was worried at the gravity of the responsibility placed on his shoulders by the Admiralty signal, which he discussed with the naval attaché, and which read simply, 'You are free to engage *Graf Spee* anywhere outside the three-mile limit'.

Given these orders, he had no alternative but to make dispositions to fight, while at the same time aiming to create a situation where the *Graf Spee* would open the engagement and where he could not be accused of rashly endangering the security of Uruguay. Accordingly he decided to move his patrol area to the north and east of English Bank, considering 'that a battle in the very restricted water just outside the three-mile limit off Montevideo was impracticable, owing to lack of sea room and the possibility of "overs" landing in Uruguay and causing international complications'. He issued tactical instructions to the *Achilles* and *Cumberland*, which had joined from Stanley, with a view to hustling the *Graf Spee* 'from area to area'. Significantly the *Ajax*'s aircraft was flown on reconnaissance with orders to keep away from the three-mile limit but otherwise to operate in the estuary.

As it happened, the status of the Plate did not become an issue because the *Graf Spee* destroyed herself, but the lessons are important. The claim that the Plate estuary was national waters was at that time only tentative, but local diplomatic and naval appreciation of its psychological importance appears to have been more acute than in Whitehall, which adopted an attitude of lofty indifference towards it, and Commodore Harwood felt that he was confronted with a difficult choice, which his orders did not completely clarify, as to whether or not he should open the engagement within the closing line of the Plate. To this extent the claim, although insecure in law, acquired rigidity as soon as the question of its being challenged or observed arose in practice.

The deficiency in communications between Whitehall and the actors would not occur today, and these legal issues would be given more serious consideration at the higher political levels. While this would diminish the area of discretion left to the local commander, it would not altogether eliminate it, because a decision upon his orders would not always be expeditiously reached, and events could overtake him.

THE ALLEGATION OF USE OF GAS SHELLS

During the naval engagement numbers of the *Graf Spee*'s crew became ill with gas poisoning in areas of the ship damaged by gunfire, and it was at first believed that the Royal Navy was firing asphyxiating gas shells in violation of the Geneva Protocol of 1925. The allegation nonplussed the British, whose immediate reaction was that it was a propaganda lie. In fact there was gas poisoning, but it was due to escape of chemicals from containers damaged by splinters, although this was not immediately discovered.

On the German side this was the first legal question to emerge. When Captain Langsdorff's battle report was received on 15 December Baron von der Heyden-Rynsch noted that the Oberkommando der Kriegsmarine had drawn attention to the apparent use of poisonous gas by the British, and that as soon as a medical report had been received from the ship's surgeon efforts should be made to set up a commission of neutral doctors to investigate. The report was received the same day, stating that the victims showed all the indications of mustard gas poisoning, but that Captain Langsdorff, on the other hand, did not believe that gas shells had been used. The German Minister in Montevideo, who was one of the new school of German diplomats, tendentiously indicated that the surgeon was specially qualified in gas defence medicine while Captain Langsdorff was not. Clearly he wished to make an issue of the allegation in order to circumvent British moves to force the *Graf Spee* to sea.

As it happened, the uncertainty of the evidence caused the point to be dropped after an initial outburst of indignation on the part of the German government, so that this legal issue did not, in fact, play an important role, although it might have.

SUMMARY

The battle of the River Plate did not end with the engagement at sea but with the destruction of the enemy brought about by the successful application of concurrent pressures, of which the law was but one. It was not the law, in fact, that was the decisive element in the situation so much as guile. But that it was a major one is beyond doubt. All the protagonists realised, if they did not express it that way, that the points of law arising in the situation were weapons in the overall armoury, to be used adroitly in combination with naval force to bring the event to the desired end.

The consciousness of the naval commanders on the spot of the significance of the legal issues as facilitating or circumscribing their tactical decisions was more developed than that of their political or naval superiors at home, and events demonstrated that their judgement of the matter, on both sides, was completely sound. The view of Commodore Harwood and of the British Minister upon the issue of the status of the Plate is particularly arresting. It was easy in Whitehall to sniff at exaggerated claims. The people on the spot had to reckon with the local consequences of flouting these claims, and the lesson is that no naval commander is ever as free in disputed waters, no matter how insecure the legal claims to them may in fact be, as he is on the high seas, and that a decision to challenge the claim is always serious and should always be made at the highest level.

CHAPTER IV

THE FORCE OF LAW IN SEA POWER

THE 'ALTMARK' INCIDENT[1]

The analysis of the River Plate affair demonstrates that the law can have a significant, even a decisive, influence upon sea power, but it would be naive to draw this conclusion independently of the politically inhibiting circumstances of the case, which were: the need to maintain friendly relations with Uruguay and the other South American countries so that their neutrality would be benevolent rather than rigorous; the existence of the Pan-American system, which meant that hemisphere susceptibilities had to be taken strictly into account; and the importance of enticing the United States into unilateral action to fend off belligerent threats in hemisphere waters so as to give that much more immunity to British and Allied merchant shipping from surface and U-boat attack. It was the total political situation which demanded respect for the rules of law and made it advantageous to manipulate them to enhance the Royal Navy's advantages, or to minimise its disadvantages.

The sequel to the River Plate action, the *Altmark* incident, reveals the diminished role of law when the political and strategic situation is quite otherwise. In 1940 Great Britain, which was shortly to contemplate a military invasion of Norway (and was in fact to mount one of Iceland, although clever diplomacy succeeded in securing Iceland's reluctant acquiescence in the *fait accompli*) was not likely to be deterred by respect for the law of impartial neutrality from a minor invasion of Norwegian territorial waters (for the limited purpose of releasing British prisoners) when in fact Norwegian neutrality was a disadvantage and not an advantage to her. The record reveals that there was no hesitation in Whitehall in deciding upon the course of action to be taken, although it was realised that it would entail diplomatic complications with Norway which might be more or less serious and hence had to be presented in the best possible legal light. Had it been thought that Norway might have been driven by the action into the Axis camp the matter might have been viewed dif-

[1] See bibliography.

ferently, but Norway's friendship could be relied upon, and a demonstration of force with a strictly limited objective might be a useful warning that the German iron ore traffic through Norwegian waters might not be indefinitely tolerated. So the law, in this case, did not influence the outcome of events but was employed in the aftermath as a justification and a palliative.

The *Altmark* drama opened in the darkness of 14 February 1940 when the *Graf Spee*'s tender, with some of the merchant seamen aboard who had been removed from *Graf Spee*'s victims, entered Norwegian waters after successfully evading Allied forces during her movement from the south Atlantic. Interrogated by the Norwegian torpedo boat *Trygg*, she said that she was a tanker bound from the United States for Germany, had complied with the Norwegian neutrality regulations by dismounting her armament, and had no prisoners aboard. Legally speaking, then, she was invoking the right of innocent passage. Admiral Tank-Nielsen, however, had read in the newspapers of the *Altmark*'s role in the *Graf Spee* affair and he reported to the Norwegian government, after his chief of staff had gone aboard the *Altmark*, that there were probably prisoners on board. Inspection of the ship was refused by the German captain on the ground that it was a State ship, and so invested with sovereign immunity—a further attempt by him to use the law as a facility in attaining his objective of completing his voyage.

Admiral Tank-Nielsen was thus confronted with a situation where he felt he could not deny passage without proof that the vessel was non-innocent, but, although suspicious, he could not acquire that proof. He resorted to the usual expedient in such cases of compromise—by prohibiting the *Altmark* from transit through the Bergen defended area, which would have the effect of forcing her near the limits of the territorial sea but not into the high seas, and would be a gesture of Norwegian independence without a fatal compromising of the Norwegian government's neutrality. In the absence of any direction from the government he resorted to the most frequent weapon of the naval officer, prudence. It was a solution readily seized upon by the naval commander-in-chief, and it was ratified in a signal to Admiral Tank-Nielsen to let the *Altmark* pass, as a State ship, outside the Bergen defended area, under escort. Hopefully, Altmark could be hustled on her way before the British government realised what was happening.

The British government did, however, gain intelligence of the *Altmark*'s passage when she was only a few hours' sailing time from German air cover. Urgent action was necessary if the *Altmark*'s prisoners were to be released, and there was no time in Whitehall for legal debate. The decision being taken to recover the prisoners, Captain Vian, then patrolling to the north of the Skaggerak, was signalled '*Altmark* your objective. Act accordingly.' The *Altmark* had been two days in Norwegian waters when at dusk she was sighted, with her Norwegian escort, hugging the coast south of Stavanger.

The preliminaries to decisive action took the form, to which we have since become more accustomed, of games with the rules of the road in an effort to detach the *Altmark* from her escort, which insisted upon interposing itself between the hunters and their quarry with a view to preventing an incident in Norwegian waters. These manoeuvres forced the *Altmark* up the Jøssingfjord, where she was followed by the escorts, the *Kjell* and *Skarv*, and two British destroyers.

It has generally been overlooked in the legal discussions of the *Altmark* case that this involved an invasion of Norwegian inland waters, and thus went beyond any question of innocence of passage in the territorial sea. The *Altmark*, when she came to a stop against the ice at the head of the fiord, fell under the same rules of the Hague Convention as the *Graf Spee*, and the Royal Navy's threat to seize her there was legally no different from any attempt to cut out the *Graf Spee* in Montevideo, where no such design could be contemplated. The captain of the *Kjell* made his protests to Captain Vian, who politely but firmly informed him of his orders. When the *Kjell*'s captain demanded the withdrawal of the destroyers and rejected a proposal for joint inspection of the *Altmark*, Captain Vian withdrew outside the three-mile limit and signalled for further instructions.

These were personally drafted by Mr Churchill after a call to the Foreign Secretary. Captain Vian was told that unless the Norwegians escorted the *Altmark* to Bergen with a joint Anglo-Norwegian guard on board he was to board the *Altmark*, liberate the prisoners and take possession of the ship pending further instructions. If the *Kjell* or *Skarv* interfered they should be warned to stand off. If they fired upon the destroyers their fire should not be returned unless the attack was serious, when Captain Vian should defend himself, using no more force than necessary. The orders concluded that Captain Vian should suggest to the Norwegians that honour would be served by submitting to superior force—an admission that honour was involved because a coup was about to be effected in violation of Norwegian sovereignty.

When Captain Vian communicated these new instructions to the Norwegians they confined their reaction to further protests. H.M.S. *Cossack* came alongside the *Altmark* and boarded her; there was a scuffle in which shots were fired, and the prisoners were released.

While it would be naive to believe that belligerents will be disposed to abide by the rules of warfare in all circumstances, it would be equally simplistic to suppose the opposite, and that even in circumstances of declared war the law will always be without influence. The truth lies somewhere between, and the effectiveness or otherwise of the law will always be a matter of the gravity of the predicament in which a belligerent finds itself and of the political circumstances in which illegal action is contemplated. And one thing at least can be said, that in none of the cases where a deliberate breach of international law has been determined upon has the decision been taken without hesitation. To that extent the law has always proved to be an inhibiting factor, although the degrees of inhibition have obviously varied.

For example, Captain Vian quite rightly felt that it would be imprudent of him to board the *Altmark* in inland waters without further orders, and the Admiralty was not prepared to issue these without the highest political direction, even though the initial orders issued to Captain Vian were sufficiently broad to cover the contingency. Two centuries of legal restraints upon cutting-out operations in neutral ports had curbed the Nelson touch to the point where the onus of breaking the law had to be placed squarely upon the politicians. In the circumstances the latter took international law lightly. Captain Vian was even ordered to take the officers of the *Altmark* prisoner to England for interrogation if no prisoners were found in the ship, and it is inconceivable that any legal pretext could have been found for this.

The justification offered to Norway for the British action was that neutrals have a right and a duty to search foreign ships in the territorial sea—which, considering the fact that the *Altmark* was a commissioned ship, was hardly plausible. If it was implausible, the corollary that self-help was available to the British because of a failure on Norway's part to discharge a duty would be unsound. The fact that the *Altmark* might have breached Norwegian neutrality would be irrelevant, and it is not even clear that she did breach it merely by transporting prisoners of war through the territorial sea, since this was not non-innocent passage *vis-à-vis* Norway. The *Altmark* certainly breached international law by taking refuge in such circumstances in internal waters, but, by the same token, so did H.M.S. *Cossack* by attacking her there.

THE WORLD WARS:
UNRESTRICTED SUBMARINE WARFARE

It is difficult to find, even in the history of the Second World War, which became the classic instance of 'total war', a flagrant disregard of the law governing warfare at sea. Disregard there was, but it was usually dressed up in legal garb, or at least there was an attempt to put the blame for events on someone else, even if the justification could not be pressed to the point of invocation of the doctrine of reprisals. For example, President Roosevelt's undertaking to convoy Allied merchant traffic as far as Iceland, thereby relieving the Royal Navy from extended commitment in the western Atlantic, was presented as an analogue of the Monroe doctrine, although it was blatantly unneutral conduct according to the classical view of impartial neutrality; and when German U-boats did the only thing they could do to intercept the convoys—that is, torpedo a U.S. Navy escort after a period of avoiding escalation—the President denounced the action as 'piracy' and proclaimed, 'We have wished to avoid shooting. But the shooting has started and history has recorded who fired the first shot.'

In this case it may well be that the United States was deliberately courting German retaliation as a means of enhancing the political conditions within the United States for hostilities with Germany. The conscientious observance of the law was less important than the internal political objectives, but even then a semblance of lawfulness had to be contrived if the objectives were not to be compromised. The policy of unrestricted submarine warfare against Japan, covered by the orders of Admiral Nimitz, may be considered to be in breach of the rules of international law, although justified as a reprisal for Japanese breach of the law. The circumstances under which these orders came to be issued were quite exceptional, in that no political exigencies called for observation of the law, while strategic and tactical considerations favoured its neglect.

Only for a short period in 1942 and 1943 was Germany in fact in a situation where the law relating to submarine warfare was equally irrelevant. So long as important neutrals existed whose hostility had to be placated or whose co-operation had to be secured, the observance of the law remained an important element in the policy of restraint. The mere fact that these conditions did prevail allowed the law to become a factor of inertia in the process of making strategic and tactical decisions, and, to the extent that it complicated the process or confused the decisions, the law influenced, and arguably decisively influenced, the struggle for naval supremacy.

The steps by which Germany was drawn into unrestricted submarine warfare are significant because the lesson is prompted that unless naval policy is co-ordinated with legal and political policy the conduct of operations is seriously affected. Until February 1915 U-boats attacked only warships, but consideration was given to attack on British merchant ships when the British blockade was drawn tightly and the German navy began to suffer from frustration. The German naval staff wished to declare a war zone around the British Isles and to sink all shipping within it. The German Foreign Office said this would be contrary to international law and would provoke neutrals, and opposed the suggestion. The Chancellor, Bethmann-Hollweg, supported the political arm of the government, but in February 1915 gave way to permit the naval staff to declare a war zone and give notice[2] that 'every enemy merchant ship found in the war zone will be destroyed without its being always possible to avert the danger threatening the crews and passengers on that account'. At the insistence of the Foreign Ministry this declaration was dressed up in the form of a reprisal, so giving it superficial legal validity and enabling German diplomats the more easily to justify it—reprisal for the ordering by the British Admiralty on 31 January 1915 that British merchant ships should on occasion show neutral colours as a *ruse de guerre*, and reprisal for Admiralty orders restricting passage through and into the North Sea by neutrals to channels where blockade supervision would be possible, and the mining of the other approaches.

The United States protested at this declaration, but only respecting neutral and not British shipping. However, the protest caused such consternation and internal dissention in the German government that naval policy became paralysed. In the following six months 150 different and often contradictory orders were issued to U-boat commanders. The submarine campaign was on again, off again. Some orders required the commander to identify neutral shipping, but these were rendered abortive by a British Admiralty directive of

[2] *British and Foreign State Papers*, vol. 110, p. 1031.

10 February 1915 that British merchant ships should as closely resemble neutrals as possible, copying any particular lighting system of neutrals, and should attempt to ram submarines. It was during this period of confusion that the *Lusitania* was sunk, causing the Kaiser to intervene in the controversy between the naval staff and Wilhelmstrasse and to order that no passenger ships should be sunk. This was regarded by the U-boat commanders as hopelessly restrictive, since they had great difficulty in identifying through the periscope one class of ship from another.

During a vital period when the Admiralty was not organised to defend British shipping against submarine attack Germany pressed that attack home in a less than half-hearted way. She felt compelled to justify submarine attacks on merchantmen as exceptional in international law, but because policy had not been firmly laid down in Berlin the justifications were various and changing, and so lost their cogency in the eyes of neutrals and the belligerent public, and even of the German politicians.

First of all, Germany announced in February 1916 that all armed merchant vessels would be regarded as warships and sunk on sight. This followed the mounting of a 4 in. gun on the stern of some British merchant ships, and was almost a necessity for survival of U-boats when the advent of the Q ship meant that a U-boat would be exposed to fire when surfaced and attempting to follow the current rules of submarine warfare. Secondly, following an American protest at the sinking of the cross-Channel packet *Sussex* in March 1916, Germany declared that its naval forces were under orders to act 'according to the recognised principles of international law' and not to sink merchant vessels without warning and without saving lives 'unless these ships attempt to escape or offer resistance'. Since all British merchant ships attempted to escape or offer resistance, the argument implied that their sinking was acceptable to international law. When the United States pointed out that British misconduct of the war could not justify German misconduct the U-boat campaign quietened down until 6 October 1916, when U-boats were ordered to attack merchant ships only after giving warning and providing for the safety of the crews. This policy was attempted for some months, but it was found that the submarine was too vulnerable to surface gunfire, ramming and the deceits of the Q ships.

By early 1917 Germany was consumed with frustration, and on 8 January the Chief of Staff of the Navy presented a memorandum which showed how the submarine could turn the tide in Germany's favour provided no restrictions were placed on its use. Next day the government endorsed the memorandum, and on 31 January 1917 a declaration concerning unrestricted submarine warfare within the declared war zone was issued, and again justified as a reprisal for alleged British violation of international law in maintaining a distant blockade and extending the categories of contraband. The tremendous toll exacted by the U-boats in the spring of 1917 is the more remarkable in view of the fact that at no time during the entire war did Germany have more than 140 submarines in active service, of which about one-third would have been on operations at any one time.

The lesson to be drawn from these events in World War I is one of administration more than of law. Naval policy had not been firmly decided upon when war broke out, and the tussle between the naval staff, preoccupied with strategic and tactical considerations, and the Foreign Ministry, preoccupied with presenting a good case in international law so as to justify a firm diplomatic stance, frustrated naval policy at a crucial moment. The lack of foresight, planning and effective liaison between the navy and the legal and diplomatic services of the government became patently obvious early in 1915, and Germany's position was seriously weakened by her constant change of ground. In fact in international law Germany had a good case. She failed to exploit it effectively in neutral eyes and eventually roused the neutrals to anger. It is worth remembering that at the time of the sinking of the *Lusitania* the United States was just as much at odds with Great Britain over violations of the law of neutrality as she was with Germany over the submarine question. It is also important to remember that Germany's submarine policy was based on reprisals, and hence on an exception to a principle, so demonstrating the powerful influence that international law, vague and uncertain as it was, exerted on the situation.

After the war the problem of the submarine was for a time caught up in the general question of disarmament, and in this context attempts were made to outlaw it. There was a universal feeling that the sinking of merchant ships without warning should be forbidden, and this feeling led to the charging of eighteen German U-boat commanders before the German courts in 1922, only three of whom were actually tried, two for sinking hospital ships. On the charge of unrestricted submarine warfare the third officer was acquitted by the German Supreme Court on the defence of superior orders.

It was again France which led the move at the Washington conference in 1923 to defeat British attempts to ban the submarine. A

United States resolution which by implication would cover submarine warfare was, however, adopted. It stated that 'for the protection of the lives of neutrals and non-combatants at sea in time of war' the following rules were to be deemed part of international law:

1. A merchant vessel must be ordered to submit to visit and search before it can be seized. It can be attacked only if it refuses so to submit.
2. A merchant vessel must not be destroyed unless its crew and passengers have been placed in safety.

The resolution then went on to state that if a submarine cannot conform with these rules it must refrain from attack; and refusal to exercise such restraint would be regarded as 'piracy'. The matter again arose at the London Naval Conference of 1930, when Great Britain again made a bid to outlaw the submarine. The result was merely a reiteration of the proposition that 'in their action with regard to merchant ships submarines must conform to the rules of international law to which surface war vessels are subject'. In particular, except in the case of persistent refusal to stop on summons, or of active resistance to visit or search, a warship, whether surface vessel or submarine, might not sink a merchant vessel without having first placed the passengers, crew and ship's papers in a place of safety—the ship's boats not being a place of safety. When the treaty of 1930 was allowed to expire in 1936 the portions respecting submarine warfare remained binding on the parties, which took steps, however, to incorporate them in a new instrument, the London Protocol of 6 November 1936, which was acceded to by Germany and Soviet Russia as well as by many other countries, so that on the outbreak of World War II there were thirty-six parties bound by the London rules.

German surface raiders, at least in the early stages of the war, scrupulously observed these rules, and the thirty-nine U-boats which were at operational stations on 3 September 1939 were under orders to conform to them. It was with disbelief, then, that the German naval staff received the British news of the sinking of the unarmed and unescorted *Athenia* on the outbreak of war, and a strong denial was made. When U-30 returned to base, however, the fact was established. A controversy stirred the government, and the result was the issuing of further orders on 7 September that passenger ships should be spared, even when in convoys. The captain of U-30 was court-martialled for disobedience of orders, although he was acquitted on the defence that he believed the *Athenia* to be an armed merchant cruiser.

On 23 September 1939 the dilution of Germany's standards began when Hitler ordered that all merchant ships which radioed their positions when stopped by German submarines were to be sunk, and that all merchant ships except passenger ships might be sunk without warning, since it was to be assumed that they were armed in accordance with a British Admiralty directive. The order was withdrawn on 3 October 1939 and reimposed on 16 October, when it was added that passenger ships in convoy could be torpedoed a short while after notice had been given of the intention to do so. Admiral Raeder wanted to go further and lay siege to England, as he put it, but Hitler, under pressure from his Foreign Office, declared himself opposed to the flouting of international law for fear of neutral reaction.

Out of this tussle resulted a compromise, as in World War I, namely the declaration of a war zone around the British Isles which all ships would enter at their peril. An international law justification for this was offered on 18 January 1940. It was argued that mining in the interests of blockade is legal; mines destroy belligerent and neutral shipping indiscriminately; the war zone was an area within which mining would be legal; what difference was there between destruction by torpedo and by mine? From 1940 to 1945 unrestricted submarine warfare became universal practice, and the only significance of the war zone was that it was an area into which neutrals ventured at their peril.

Analysis of the conduct of the enemy against the background of international law can be a valuable means of ascertaining his belligerent policy, and so countering it, but there is a danger that a number of breaches of the law will be taken to indicate a policy of disregard for it, and the dispositions taken to deal with this policy may to that extent be mistaken and serve to hasten the dissolution of the law's authority. During 1939 and 1940 the M Branch in the Admiralty collected evidence of German disregard of the London Protocol and early jumped to the conclusion that Germany had no intention of observing the requirements of that instrument, without adverting to the possibility that there might, in fact, be disagreement about the matter in Berlin. On 6 December it was concluded that 'as time has advanced the proportionate number of illegal sinkings or attacks show a decided and consistent increase over the period reviewed'.

Illegality was attached by the Admiralty to any submarine attack made without previous warning to stop (thirty-six cases), mining in an unnotified area (sixteen cases), and neglect to take adequate steps to secure the safety of the passengers and crew (eighty-four cases). In addition, forty-seven neutrals were attacked. On 2 March 1940 the number of illegal attacks on British ships was an additional fifty-eight, and on neutral ships an additional ninety-eight. This appraisal led to the consolidation of the policies of arming British merchantmen, convoying them, and offering convoy protection to neutrals.[3]

At Nuremberg Admirals Raeder and Doenitz were among the major war criminals, and among the charges laid against them were waging unrestricted submarine warfare and violation of the London Protocol in the declaration of war zones. The prosecution assembled a great amount of evidence on these charges and the case was fully argued. After hearing Doenitz's defence that it was the British Admiralty that had taken British merchant ships out of the protection of the London Protocol, the tribunal held that 'in the actual circumstances of the cases, the Tribunal is not prepared to hold Doenitz guilty for his conduct of submarine warfare against British armed merchant ships'. So on this charge there was an acquittal. However, the tribunal held that international law created no exception for war or operational zones. In any such zones the ordinary rules should be followed. On this charge Doenitz was found guilty.[4]

EVALUATION

What emerges from the study of these occasions when the rules of international law were deliberately ignored in the pursuit of strategic and tactical objectives is that the circumstances in which this neglect is expedient or even possible are restricted, and that they have never arisen immediately upon the outbreak of war, nor even in its early stages, except when the action taken, as in the *Altmark* case, is of a highly limited character and constitutes no threat to the integrity of the victim—in that case Norway. Before international law has been discounted there has always been a graduated escalation of the war, to the point where no important neutrals stand aloof from the conflict, and the military situation has become so desperate that limi-

[3] Adm. I, 10244.
[4] *Trial of the Major War Criminals before the International Military Tribunal, Nuremberg* (1948), vol. 22, p. 558.

tations on the conduct of operations have ceased to be of persuasive value or political importance. Had Germany proceeded instantly to unrestricted submarine warfare in both World Wars she might have struck a decisive blow for victory, but the necessity for such extreme action was not then apparent and victory was not invested with the drastic qualities of national survival that were subsequently to become associated with it. Observation of the law remained an important condition of hostilities, and when its importance began to be questioned there was a period of inevitable internal struggle between those departments of State which resisted the flouting of the law and the armed forces who said the war could not be won unless the restraints were removed. The confusion of policy during this interim period seriously impaired the German navy in its conduct of the war. The United States found itself in the fortunate position of being able to proceed to a position where the law relating to submarine warfare was irrelevant without the indecision of this interim period, because the escalation had already been brought about by Germany's own conduct.

There was, during the early stages of the Cold War, a supposition that a future war between the nuclear Powers would be instantly absolute, with a total nuclear exchange. Obviously, if this occurred, all restraints on conduct would be removed, including the law. In these circumstances there would probably not be much point in discussing the influence of law upon sea power, but by the same token there would not be much point in discussing sea power either, since a nuclear exchange of this magnitude leaves little of the objectives of power or the instruments for its exercise. More sober assessments have discounted the probabilities of this instantaneous Armageddon and have accepted that even war between the major Powers is more likely to escalate progressively in terms of the commitment to desperate measures, as in 1914–15 and 1939–40. The law will thus continue to play its classical role in naval warfare until it is overtaken by this progression. The circumstances in which the law may become irrelevant are, therefore, unlikely to exist even in the early stages of a global conflict.

But if one discounts the likelihood of a global conflict at all, the chances for the law to influence the conduct of naval operations are obviously enhanced, since now the circumstances when it might become irrelevant are difficult to envisage. This does not mean that the rules of law will always be observed, for there will be situations where gains will be sought at the expense of the law. But inevitably they will be limited situations where the goals are restricted and the risks of escalation to a point undesired by the actor can be discounted. These will be actions of the *Altmark* character, one example being the Israeli helicopter raid on Beirut airport in December 1968, which was designed to intimidate the Lebanese government from continuing to allow its territory to be used as a base for guerilla operations against Israel, and others being the Israeli seaborne commando raids. Such raids, or the cutting out or destruction of ships in ports, are quite within the range of foreseeable options to countries at tension with one another.

The point, then, is not whether the law is breached but how it enters into the decision to breach it, what value it has in the circumstances compared with other values, and what influence it is allowed to have. It does not cease to be the law merely because it is relegated to a low level of priority, but neither should it be presumed that it will be so relegated.

CHAPTER V

LAW AND THE THEORY OF GRADUATED FORCE

Naval planning, while obviously concerned with the professional requirements of the global balance of deterrence, assumes, because of the very effectiveness of that deterrence, that actual conflicts at sea will be limited, at least initially. And while the United Nations exists and continues to exert its present measure of influence the chances of their remaining limited are high. Limitation implies restriction and prohibition, and these are features of law, which, to put it simply, has the unique capacity of characterising conduct and of measuring the scale of reaction to the threat or use of force. Rights and wrongs play a powerful part in the behavioural give-and-take that is significant of the use of sea power. A theory of the role that international law plays in contemporary naval planning is therefore possible, and is indeed central to naval doctrine.

The assumption behind the United Nations Charter is that the parties to a dispute will never resort to force but will resolve the dispute peaceably through the machinery of the United Nations or otherwise. If the assumption were correct there would be no need for navies, but since they do exist and are used, some less ambitious concept of law for the regulation of the use of force at sea must be resorted to. The function of law is not only to suppress the unlawful use of force but equally to invest States with rights to territory or jurisdiction, which often in this imperfect world cannot be guaranteed except by the use of force. This internal contradiction of the international legal system is resolved by the notion of self-defence, but resolved in a very unsatisfactory way because, when both sides to a dispute invoke the right of self-defence in assertion of their mutually contradictory territorial claims, it is unclear where the rights and wrongs lie.[1] At the same time it is a matter of common sense, as well as of law, that a use of force quite beyond the scale of what is required in the circumstances to maintain a claim effectively cannot be described as self-defence.

[1] Subject to the presumption of the lawfulness of possession. See R. Y. Jennings, *The Acquisition of Territory*, Manchester, 1963, in this Schill series, at p. 86.

Since aggressors hardly ever recognise themselves for what they are, and nations in conflict tend to believe that they are engaged in self-defence, naval operations will continue to be invested with the legal characteristics of self-defence. In a way it has always been so, but today there is the important difference that the law has changed since 1945 so as to deprive self-defensive operations of the benefit of the belligerent freedoms that classical international law endorsed for cases of naval warfare. There are now limitations upon what forces engaged in self-defence may do and where they may do it, for self-defence is not a release from all constraints but is measured reaction necessary to the occasion and proportional to the threat.

The framework for all this is Articles 2(4) and 51 of the United Nations Charter. The first forbids the use of force directed against the political independence and territorial integrity of another State, and the second reserves 'the inherent right of individual or collective self-defence against an armed attack'. If naval planning staffs had to digest the amount of ink that has been expended on the meaning of these two articles and the links between them they would never mount any operations. It is necessary to cut right through this thicket and clutch two central features that are politically irremovable, however much they may be gnawed into by legal exegesis. These are, first, that Article 2(4) is a catch-all clause which forbids the use of actual force altogether, and that such arguments as were floated during the Cuban 'quarantine' crisis—that interference with ships is excluded from it because not directed at political independence or territorial integrity—will not convince many delegations in the United Nations who like to see things in simple terms when they have no motive for complexity or sophistry; and secondly, that nations will invoke self-defence, and mostly get away with it, whatever the quibbles of the lawyers about whether the rights arising under Article 51 are limited to cases of clear violations of Article 2(4), or whether Article 51 is in substitution for older doctrines of self-defence, qualifies or modifies them, or is the sole source of the right of self-defence.

As a practical guideline naval planning staffs should take it for granted that the employment of force, as distinct from its manifestation—or of violence, as distinct from intimidation, if one likes—will be regarded as overstepping the boundaries of the legitimate, except when resorted to in self-defence. The real problem is what is meant by 'self-defence against an armed attack'.

This guideline expresses the law in tactical terms convenient to the theory of graduated force, which is a theory based upon the

LAW AND THE THEORY OF GRADUATED FORCE

assumption that any progression to an increased level of power will occur only in response to a failure on the part of the other protagonist to yield at a lower level. Both sides in this escalatory process can claim to be exercising the right of self-defence, and both may believe it. Provided that the process is controlled, the action and reaction can be made to appear legitimate, and the chances are that the objective—whether it be the balance of deterrence or persuasion of lesser Powers—will be attained without violence actually occurring, or, if it does occur, that it can be contained in terms of time, areas and levels. So long as confrontation can be conducted by legal means—as, for example, in taking advantage of the rules of the road to gain ascendency by interposition, thereby furthering the disputed interest by making it difficult for the opponent to challenge it—the law benefits the more adroit of the two parties.

This may result in the outwitted seeking to recover equivalence by resort to force: perhaps, in the first instance, collision; perhaps, in the second, gunfire. The objective of each side will be to put the onus on the other of breaching the law by taking the initial steps in the use of force, so that the victim can invoke the right of self-defence against an armed attack.[2] Once the benefits of self-defence accrue to a party, the idea that the measures of defence must be proportional to the assault does not mean that the victim must fight his defensive battle on the opponent's terms, but on the contrary warrants his moving to a higher mode of weaponry and to a greater degree of firepower. At the same time, if the political advantages of legality are not to be sacrificed, the level of response, while it may be further up the scale of force, must not be altogether disproportionate to the threat. It follows that at each level the graduations of force must be discriminating, and therefore deliberate, with clearly defined and limited goals in view.

THE CATEGORIES OF GRADUATED FORCE

At one time naval doctrine envisaged deterrence as a static situation maintained by the fact that appropriate weapon systems existed and were properly deployed. It was assumed that if an aggressor was undeterred by that fact the transition from peace (or at least from political tension) to nuclear war would be immediate. Experience gained during the several occasions when the United States and the

---

[2] See, for example, D. W. Bowett, *Self-defence in International Law*, Manchester, 1958, chapter IX, p. 182, 'Self-defence under the charter of the U.N.'

I.L.S.P.—3*   55

Soviet Union confronted each other in a struggle to achieve policy objectives—notably the Cuban quarantine situation in 1962—and reflection upon the way in which power could be exercised so as to influence events without resort to the ultimate crisis of an unrestricted nuclear exchange, led to the more subtle concept of graduated escalation. This concept excludes the notion of instant recourse to the final weapon system in the event of provocation, and it is resolved into three propositions, namely:

1. The practice of deterrence is reflected in a theory of escalation.
2. A theory of escalation presupposes adequate provision for naval operations at various levels of capability, ranging from initial response to nuclear exchange.
3. The concept excludes the relevance of the traditional boundary between 'peace' and 'war', upon which, of course, traditional international law is postulated.

The levels of escalation are classified by naval doctrine into four, namely:

1. *No-tension or low-tension conditions.* Naval operations at this level are designed to achieve a high state of efficiency, to make manifest the capability of maintaining the deterrence, and to demonstrate the effectiveness and cohesion of collective defence arrangements.
2. *Rising tension.* At this level naval operations may involve the purposeful application of limited force, either to achieve political objectives or to defeat another's political objectives by reinforcing the *status quo*. It follows that naval planning must anticipate the need for rapid adjustment to the scale of operations required, and that these be restricted in detail by means of rules of engagement so as to maximise the chances of attaining limited political objectives while minimising the chances of progression to the next level of force.
3. *High-level tension.* At this level all available resources are activated and the scale of operations involves considerations of concentration, intensity and duration. Again, political objectives and restraint on further progression are embodied in strict control through rules of engagement.
4. *Hostilities.* While the use of weapons is conceivable in high-tension conditions, it is thought that the manifestation of power and intent will be characteristic of the degree of the use of force, and that the fourth level alone will involve the employment of

weapons. Again, it is possible to envisage limitations on the use of destructive force so as to inhibit further progression to nuclear exchange.

It follows from the concept of graduated force that control and limitation are the primary characteristic, and that the law is an element expressing it. It follows, too, that the means of exerting graduated force appropriate to the various levels should be sufficient for the adequate pursuit of the political goals of the operation while at the same time being capable of confining the operation within the requisite limitations, including those expressed in notions of law. Appropriate to the levels of escalation, forces can be classified as follows:

1. *The initial response.* Single units or small numbers of units of low-capability general purpose, excluding ASW.
2. *Reinforcement.* High-capability surface ships suited to area defence, including, where appropriate, ASW and some backing with submarines, and afloat support.
3. *Higher-level operations.* Area control forces of all capability, with the function of controlling an area of sea.
4. *Strategic nuclear response forces.*

The central feature of Western thinking about the role of international law in graduated force is that self-defence is hardly ever likely to succeed as a characterisation of the initial act which sets in motion a process of escalation. If a legal justification is to be found for the instantaneous resort to a high level of force expressed in sea power it should be sought elsewhere than in the principles of necessity and proportionality. The fact that Article 51 did not make an appearance in the justification of the Cuban quarantine is an indication of this. In fact the device of the quarantine was resorted to not because it was the most legal method available but because it was the most strategically and tactically sound and the least risky of all possible measures. The law played a role in convincing the Russians of its limited purpose, but not much in the concept or even in the motivation.

Another important feature is that the introduction of naval forces is inseparable in escalation theory from diplomatic activity and is not a substitution for it. But negotiations have not always marched hand-in-hand with naval power—witness the Corfu Channel incident—and the possibility always exists of probes unaccompanied by threats, palliatives or proposals, or of abstract gestures in demonstration of the intention to exercise rights, as in the passage of the Lombok Strait in 1964 by H.M.S. *Victorious* and her escorts during Indonesia's confrontation with Malaysia.

It is possible, of course, that all this is only Western ideology, and naval planning staffs may have to take account of the possibility that the Soviet Union does not see the process in this way and may not play according to these rules. Russian writings pay little attention to the proportionality principle and express some contempt for the whole notion of limited war; Russian force, when actually used—which is, admittedly, rarely—is ordinarily overwhelming and never tentative. The nearest that Admiral Gorshkov comes to recognising that self-defence has a conceptual role to play in his study in *Morskoy sbornik* (1973)[3] of how international law affects Soviet naval thinking is in the following passage:

Only our powerful armed forces capable of blocking the unrestrained aggression displayed today all over the world can deter the aggressiveness of imperialism. In addition, of course, to the Strategic Missile Troops, it is the Navy which is this kind of force, capable in peacetime of visibly demonstrating to the peoples of friendly and hostile countries not only the power of military equipment and the perfection of the naval ships, embodying the technical and economic might of the State, but also its readiness to use this force in defence of the State interests of our nation or for the security of the Socialist countries.

There is not much deference to necessity and proportionality discernible in this summary of Gorshkov's theories.

THE CONCEPT OF SUPERIOR FORCE

If one of two parties engaged in confrontation is significantly weaker than the other it is incapacitated from defending the national interest, so that in a dispute over legal rights the superior force has the advantage of effecting a *fait accompli* without the risk of effective retaliation. The concept of superior force is essential both to the theory of graduated escalation and to that of legal self-defence: to the one because the disposition of an opponent to move to a higher level of force can be inhibited by the threat of more massive response; to the other because the availability of superior forces dictates the proportionality of defensive reaction, if it does not altogether sup-

[3] See chapter I above, p. 13.

press the use of force. Navies that are concerned with law-enforcement or law-and-order operations must have superior force available—if not on the spot, then by way of rapid reinforcement.

In the circumstances of declared war only honour or prudence could affect the determination to engage a superior enemy. But declared war has always been the exception rather than the norm in the history of sea power, from the days of Elizabeth I, when the legality of the depredations of her sea-rovers was a central issue in peaceful relations with Spain, to the innumerable instances in the nineteenth century where the naval Powers sought to influence events by establishing a naval presence. The primary rule of this type of diplomacy is that the presence must be sufficient to overawe opposition or to defeat it if encountered.

Usually the law will be a sufficient guarantee that the objectives of sea power will be achieved without violence, but this assumption must be matched with readiness for conflict if the manifestation of power is resisted, and with superior force to diminish the likelihood of its being resisted. A classical illustration of this rule is the confrontation between H.M. battleship *Royal Oak* and the Spanish Nationalist cruiser *Almirante Cervera* on 6 May 1937.[4] The cruiser's objective was the seizure of Spanish merchant ships carrying 2,500 Republican refugees from Bilbao. The battleship, escorted by two destroyers, interposed herself between the cruiser and the merchant ships. The legal situation now involved a contradiction between two groups of rules. From the Spanish Nationalist point of view there was jurisdiction over Spanish flagships on the high seas, which no other nation was entitled to resist (although, admittedly, the rules had become confused because of international action taken to confine the hostilities to Spanish territorial waters and the refusal of belligerent rights). From *Royal Oak*'s point of view the right of interposition followed from the manipulation of the rules of the road. If the *Almirante Cervera* could not board the merchant ships because the battleship was always in the way, or fire into them because they were shielded, her options were to yield to superior force, hold her course to the point of collision, or engage in some heroic but profitless demonstration of honour. By definition cruisers which ram battleships lose, and are imprudent if they engage them. One of *Royal Oak*'s escorts signalled that the *Almirante Cervera*'s torpedo tubes were unloaded, which demonstrated that the cruiser lacked the immediate capability of eliminating superior force and thus the inten-

[4] Cable, *Gunboat Diplomacy*, p. 101.

tion to do so. What is significant is that the escort took that possibility into account.

Predictably the parties to this confrontation confined themselves to legalities. The *Almirante Cervera* signalled to *Royal Oak*, 'I have orders from my government to stop any Spanish ship leaving Bilbao. I protest if you stop me in the exercise of my rights.' *Royal Oak* replied, 'I have orders from my government to protect them on the high seas.' These legal exchanges were the sum total of naval action, but it is important to observe the operation of the principle that in a case of conflict of legal rights the peaceful resolution of the conflict is likely to depend upon the availability of superior force and the readiness to use it. The basic rule was restated shortly afterwards in the following recommendation of the admiral commanding to the Commander-in-chief, Home Fleet, who forwarded it to the Admiralty: 'To avoid "incidents", i.e. the Spanish warship opening fire on a British merchant ship, or warship, the British warship present must be unquestionably more powerful than the largest Insurgent ship'.

The *Royal Oak* incident demonstrates that a situation can be contained and policy objectives secured by a demonstration of superior force. If the demonstration is supported by a solid legal posture the onus is placed on the other party, even when the overall legal situation is controversial, of moving to a condition of still higher level of force, wherein the legal situation is likely to become even more controversial. Escalation of force is normally accompanied by escalation in legal ambiguity. The decision to move to a higher level of force is never one to be taken lightly, and the accelerating insecurity respecting one's position that inevitably results from the progressive dissolution of the boundaries of legal clarity is itself a curb upon the policy makers.

Since an instantaneous resort to nuclear weapons is discounted as a likely expedient, even in Great Power confrontations, the theory of graduated force applies in all conceivable situations of the exercise of sea power, whether they be global or local, involving the Great Powers or trifling ones. The end of escalation may, indeed, be nuclear holocaust, but it is unlikely to be immediately reached, and at any level short of it the exercise of sea power will be inherently limited, and hence affected by the law, which aims at limitation and seeks restraint. All naval operations are, to this extent, limited and all wars are limited wars. In the system of global deterrence the law offers a set of rules which might, indeed, be swept aside but which, so long as the disposition to avoid nuclear confrontation exists on both sides, limit the options open to a protagonist which fears retaliation.

The game is one of bluff, as it always has been in conditions of tension previous to the outbreak of war. Neither the potential assailant nor the potential victim can be quite certain that a threat will not be followed by attack or that an attack will not be resisted to the point of mutually assured destruction. The difference between nuclear deterrence and previous conditions is that the calling of the bluff will inevitably lead to intolerable damage to the assailant as much as to the victim. It is therefore essential to convince a threatening nuclear Power that if its threat is executed it will be met with resolution. Sea power properly used can invest the resistance to threat with sufficient credibility to make the risk to the assailant unacceptable. The rules of law enhance the deterrence by establishing the boundaries of conduct within which power can be demonstrated without inducing panic or provoking incidents likely to lead to instantaneous violence.

There have been threats of nuclear warfare since the balance of deterrence was consolidated, but, except perhaps in the case of the Cuban quarantine crisis of 1962, they have been discounted because the retaliation would be totally disproportionate to the interests involved. For example, Krushchev thundered at the time of the American naval landing in Lebanon in 1958 that the intervention had brought the world 'to the brink of catastrophe', and he improvised naval manoeuvres in the Black Sea. The threat lacked credibility, for the Soviet navy remained remote and impotent. It is only when the balance of deterrence is itself threatened that the nuclear threat is taken seriously, and both sides have recognised in the rules of law a mechanism for controlling the escalation of force so that the balance will not be threatened.

It is from this point of view that the Cuban quarantine case is relevant. The main legal justification offered for the United States' action in intimidating the Russian merchant ships carrying missiles to Cuba so that they turned back was the Inter-American regional system rather than unilateral self-defence. There were obvious difficulties about any legal doctrine justifying the molestation of foreign ships on the high seas, and so it was encumbent on the United States planners, who included a fair measure of international lawyers, to devise a use of sea power that would convince the Soviet Union that vital American interests were engaged to the point where the landing of further missiles in Cuba would be resisted by whatever degree of force would be necessary, but also that this was the sole objective of the operation, which therefore involved a threat neither to the territorial integrity of Cuba nor to Russian communications with Cuba. To demonstrate that the action was not bluff, but also that it was strictly limited, it was necessary to mount a large-scale naval operation, be resolute in the interception of Soviet missile-carrying ships, but scrupulous in observance of the freedom of the seas in the case of other Soviet ships.

As it happened, it was convenient that a Soviet ship *en route* to Cuba without missiles was the first to reach the quarantine screen and was not intercepted, and also that the missiles were being transported in crates on deck so that full intelligence respecting the ships which needed to be stopped was available. This made it possible to convince the Russians that the objective was in fact limited to what was essential to the balance of deterrence. At the same time, it was necessary to deploy sufficient force to nullify the threat posed by the Soviet fleet units which entered the Caribbean in a demonstration of the freedom of the seas. This was an easy task, since the nineteen Soviet submarines which were deployed could be easily dealt with, and the approaches to Cuba are quite unsuited to submarine escort of merchant ships. The only realistic option open to the Soviet Union was to escalate to a higher and different mode of threat and to extend the boundaries of the issue beyond the limits of a local naval confrontation, for which the Red navy was not equipped but for which the United States Navy was resolutely prepared—a resolution which extended even to the Royal Canadian Navy.

There may not seem to have been much law in this singular event, but poker is not played without rules. The fact that the lawyers were prominent in the group surrounding the President during the crisis is sufficient testimony, of itself, to the influence of law upon events, and it is known that the legal consultations covered both the overall framework within which action was taken, including the justifications and presentation for world opinion, and the technical details of visit and search, boarding and the degree of force to be used to compel submission. It is at this lower level that the law took on more concrete characteristics and was not mere political window-dressing.

The Cuban quarantine was a highly successful exercise of definitive sea power, since it achieved its objective of elimination of a threat to United States territorial integrity without actual hostilities. Admittedly, Mr Krushchev's motives in putting the missiles in Cuba may have been only a matter of tit-for-tat, but it had graver psychological if not actual consequences for the balance of deterrence than he anticipated. The United States reaction was designed to reinstate the balance upon the conventional supports which had been established during the period when the nuclear weapon and the system of alliances evolved.

The incident demonstrates that the only options available to a nuclear Power which cannot match the sea power of its adversary are submission to the force of events or retaliation in an altogether different environment, where the risks of inevitable and unacceptable destruction to both sides are obviously much graver. The lesson is that it is possible for the nuclear Powers to confront one another upon the sea and seek by the exercise there of superior power to gain objectives which are challenged by the other protagonist. The ascendency of one Power over the other in this limited exercise of sea power is not only a matter of superiority of numbers or weapon systems or resolution but also one of graduated force, wherein the law conditions the modes whereby the force can be exercised without it becoming unacceptable.

The other lesson of the Cuban quarantine is that the exercise of sea power is apt to be strictly localised and governed by various rules of law respecting the areas of national and international jurisdiction. If the response is made in an area removed from the scene of an initial thrust, and in an altogether different mode, this would represent a degree of escalation that would not only be excessively dangerous but would tend to lack the characteristics of self-defence, thereby depriving the responding State of the political advantages of apparent legality. The essence of limited hostilities is that if they are to be rationalised on the theory of self-defence they will be limited as to theatre as well as to type, and this restriction is necessary if the progression to general war, which would in previous epochs have been thought inevitable once the process of escalation had commenced, is to be discounted in advance.

The only occasions since 1945 of instantaneous resort to the higher levels of naval warfare without the processes of graduated escalation occurring have been, apart from Korea, the Middle East wars and the Indo–Pakistan war, and only in the latter case has the conflict been allowed instantly to spill over on to the high seas. Elsewhere a classic pattern of graduated escalation, often logically connected with precisely defined areas of legal jurisdiction, is ordinarily discernible. The progression up the ladder may be rapid, as in the case of the battle of the Paracels, or it may be prolonged, as in the case of the naval war in Vietnam, where the striking at the North Vietnamese patrol base after the *Maddox* and *Turner Joy* incidents[5] was of a very limited character. The U.S. involvement in Vietnam arose out of the incidents. Although of a limited character, they initiated a progression that led eventually to the mining of Haiphong eight years later, which was a use of force that had been ruled out as inappropriate to the legal level of operations in 1968. In the confrontation with Indonesia the level of response was successfully kept low. Fishery disputes provide the classical instances of progressive use of force extended in time, the 'cod wars' being pre-eminently interesting in this respect.

PROPORTIONALITY OF RESPONSE

Vague as they may be, the boundaries of legitimate self-defence are inherent in the concept itself, and have been traditionally reduced to 'necessity and proportionality'. It is a matter of judgement in concrete instances what level and mode of response are proportionate to the assault, and all attempts to standardise the guidelines have proved unsuccessful because, as in the case of any other general principle of legal conduct, so much resides in the contingencies of a situation. The very notion of graduated escalation embodies the idea of a superior level of response so that proportionality is obviously not equated in naval thinking with equilibrium of action and reaction. But the pattern that has developed since the Second World War verifies two principles of conduct which express the doctrine of proportionality.

The first of these principles is that response, if possible, should be in the same mode. That is, harassment by manoeuvres is met with evasion or counter-harassment and not by gunfire. Where gunfire has been used, as in the fishing disputes, it is not met with counter-gunfire except where this is immediately necessary. Surface force is not responded to by submarine or air attack but is met by counter-surface force. There are exceptions to the pattern which are also justified by proportionality. For example, mining shifts the use of sea power into a different and more dangerous mode. It was ruled out by the United

[5] On 2 August 1964 the U.S.S. *Maddox* replied with gunfire to an alleged attack of North Vietnamese torpedo boats. At night, on 4 August, both *Maddox* and her consort, the U.S.S. *Turner Joy*, claimed to have been near-missed by torpedoes. For details see United States Naval Institute *Proceedings*, May 1972, p. 69.

States in 1968 in the case of Haiphong as a disproportionate exercise in self-defence in the conditions of warfare then prevailing. It was resorted to in May 1972 as necessary to restrict the overwhelming logistical support available to the forces of North Vietnam because other methods were inadequate, and it was thought then to be proportional because of the accelerated scale of supply to North Vietnam and of the North Vietnamese attack. But the restraint upon retaliation in a different mode remains a feature of the theory of self-defence in escalation policy.

The second principle is that response is confined to the geographical area of the attack. When the U.S.S. *Pueblo* was seized by the North Korean navy on 23 January 1968 while carrying out electronic surveillance the United States had the possibility of retaliation by seizing North Korean ships anywhere in the oceans; Portugal had the same possibility of seizing Indian ships when Goa was seized. All self-defence operations have in practice been localised, and from this experience it is possible to consider whether international law restricts naval operations in self-defence to the areas of national jurisdiction of the protagonists, and to those parts of such areas where the assailant's force is employed.

THE DEGREE OF INITIAL FORCE

When the captain of a fishery protection unit of a middle-grade naval Power signalled that a foreign fishing boat was defying arrest, and sought instructions, the naval authorities referred the matter to the political branch of government, and eventually the Cabinet was called together. A Cabinet Minister was reported to have enquired what the navy had guns for, and what had happened to the Nelson touch? Politicians expect navies to resolve the political predicament by decisions that they themselves are reluctant to take; navies know that if the decision is politically wrong heads will fall.

The question of opening fire in law-enforcement operations is a matter of great concern to naval staffs, and the tenacity of the law in this regard is not always sufficiently recognised. The only proper assumption to make is that fire is not to be opened until every other tactical expedient to effect arrest or resist threat has been tried, and patiently pursued, in vain; and that even then only the minimum degree of firepower is to be used. Otherwise the law-enforcement unit may be held to be in breach of international law.

During the Prohibition era a United States coastguard vessel pursued the Canadian-registered *I'm alone*,[6] which was engaged in liquor smuggling into the United States, and since it could not overhaul the quarry opened fire and sank it. The resulting dispute went to arbitration, and the tribunal laid down the law for naval guidance as authorising the use of necessary and reasonable force in visit and search, and if sinking should accidentally occur as a result the pursuing vessel might be entirely blameless. But the facts of the case were held not to justify the sinking.

During a dispute between Denmark and the United Kingdom over the fishing limits of the Faeroes, the Danish fishery protection vessel *Neils Ebbesen* put a boarding party on to the trawler *Red Crusader*,[7] which was alleged to have been fishing within those limits. The skipper of the *Red Crusader* succeeded in locking up the boarding party, and he sought to escape into the high seas, followed by the *Neils Ebbesen*. After half an hour the *Neils Ebbesen* fired one round of 127 mm shot astern of the trawler, and another ahead, while signalling to heave to. Fire was then opened on *Red Crusader*'s radar scanner and lights, and eventually a round of 40 mm hit the stem. All firing was by solid shot and took place in Danish territorial waters. The firing ceased, and *Red Crusader*, followed by the *Neils Ebbesen*, headed for British territorial waters. H.M.S. *Troubridge* interposed herself between the two vessels, so, according to Denmark's protest to the United Kingdom, permitting *Red Crusader* to escape.

In a diplomatic exchange between Denmark and the United Kingdom the latter claimed the cost of repairs to *Red Crusader*. The matter was referred to an international commission of enquiry, which found that the captain of the *Neils Ebbesen*

exceeded legitimate use of armed force on two counts: (*a*) firing without warning of solid gunshot; (*b*) creating danger to human life on board the *Red Crusader* without proved necessity, by the effective firing at the *Red Crusader* . . . The Commission is of the opinion that other means should have been attempted, which if duly persisted in, might have finally persuaded Skipper Wood to stop and revert to the normal procedure.

The commission found that the captain of H.M.S. *Troubridge* had made every effort to avoid any recourse to violence between the

[6] *Annual Digest of International Law Cases*, 1933–4, case No. 86. *I'm alone* reference R.I.A.A., vol. III, p. 1616 (joint final report), and in *A.J.I.L.* 29 (1935) p. 329; also R.I.A.A., vol. III, p. 1613 (joint interim report), and in *A.J.I.L.* 29 (1935), p. 326.

[7] For exchange of diplomatic notes in this case see Sir Francis Vallat, *International Law and the Practitioner* (Manchester, 1968), in this Schill lecture series, p. 79, and *I.L.R.*, vol. 35, p. 485 (1962).

Neils Ebbesen and *Red Crusader*. 'Such an attitude and conduct were impeccable.' The matter was settled after the commission's findings by a withdrawal of claims and waiver of rights of both parties.

The difficulty in drafting fishery protection instructions is that the question whether the use of weapons is 'excessive' remains a matter of judgement on the part of the captain. The *Red Crusader* case suggests that every device, including, presumably, harassment by navigational means, must be employed and for a sufficient period of time before force is justified. This puts the commander in a difficult position, for harassment can lead to situations where the rule of the road becomes unclear, and a collision may result.

In fact fire has been opened on several occasions in recent years. The United States protested to the Soviet Union at fire being directed at the American merchant ship *Sister Katinge*[8] in 1964, sixteen miles from the Russian coast, after the captain of that ship had quitted Novorossisk without clearance following an altercation with the Soviet authorities. The Russian action was characterised in a State Department note as an 'excessive method' of effecting arrest. One of the most energetic fishery protection actions carried out in recent years was that of Argentina respecting the Soviet fishing vessels *Pavlovo* and *Golfstrim* in 1968.[9] Argentina in 1967 enacted legislation drawing a 200-mile territorial sea from a baseline, and applied thereto a fishery law which requires all foreign fishing vessels to take out a licence and pay royalties in respect of catches within the territorial sea ($500 and $10 per ton). At the same time an agreement with Uruguay enclosed the River Plate, so that the 200-mile line is drawn on the outer side of this baseline. However, no agreement with Uruguay existed respecting the point at which the northern boundary of Argentinian waters was to be fixed, and administratively Argentinian authorities presumed this to be the Uruguayan three-mile limit. In the rectangle thus formed by this northern limit, the closing line and a perpendicular line drawn from the centre of the closing line the two Soviet vessels were detected fishing on 22 June 1968.

When the Soviet vessels resisted an order to stop made by the Argentinian destroyer *Santa Cruz*, and moved towards the high seas, the *Santa Cruz* fired five rounds of explosive shells, as a result of which the *Golfstrim* suffered two holes of 45 mm in the bow, three metres above the waterline, and a hole of 0·5 m below the waterline to port. Four cabins were destroyed. The two ships were then

[8] *Revue générale de droit international public*, vol. 68 (1964), p. 938.
[9] Not reported; private source.

escorted to Mar del Plata, where they were fined $25,000 and detained for twenty days until the fine was paid under protest by the Soviet shipping agency. The Soviet embassy in Buenos Aires delivered a note of protest against 'the illegal action of the authorities of the navy'. When a verbal reply was communicated to the effect that the matter was now one for the Argentinian courts no further Soviet protest was made. The Soviet took out the necessary fishing licence, and there the incident ended.

The fact that fire may have been opened without other possibilities of law enforcement being exhausted does not mean that this action is endorsed by international law, and the burden of proving the necessity of resort to weapons rests on the assailant. Some domestic legal systems may, indeed, contain no authorisation to open fire at all, and this seems to be the situation at common law. In 1841 the Admiralty lawyers advised their Lordships that there was no law or customs regulation authorising the firing with shot at any vessel 'quitting any port or harbour' in violation of the customs laws.[10] They said that the only law upon the subject of firing was the Smuggling Act of 1692, by which it was enacted that in case any vessel liable to seizure or examination under any Act for the prevention of smuggling should not bring to on being required to do so, or being chased by a ship of His Majesty's navy, it should be lawful, following warning shots, to fire into that vessel. On the other hand, in 1877 the Law Officers of the Crown advised that a foreign ship abducting British convicts could be stopped anywhere in the high seas, and 'in case she could not be stopped without resort to such a course we think it was lawful to fire into her'.

The apparent disparity between the two opinions calls for examination. A naval officer is not invested as such with any powers over civilians. His powers of arrest, unless enlarged by statute, are those of any citizen at common law. If he sees a crime being committed he may be competent to effect arrest and to use the requisite force, which might have been the case with the abduction of the convicts but would not be the case with breach of the customs law. The problem is that a naval officer does not go about veiled extraterritorially in the common law, so that his powers of arrest, and hence of force, outside his own or another national ship are questionable. The statutory draftsmen of the eighteenth century understood very well that they had to write in the power to open fire, and in some

[10] See O'Connell and Riordan, *Opinions on Imperial Constitutional Law*, London, 1971, pp. 122, 129.

common-law countries this is still done in fishery protection regulations covered by statute. Outside these rules the right of a naval officer to open fire at all is still questionable.

The English Law Reports contain three celebrated cases of Royal Naval captains being civilly sued for trespass or conversion in execution of their orders.[11] The navy has sheltered behind the common-law doctrine of Act of State to remove such cases from the jurisdiction of the courts, but that doctrine depends for its operation on nationality and location, and cannot be assumed always to be available. These internal legal difficulties suggest that naval staffs should ensure that there is proper domestic legal coverage for the operational orders they issue. In this day and age of human rights and civil liberties the Nelson touch may be no defence.

EVALUATION

Inherent in the concept of self-defence, then, are restrictions on the character of operations, the uses of operations and the weapons to be used in operations. Naval planning staffs must, it follows, consider the appropriate vehicles for initial thrust or response, the appropriate weapon mix, and the appropriate terrain of confrontation. To these it is now necessary to turn.

[11] *Buron* v. *Denman* (1848), 2 Ex. 167; *Walker* v. *Baird*, [1892] A.C. (P.C.) 491; *Carr* v. *Fracis Times & Co.*, [1902] A.C. 176.

CHAPTER VI

SELF-DEFENCE AND
WEAPON CAPABILITY

HOSTILE ACT AND HOSTILE INTENT

The basic assumption in escalation theory is that force will be progressively applied to achieve or defeat political goals without resulting in hostilities; and that if hostilities do occur they can be brought to a successful termination without progression to another mode of warfare or to other areas of conflict. Intrinsic to this assumption is the requirement, to put it simply, that the other side fires first, for then the use of force can be presented as self-defence. In fact the use of firepower, mainly in the form of gunfire, during the past twenty-five years has been so frequent that one can have little confidence that the resolution of disputes by the use of sea power will not result in the actual employment of weapons. The rules of the game thus require that the burden be shifted, if possible, to the other side in the event of a confrontation of warships, or at least that the opening of fire be necessary to enforce the law, as in the case of fishery disputes or protection of the revenue.

Technology has made of this a potentially lethal game, for weapon systems are so instantaneously activated, and homing or guidance systems are, in theory at least, so accurate and their terminal impact is so destructive, and the design of modern warships affords so little possibility for damage control, that the victim may well be deprived of the capacity for self-defence, and the assailant of the capacity for graduated force. The homing torpedo made navies aware of the problem early after World War II, and the progressive reduction in the detection rate in ASW as submarines have become quieter and take greater advantage of temperature layers so as to escape sonar waves—these factors have made naval staffs apprehensive of the problem of defence against a first strike. The fact that missiles presented an analogous problem became obvious during the late 1950s, but naval staffs seem to have been surprised and alarmed when in 1967 the Israeli destroyer *Eilat* was sunk by Styx missiles fired from a *Komar*-class patrol boat alongside in Alexandria harbour.

This brings operational analysis to the question of what constitutes an 'armed attack' within the meaning of Article 51 of the United Nations Charter. Is there room at all for any distinction between attack and imminent attack? Does the article exclude all anticipatory action in self-defence, when to await the launching of a controlled projectile from a potentially hostile contact may deprive the victim of the capacity of self-defence? In naval parlance the expression 'hostile act' is used instead of 'armed attack', and 'hostile act' is distinguished from 'hostile intent'. 'Hostile act' is apparently a broader concept than 'armed attack', for a hostile act may be committed which is not actual attack. For example, it might be thought that the pointing of guns or the locking on of fire-control radar would in certain circumstances amount to a hostile act, although it could not be said to amount to an armed attack. In naval parlance, therefore, the line between 'hostile act' and 'hostile intent' may not be as clearly defined as Article 51 would seem to require, if it is to be read literally.

Until the *Eilat* incident naval thinking assumed that hostile intent in times of limited war or high tension could be manifested or assumed only when a hostile act was actually committed. Hence operational orders tended to limit the expression 'hostile act' to the actual employment of a weapon. Following that event naval speculation experimented with clarifying the ambiguous borderland between 'hostile intent' and 'hostile act', so as to encompass the possibility of anticipating immediate attack so that the tactical advantage would not pass irrevocably to the potential assailant. This has usually taken the form of attempting to indicate the tactical indices of the point at which 'hostile intent' is ordinarily translated into 'hostile act', including combinations of such matters as the unhousing of a missile or the locking on of a fire-control radar in a firing position.

The legal and tactical possibilities of this approach to self-defence from the point of view of tactical indices will be examined after the problem has been expounded in the contexts of submarine and surface-missile attack.

Three expressions require definition for an understanding of the significance of these tactical indices. In an *active* mode power is emitted from a radar sensor set; the target reflects some of that power back to the originator, who then marks the time taken and the direction (the time taken giving range). In a *passive* mode the radar or sonar set collects energy not self-emitted. This energy comes from the target itself—for example, noise, radio, radar transmissions. The term 'locked on' is often used loosely, but it refers basically to the radar component of a fire-control equipment which is controlling itself to keep the target in the middle of the beam. When the radar has locked on to the target the fire-control problem can be solved, and where appropriate the gun or launcher can be aimed off, taking into account the movement of the target. In one method the set transmits an eccentric beam, and the returning target echoes are compared in a phase comparison technique to indicate in which portion of the beam the target is situated. The information is then used to direct the radar scanner in the direction of the target.

SUBMARINE THREAT AND ASW

In evaluating the question of the tactical indices of hostile intent in the case of submarines it is necessary to consider first the modes of submarine attack and detection, then the procedures of detection and positive identification, and finally the tactics to be adopted.

THE MODES OF SUBMARINE ATTACK AND DETECTION. Submarine sensors include vision, radar, electronic counter-measures (ECM) and sonar. Visual apprehension by means of the periscope when submerged remains the primary and the most reliable method of identification and classification in daylight. Submarine periscopes have kept pace in their development with the speeds and tactics of surface and air vehicles, so that the World War II balance of probabilities of sighting between submarines and surface vessels and aircraft has remained constant. Radar is an aid in air defence but is seldom used in tactical situations by submarines, which prefer to use passive sensor devices. Radar suffers from disadvantages which are to be discussed later. ECM is an important sensor in submarine operations because of a range advantage of about 2:1 over radar. By this means information on frequency, bearing, range indication and radar type is normally acquired. The most important submarine sensor is the sonar, which is limited by three physical laws: (1) range is inversely proportional to intensity; (2) directivity is dependent on frequency and hydrophone configuration, so that the lower the frequency the larger the aerial array required; and (3) wave distortion of sound rays occurs owing to oceanological patterns, namely density and temperature changes.

All these sensors suffer from inherent limitations. The factors affecting the periscope are its distinctive wake in calm seas at even moderate speeds; the curvature of the earth; upper lens fouling from ocean surface pollution, spray and swell; and vibration, particularly at high speed. The effectiveness of the searching radar depends upon sea-surface conditions. In a calm sea a periscope can be easily detected by radar, but in heavy weather would be lost in the sea-surface echoes painting on the radar screen. ECM normally provides information on frequency, bearing and other characteristics, but is unreliable with respect to range, owing to the necessity to estimate the power output of the aircraft or ship detected, which is often varied as a tactical means of confusing submarine operators. The capability of the sonar has hitherto been restricted by a lack of adequate scientific knowledge of areas of the sea, as well as by technical limitations. Passive sonar arrays are dependent on a quiet listening background, and so submarines have evolved techniques of minimising self-noise so as to increase their listening effectiveness and decrease their chance of being detected by a passive enemy sonar.

ASW is conducted by surface vessels, fixed-wing aircraft, which are valuable against snorting submarines (i.e. submarines employing a snorkel) but of limited use against high-speed nuclear vessels, and the rotary-wing aircraft which were a significant advance in anti-submarine warfare. A helicopter can assume an active or passive sonar role by lowering a listening device into the sea, and it is currently invulnerable to submarine counter-attack. It is limited by weather conditions and in sonar range. Shore-control fixed acoustic arrays are not so effective as was originally hoped, owing to high background ocean noise level and general ignorance of sonar transmissions through ocean patterns, though they are a significant factor, and raise important naval implications for proposals to 'internationalise' the deep sea bed. The siting of such arrays on one's own continental shelf might be a defensive action, but if they were placed around a foreign naval base, and even upon a foreign continental shelf, they might be offensive in purpose.

DETECTION AND POSITIVE IDENTIFICATION. Since self-defence measures centre upon distance and evasion, the first requisite of their success is early detection of a threat. Modern methods of detection have impaired the traditional ability of warships to make surprise appearances over the horizon, and early warning equipment, including the use of satellites, has vastly enhanced the possibilities of early intelligence. Whereas before the Second World War naval forces had to make their intentions known before they could be considered a threat, today NATO and Soviet forces are plotted by each other even when not visible, on the assumption that each is a menace to the other. But it is not always thus. Many navies lack the equipment and training for long-range, accurate intelligence, while submarines in present circumstances are not easily tracked and may be detected by an escort's sensors only when the range is dangerously close. Detection is a combination of the physical and intellectual. Data acquisition by means of equipment is followed by data processing, and a certain sophistication of judgement enters into the picture, which requires standardised methods of evaluation of the indices of positive identification and hostile intent. The scheme in the case of ASW is set out as follows.

Contact with a submarine may be made by surface vessel, another submarine or aircraft. The first two rely principally upon sonar, which may be either shipborne or in the form of a towed array. Such arrays are of two types, search and tactical. The former are streamed at depths to more than 1,000 metres and at distances of several miles, and have detected submarines at astonishing ranges, while the latter are lighter versions streamed at much less than one mile and with much shorter detection ranges. The disabilities of towed arrays are that efficiency is inverse to speed, launch and recovery times are long, and changes of course are restricted.

Sonar being directional, the procedures of detection and localisation are phases only. In the case of aircraft used in an ASW role, however, the procedures vary as between detection and localisation, through the following means:

1. *Detection*

(a) *Radar.* Its use depends on the conditions at the time, but because it operates in the active mode it warns the submarine of its presence. Radar is effective only when a submarine is displaying one or more masts above the surface.

(b) *LOFAR* (low-frequency analysation and recording). This is contained in a sonobuoy dropped from the aircraft which transmits its contact information to the aircraft. It gives no information to the submarine of its presence.[1]

---

[1] LOFAR is a means only of detecting the presence of a submarine, not of locating it. It is non-directional, that is, it does not give a bearing on the submarine. A forthcoming development of the sonobuoy is directional, and is thus partly an aid to location as well as to detection.

(c) *ECM* (electronic counter-measures). This is useful only when the submarine transmits on radar, or radio, which is rare.

(d) *Visual.* The submariner should sight the aircraft before his periscope is itself seen.

(e) *IRLS* (infra-red line scan), which may be operated from a satellite and operates on detection of heat levels. It may be the major development in ASW of the future, though it has limited value against deeply submerged submarines.

(f) *Sniffer (ETI).* A code name for an exhaust trail indicator which detects the exhaust emitted by a snorting diesel submarine.

2. Localisation

(a) *CODAR.* A phase of the dropped sonobuoy which is localised to less than four miles. Both LOFAR and CODAR are contained in a sonobuoy operating on the passive mode, and known to the Western navies as JEZEBEL. It detects in its true mode the low-frequency sound emitted by a snorting submarine. The difference between LOFAR and CODAR consists in a shift from a low-frequency spectrum which has lower attenuation in the water, and so a longer range, to a higher-frequency spectrum with better direction but shorter range.

(b) *Sonobuoys,* which may be passive or active.

(c) *MAD* (magnetic anomaly detection), a passive device for close-range detection depending on the changes induced in the earth's magnetic field by the submarine. The aircraft must almost fly over the submarine for it to be effective.

The United States Navy *Tactical Aid* (TACAID) lists six ASW situations in times of ostensible peace, with directions as to the action to be taken respecting each. This must be taken as a guide to the practice of States, since it has gained general naval currency, and is familiar to and apparently acquiesced in by the Soviet navy. These situations are:

1. Where a submarine is detected in the act of attacking 'friendlies'.
2. Where a submarine is detected in the act of launching a missile.
3. Where 'friendlies' are detected in the act of prosecuting a submarine contact and the question of joining in arises.
4. Where an unidentified submarine is detected in inland waters.
5. Where an unidentified submarine is detected in territorial waters.
6. Where an unidentified submarine is detected on the high seas.

There is a scale of levels of response laid down, depending upon the situation. Obviously action will be immediate in the first two situations, and the transition from interrogation to attack may, in the nature of the distinction between inland waters and the territorial sea, be more immediate in situation 4 and in situation 5.

The principal difficulty in submarine contacts is that of positive identification, and it is for this reason that procedures must be followed carefully to avoid a threat to submarines exercising the freedom of navigation and not themselves in a threatening posture. The NATO and United States naval procedures depend on a classification scale of four levels, each of predetermined criteria, as follows:

1. *Non-sub.* This is where sensors have not provided evidence of a contact but the indications point to it not being a submarine.
2. *Possible sub.* This is where sensors have provided some evidence of a contact, and the category is subdivided into four confidence levels based on the information received and the number of sensors in contact according to a classification code.
3. *Probable sub.* This is where at least two sensors provide certain classes of information which lead to the evaluation concluding that there is a probable submarine contact.
4. *Certain sub.* This is where visual identification makes for certainty.

Once a submarine contact is made, the next step is to follow up with all available sensors to attempt to achieve either a 'certain sub', or a 'non-sub', classification. Sensors available to the escort vessel are mainly centred around the active sonar set. The type of echo is an indication, and a 'woolly' echo would suggest an object less solid than a metal hull. Wrecks lying on the bottom are charted, so far as is possible, but the task of choosing between an uncharted wreck and a bottomed submarine is difficult. 'Doppler', the change in sonar echo pitch due to target movement, is an excellent classification aid, but many a submarine contact has turned out to be a whale. A well trained and well maintained submarine would not normally make a noise to give a clue to its existence—such as hammering or running noisy machinery—while it knew an escort to be investigating it.

Fixed-wing ASW aircraft have the advantage of not producing background noise in the water close to their sonobuoys and so have developed passive classification aids. Hence LOFAR print-outs of a submarine's noise characteristics will often give specific detail of the type of submarine being tracked. Provided the sonobuoy is operating under good conditions, this type of information can lead to positive identification of a submarine. Once the type is ascertained, nationality may be automatically attributed.

SUBMARINE AND ASW TACTICS. The tactics used in any situation will depend on the priorities detailed in the respective war orders of the participants. Traditionally the submarine has been better employed in sinking or damaging the heavy units of the opposing fleet—this includes the merchant marine, particularly tankers. Opposing escorts have usually concentrated on the 'safe and timely arrival of the convoy', with the destruction of enemy submarines a welcome bonus but subsidiary to the main task.

A submarine's opening tactic will usually be to locate the enemy force. To achieve this it will combine the shore intelligence transmitted to it with the radio, ECM and sonar interception it is able to achieve at sea. It will change depth to use surface or deep sonar channels, alter course and speed to close possible targets, always attempting to avoid detection by enemy air, surface or submarine units while achieving its primary aim.

The protecting units, on the other hand, will make every effort to harass, decoy and intercept the submarine before it attacks. Where detection is made, the heavy units will usually be re-routed while the escorts intercept and attack the submarine. Identification problems of determining that the submarine is, in fact, enemy are normally avoided by ensuring that no friendly submarines are in the areas in question. Where friendly and enemy submarines are both in the same area of water the problem of identification is most difficult— almost impossible—and the friendly submarine will probably be ordered to surface, thus rendering it ineffective in the action and also vulnerable to attack.

While the surface vessels in the past normally had a speed advantage over their submerged adversaries, the nuclear-propelled submarine has reversed the situation. This vessel can cover large areas of the ocean in the search for targets, and carry out multiple attacks once the target is located. Another aspect is that missile-firing submarines may launch at a range well outside effective sonar detection, which means that they may never come within the defended ocean area. In this case the combination of advanced friendly submarines and heavy maritime aircraft cover is the common tactic to prevent launching; anti-aircraft guns and missiles are used to intercept missiles in flight before they reach the target area.

SELF-DEFENCE AND TACTICAL INDICES IN ASW. The legal situation respecting submarine warfare as expounded by the Nuremberg tribunal in the Doenitz case[2] could not be more explicit or more simple: the submarine is subject to the same rules as a surface ship provided that its operations are governed by no greater risks. When the enemy's merchant ships are convoyed, or when they are instructed to defend themselves by any means against submarines, or when the submarine is exposed to disproportionate risk of air attack (to which it is highly vulnerable) by surfacing to save passengers and crew, the submarine is exempted from the provisions of the London Protocol of 1936,[3] which is therefore of legal relevance only in the situation where the submarine can act with minimal risk on the surface. Since in practice that situation is hardly ever likely to occur in time of war, whether general or limited, it must be admitted that the only legal restraints upon submarine warfare are those common to any vehicles of sea power, namely self-defence.[4]

The problem from the point of view of the submariner is that a submarine is not a vehicle adapted to self-defence operations. It cannot operate on the surface without disproportionate risk and it cannot respond to attack upon itself or those it is protecting except by torpedo; and the alternative to the use of torpedoes is withdrawal or manoeuvre. The problem of ASW is to ascertain that a submerged contact, once the level of positive identification has been obtained, has a hostile intent which may be translated into a hostile act. It may be determined, from the plotted track of the submarine, whether it is in transit and only accidentally in the operational area, or whether it is tracking the surface forces or the shipping which the ASW escorts are protecting. But no amount of evaluation will determine whether the submarine is exerting pressure on the surface forces by manoeuvre or preparing to attack, for it is impossible for anyone outside a submarine to know its state of readiness. A raised periscope could merely be observing the surface scene as a seamanlike precaution to avoid collision, or it could be taking a final range and bearing prior to firing a weapon. Submarines generally avoid the use of radar, but detection by an escort of the use of radar by a submarine could be unimportant; or it could be the final check of range before firing. In the case of sonar, the most important sensor in ASW, a surface vessel will have no indication of whether a submarine is

---

[2] See above, p. 50.   [3] See above, p. 48.
[4] See the Peleus case, *Law Reports of Trials of War Criminals*, vol. 1, H.M.S.O., London, 1947, p. 1.

tracking it on passive sonar. The surface vessel can only assume, when it makes a submarine detection, that the submarine is likely to have been tracking it for some time and might already have made all preparations to launch its attack.

Except in time of open naval hostilities, such as the Indo–Pakistan war of December 1971, the operational use of submarines thus presents dilemmas to both the submarine and the ASW forces. If there are no valid indices of the translation of hostile intent into hostile act on either side, the criteria for self-defence are deficient. Deployment of submarines in the operational areas of surface forces in time of high tension can therefore be met only by systematic prosecution of harassment tactics on the part of the ASW escorts to keep the submarine out of torpedo range of a convoy. The balance of self-defence may thus depend upon the respective levels of professional proficiency of the rival forces.

A CASE STUDY: THE SPANISH CIVIL WAR. On 12 August 1937 the Admiralty advised the Commander-in-chief, Mediterranean, that it had secret information that Italy intended to start unrestricted submarine warfare, and the following day the French ship *Pavane* was attacked by a submarine off Tunis. In the following few days two Spanish ships, the *Cuidad de Cadiz* and *Armira*, were sunk in the Aegean, and on 31 August attacks began on Russian ships when the *Timiriasev* was sunk off Algiers, the *Balgoev* and the *Molakieff* off Skyros, while the Greek-owned British tanker *Woodford* was sunk off Valencia. In all these cases no attempt was made to rescue survivors.

The fact that this conduct was manifestly in breach of the law did not imply that the Royal Navy was released from constraint, although it did mean that it was in a situation of high tension where active measures of self-defence were necessary. The rules that now came into play in the conduct of its operations were the traditional ones of necessity and proportionality. On 31 August–1 September 1937 H.M. destroyer *Havock* was, according to the warning of a look-out, near-missed by a torpedo while on the Non-intervention patrol and while its anti-submarine operators were not closed up. Doubts have been expressed as to the reality of the attack, just as they have been expressed as to the reality of the attack upon United States destroyers in the Gulf of Tonkin in 1964, but, be that as it may, the *Havock* immediately turned to port, activated the ASDIC and gained contact. Shortly afterwards a submarine was sighted in the darkness on the surface about 400 yards away, and it dived. ASDIC contact was lost and was not regained for three and a half hours, when the *Havock* attacked with a full pattern of depth charges. The rest of the flotilla arrived shortly afterwards and a sweep was made, but contact was not gained until 12.27 that day, when the *Hardy* was ordered by the Rear Admiral (Destroyers), Rear Admiral Somerville, to drop one depth charge in an attempt to force the submarine to the surface, but to take no other action. At 12.45 a signal was received from the Admiralty ordering that no attack was to be made because of the lapse of time. Count Ciano in his diary identified the submarine contacted as the *Iride*.

The interaction of legal and operational considerations in this incident are particularly revealing. From the professional naval point of view the failure of the *Havock* to maintain contact painfully shattered illusions as to the effectiveness of ASDIC in wartime, and the initial disposition was to believe that the captain of the *Havock* was to blame for not prosecuting his first attack sufficiently. At the board of enquiry held at Gibraltar the understanding seems to have been that he had the full endorsement of the right of self-defence and should have exercised no restraint. It was acknowledged, however, that as time wore on the right waned, both because of doubt whether the regained contact was in fact the culprit and because, even if it was, retaliation would be more difficult to classify as self-defence. Again the parallel between this situation and the air strikes at the North Vietnamese bases that followed the Gulf of Tonkin incident is to be noticed.

New orders to the fleet were required by the incident. The Commander-in-chief, Mediterranean, instructed Rear Admiral Somerville that any contact was to be followed until it surfaced and could be identified. (Submarines in those days had limited underwater endurance.) On 18 August 1937 general instructions were issued by the Admiralty that a submarine detected submerged within five miles of a torpedoed merchant ship was to be hunted and sunk, as also any identified submarine within this distance which dived. This solution is of particular legal interest. It implied that a hostile act had to be committed before attack was authorised; but when it was committed a type of war zone would exist for five miles around the scene of the act, within which any submarine could be destroyed. Modern naval doctrine, which has examined intensively the problem of the submarine threat in time of tension but not war, has failed to come up with solutions very different from this one.

The Spanish Civil War is the only occasion when submarines have been used outside the conditions of open warfare at sea, and they were used here because their anonymity made their attacks non-attributable. This is why at Nyon these attacks were characterised as 'piracy'. The use of submarines drove home two lessons: on the side of the assailant that they involve a dangerous level of escalation because the force they exert can only be extreme, and that anonymous though they may be their masters court the risk of violent reprisals (Mr Eden's proposals for bombardment, for example); and, on the side of the victim, that positive identification is difficult and that unless the response to their attack is immediate, and contact is maintained, the necessity of self-defence quickly vanishes and the risk of attacking an innocent submarine arises. The freedom of the seas exercised then, and does today, a restraint upon ASW vessels that makes reaction to a hostile submarine threat very difficult to counter in practice, but equally makes the submarine a very dangerous vehicle of sea power in time of limited hostilities.

MISSILE THREAT

The tactical problem of self-defence posed by the missile is one of estimating the risk of awaiting the launch of a missile, and thus of calculating the time scale of reaction and interception. A missile travelling at the speed of sound and launched at a range of fifteen miles will take about seventy-five seconds to reach the target. It will take the target's radar scanner some seconds to detect the missile, and it will take additional time to evaluate the situation, decide on counter-measures and release the target's missiles on an interception course. It now becomes a question of calculating the chances of the target being hit, supposing it cannot intercept the missile much outside the radius of damage, and of determining whether missiles shall be fired at the threatening vessel, which will be possible in the time scale before the target's own missile system becomes totally engaged in interception of the incoming missile. The question for discussion is whether this is the only measure of 'pre-emption' permitted by international law.

In the case of long-range missiles of up to 100 miles the problem is more difficult, for, owing to the curvature of the earth, these may be most effectively used against surface targets when guided from aircraft after launch, or in the future from satellites. In this case the guidance radar will be flooding the target area with illumination, and the echoes from the target will be intercepted by the missile. There is no ECM method whereby the target can detect that a missile is being guided, but the missile may be tracked once it is launched. In this case the time scale for reaction and interception is much larger, and measures can be taken against the aircraft if it has been positively identified. At present there is little disquiet respecting the capability of long-range surface-to-surface missiles, because of the greater range of possible failure, and it is sufficient for immediate purposes to investigate the question of self-defence against short-range missiles.

The future problem may centre on the infra-red homing of missiles, which eliminates the radar guidance system, and hence the detection of intent to launch. But the acquisition range of such a missile is short, owing to the rapid attenuation of heat, and at present the attacker would have to close the range to the point where the target's own means of reaction would be more effective.

Naval proposals to resolve the problem have taken the form of indicating the indices of translation of 'hostile intent' into 'hostile act'—for example, a combination of several factual circumstances, including identification by means of ECM when the potential attacker's radar guidance system has 'locked on' to the target, supposing that the missile is 'beam-riding'. It has been argued that this is the moment of 'armed attack' and the moment when measures of force in self-defence may be undertaken.

EVALUATION: THE CONCEPT OF INITIAL CASUALTY

Experimentation with technical and tactical indications of the translation of 'hostile intent' into 'hostile act' is generally thought to have been unsuccessful because the indices, from a purely naval point of view, do not yield a sufficiently fine definition or operate with the requisite certainty. Some of these indices, such as the opening of a missile housing on a patrol boat, depend on visible apprehension, which is unlikely to be available; others depend on electronic information which, especially in a moment of excitement, but always in conditions of atmospheric or sonar aberration, may, because of anomalous propagation or human error, give false or ambiguous responses that may be taken as indications of enemy action. Sonar classifications, in particular, are unreliable. And since a combination of indices is relied upon, their coincidental detection is likely to be fortuitous rather than assured.

In the absence of more precise tactical indications of an intended hostile act, naval thinking is returning to its point of departure some twenty years ago, that weapon systems may be activated in self-defence only in response to the discharge of a projectile by the other side. The implications are that in the exercise of sea power one must expect to sustain an initial casualty before going into action under the cover of self-defence; that a single-unit operation will be ruled out because the fragility of modern warships, which are built to evade and not to sustain damage, makes them excessively vulnerable to any form of first strike; and that the fact that the threat the unit poses could be eliminated in one blow may tempt a degree of escalation that would not be contemplated if other units were present and available for instant and overwhelming retaliation. It follows that the conclusions reached on the problem of self-defence will dictate the scale of superior force, together with the attendant fleet dispersal and logistic considerations.

It does not follow from these conclusions that an initial casualty will in fact be necessary, or that reluctance to contemplate it will seriously inhibit resort to sea power. The tactical doctrine of pre-emption is based on the hypothesis, which the *Eilat* sinking is alleged to verify, that the ship against which a missile is launched has little chance of survival. It must be remembered, however, that the *Eilat* sinking occurred in conditions exceptionally favourable to the attacker, including launch from a craft alongside in harbour, when the respective positions of launcher and target could be fixed with minimal error, in the most desirable weather conditions, and against a ship which had no capability of intercepting the missiles except gunnery. The same is, by and large, true of the more recent occasions of instant destruction by missiles, notably the sinking of the Pakistan destroyer *Khaiber* and of the South Vietnamese frigate at the Paracels. Although surface-to-surface missiles constitute a serious threat, they are in fact not so reliable as to imply the automatic destruction of the target. The failure rate in launchings is high, the chances of interception by the target's surface-to-air missile system are good, the decoys are reasonably effective, and evasive tactics of the target are helpful. And while these are considerations which time and technological developments will alter, the statistical chances of success in an opposed missile strike are never likely to be so high as to preclude altogether the risks of using sea power.

As for submerged attack, the chances of torpedo strike will always remain high, but torpedoes will always have a finite range which is unlikely to exceed the range of detection. If detection is prompt and the escorts are skilful in fending off the submarine so that it does not get within range of the target, and in evading or decoying a torpedo launched at themselves, the risks of a submerged first strike likewise are not likely to be so high as to preclude resort to sea power.

If attack upon a contact which is believed to be hostile is to be ruled out because other alternatives are available, it is necessary that these alternatives be effective; they are all reducible to the question of the standard of naval proficiency, and the high state of readiness, training and maintenance. The requisite level of proficiency is unlikely to be reached where Treasury policy inhibits practice; and parsimonious governments have the choice of abandoning any ambition of peace-keeping and law enforcement at sea, let alone of coercive use of force, or of depriving their naval forces of the one capacity for self-defence and balanced escalation which the law appears to allow them.

CHAPTER VII

LEGAL RESTRAINTS ON
WEAPON SYSTEMS

MODES OF WEAPONRY

Because limited war is susceptible of tight control it is possible for it to be conducted at a high level of violence but in a low mode of weaponry. The concepts of necessity and proportionality appropriate to the theory of self-defence regulate the progression to the higher modes of weaponry and tend to exclude them at the level of initial response. The fact that low-level weapon systems are essential to the notion of limited war, and that doubt arises respecting the circumstances of resort to the higher levels, has a bearing on operational planning, on the drafting of rules of engagement and ultimately on procurement policy. This is especially the case where neutral rights are likely to be seriously affected. The supposition underlying much naval planning since 1945 that naval warfare will involve total war at sea, in which the most destructive category of weapons will be used, has been largely belied by events. The submarine has been used only in the instances of open warfare in the Middle East and between India and Pakistan, and missiles only where there was no risk of effective retaliation (except in the October 1973 Middle East war, when there were exchanges of Gabriel and Styx[1] missiles leading to the destruction of the Syrian vessels without damage to the Israeli ones). The most protracted and extensive naval operation has been that of the Vietnam War, which according to all naval hypotheses was of the most improbable type. The primary—indeed, almost the only—weapon used there was the gun, although in theory a fleet could not establish a gun line in face of land-based missiles.

By characterising conduct as self-defensive, and thus making it tolerable to political judgement, the restrictions of the law obviously play their part in defining the scope of operations by reference to the mode of weaponry.

It is not proposed to discuss here the question of the legality of the use of nuclear weapons as such, since it is a topic so politically

[1] See p. 88 below for types of missiles.

charged and jurisprudentially so complex that it escapes the confines of the present investigation, and also because, if it came to the point where strategic nuclear weapons were resorted to, the boundaries of limited war would have been passed and the law would have little relevance. But the law is very relevant to the question of the resort to weapons and to delivery systems which are intended to be used in a discriminating fashion against restricted targets for limited ends, whether or not they are capable of carrying either conventional or low-yield tactical nuclear warheads. The requirement of maintaining satisfactory relationships with important neutrals so as to gain political ascendency over an opponent is always present in conditions short of total global war, and the need to respect neutral persons and property and to distinguish between military and civil targets constitutes a curb upon the deployment and use of particular types of weapon. Three such types will be discussed: missile attack, naval gunfire support, and mining.

MISSILE ATTACK

The employment of naval missiles represents a high stage of deliberate escalation, and the fact that they are being resorted to with greater frequency and diminishing discrimination in the definitive use of sea power suggests that we have moved into an altogether different and more dangerous milieu of limited war than we have hitherto experienced. Since the sinking of the *Eilat*, missiles have been used in the Indo-Pakistan war of December 1971, the Middle East war of October 1973 and the battle of the Paracels in January 1974. In all these engagements the destructive capacity of the missiles and the vulnerability of targets which lacked the means of effectively opposing them were clearly demonstrated. But equally it has been demonstrated that neutral shipping is put at much greater hazard during a missile engagement than during an exchange of naval gunfire, apparently because of the capricious behaviour of the missiles and malfunction or inadequate operation of the guidance systems.

On the night of 8 December 1971 *Osa*-class patrol boats of the Indian navy fired Styx missiles at targets in Karachi, which included the oil tank farm at Keamari. The British S.S. *Harmattan* was hit by a Styx missile and set on fire while at anchor in the roadstead between four and five miles offshore, and a small Greek ship, the *Gulf Star*, was hit by two Styx missiles and sunk. On the night of 3–4 December there was an engagement about twenty miles from

Karachi in which the Pakistani destroyer *Khaibar* was sunk by Styx missiles fired from an *Osa*-class boat. On that night the Liberian-registered S.S. *Venus Challenger*, whose estimated date of arrival at Karachi was 5 December, disappeared. On 5 January 1972 her wreck was discovered by the Pakistan navy 26·5 miles from Karachi. She lay in shallow water on an even keel with derricks visible about six feet above mean high tide, and bore evidence of having been struck forward of the bridge by a missile, with consequent heavy damage. Subsequent investigation showed that she was lost on the night of the sinking of the *Khaibar* and that the wreck had been first sighted two days later. There were no survivors, and the government of Liberia issued a death certificate on the entire crew. The vessel was apparently unable to send an S.O.S. before catastrophe hurtled down upon her.

In Syrian ports in October 1973 several neutral ships, including Greek and Russian ones, were heavily damaged by Gabriel missiles fired into the roadsteads from about ten miles offshore, and apparently aimed at docks and oil tanks by patrol boats of the Israeli navy.

The threat posed by naval missiles to neutral shipping is serious and verified by events, and it is pertinent to examine the question of protection of the innocent from injury both inside and outside the target area. In particular, specific questions arise as to whether the existing rules of international law relating to discrimination between military and civilian targets can be observed in the event of the use of naval missiles, and whether the immunity of neutral shipping from attack can in practice be respected. In the case of submerged missile launchings it must be considered whether this is not tantamount to unrestricted submarine warfare in a new guise.

Tactical missiles generally have an aerodynamic form and are usually known as cruise missiles. They are self-propelled; launched from platforms in the air, afloat, under water or on land; and may be guided in some way or other against aircraft, ships or any other target. The missiles used in warfare at sea may be divided into surface-to-surface missiles (SSM), surface-to-air missiles (SAM) and air-to-air missiles (AAM) (used between belligerent aircraft). Submerged launched SSM, of which Soviet submarines are now capable, are designated SLSM. The SAM often has some surface-to-surface capability.

The SSMs are further divided into short- and medium-range types (long range being reserved for ballistic missiles which are directed at targets whose location is known exactly and is constant through the time of flight from vehicles whose position is fixed by inertial navigation, or from fixed installations). The short-range types operate within radar horizon, and, like Styx, Exocet or Gabriel, are therefore guided from the launching vessel to the target. The medium-range types operate beyond the radar horizon and, unless guided from aircraft, employ terminal homing systems. They are all, at present, Soviet weapons,[2] i.e. 'beyond-horizon' developments of Styx or Shaddock, with an estimated range of 200 miles and a speed of 0·95 Mach. The terminal homing systems of such beyond-horizon missiles may consist of either radar transmission from the missiles or infra-red homing whereby the missile detects a heat source and locks on to it, or both in some form of combination. (Owing to the rapid attenuation of heat the acquisition range of heat-seeking homing devices is short, so that infra-red homing would be used only in the final stages of flight.)

In the absence of aircraft to act as a command link to guide the medium-range missile to the target by the semi-active homing method, the missile is set free after launching to scan the target acquisition area, which is predetermined for it by range gate and lateral limits. These restrict the search for the target to a band of sea some distance, say 150 miles, ahead of the launching vessel. Within that band the missile will home upon whatever activates its sensors, that is, the largest radar reflection area in the case of active radar homing and the greatest heat emission source in the case of infra-red homing. During the lapse of time between detection and identification of the target (which can come only from intelligence outside the launching vessel and may already be out of date) and the locking on of the terminal homing system the target may have moved out of the predetermined belt; or a larger ship, perhaps a neutral tanker whose whereabouts was not included in the intelligence, may have moved into it. In this event the missile may acquire the wrong ship. Furthermore, if the incoming missile is successfully opposed by the target—and the chances of this happening in the case of a warship with the proper ECM and other devices are high, at least in the case of missiles other than the short-range surface-skimmers which are difficult to track—the missile may be diverted and scan the wrong sector of sea, so homing on another target.

The sinking of the *Venus Challenger* in 1971 may have been due

[2] Although the U.S. missile Harpoon will have beyond-horizon autonomous homing capabilities.

to the *Khaibar* transmitting false information so as to confuse the guidance system of the *Osa*-class boat which launched the Styx missiles, or to a failure in that system. If this sort of disaster can occur when the missile is guided throughout flight, how much greater are the chances of it occurring when the missile is self-homing? And the chances are very much greater again when the launch is from a submerged submarine, for in that case the intelligence on which the submarine relies is more likely to be inadequate owing to the difficulty of communicating with a submarine at lower than periscope depth.

The approximation of the use of the cruise missile to unrestricted submarine warfare is thus evident, yet in his study of the law as it relates to naval warfare in the eleventh of his articles in *Morskoy sbornik* (1973)[3] Admiral Gorshkov does not advert to this. On the contrary, he exhibits no reticence respecting the future employment of the weapon, saying that 'cruise missiles have become a most important weapon for destroying surface targets. Their appearance has introduced fundamental changes in the organisation of a naval engagement and permits the delivery of powerful and accurate attacks from great distances against the enemy's major surface ships.' It is accuracy that is the point at issue, and it is of a lower order than Admiral Gorshkov admits; nor is it likely to be augmented by technical developments in radar and heat-seeking, simply because of the physical limitations of these acquisition systems. (The alleged accuracy of multiple re-entry vehicles of United States ICBMs, which home on the targets by means of their own television acquisition systems, suggests that the problem of the accuracy of naval cruise missiles might be solved in this way, but there is no evidence that more than theoretical consideration has been given to this possibility, or to the possibility of satellite guidance.)

Where does this leave us? Except at the highest level of escalation and in global total war, when the neutral can be politically discounted, it is inconceivable that the present generation of beyond-horizon cruise missiles could be used responsibly in limited war. The wide spectrum of doubt respecting the occasions and mode of their use make the planning for their deployment exceptionally difficult, and to this extent the requirement to respect the neutral, which gains normative form in the law, has a bearing upon procurement policy, not to speak of the writing of rules of engagement.

At the same time it is a distressing symptom of the tolerance

[3] See above, p. 13.

89

currently accorded to high levels of violence that incidents such as the destruction of the *Venus Challenger* are apparently shrugged off by neutral governments which ought to have a vital interest in the security of their shipping. The fact that Russian ships have been among the first generation of neutral victims may cause Admiral Gorshkov to pause. The least that can be urged is that the problem of the cruise missile be taken up in the disarmament machinery before it is too late—before, that is, as a result of proliferation by gift or sale, these weapons are in the hands of many navies which belong to relatively insignificant nations in highly volatile areas of the world and on the flanks of the major shipping routes.

NAVAL BOMBARDMENT AND THE HAGUE RULES

The Convention respecting Bombardments by Naval Forces in Time of War adopted at the Hague in 1907 forbids the bombardment by naval forces of ports, towns, villages, houses or buildings which are undefended.[4] However, this prohibition does not extend to military works, arms depots or installations used for the purposes of an enemy army or navy. The naval commander may destroy these if, after summons and appropriate delay, they are not destroyed by the enemy; and no responsibility for involuntary damage which is occasioned by such bombardment arises. Even when military necessity requires immediate bombardment, undefended towns remain immune. All efforts must be made to avoid damage to buildings of cultural, artistic, scientific or benevolent character, and these are to be identified with visible signs by the inhabitants.

Needless to say, these provisions were drafted for tactical situations which have long since become irrelevant, but the central principle which they enshrine, namely the obligation to restrict shelling to military targets and to avoid unnecessary damage to civilians, re-

---

[4] The Nuremberg tribunal held that the Hague Convention on the laws of land warfare were binding as customary law, notwithstanding that they contained a 'general participation' clause. (*Judgement of the International Military Tribunal for the Trial of German Major War Criminals, Nuremberg*, p. 65.) The thought has been expressed by R. R. Baxter that the Hague Convention of 1907 (*British and Foreign State Papers*, vol. 100, p. 401) relative to the laying of automatic submarine contact mines (*ibid.*, p. 389) and concerning bombardment by naval zones in time of war have 'largely passed into desuetude' because of technological developments, and 'any customary international law which they may have created died with them'. ('Treaties and custom', *Recueil des cours de l'Académie de droit international de la Haye*, vol. 129, 1970, p. 97.) This must be regarded at least as controversial.

mains as the dominant consideration in the drafting of rules of engagement for modern situations.

It must not be forgotten that claims respecting damage to or destruction of civilian property owned by nationals of States other than the combatant parties may be made, so that the legal issue is not one merely as between those parties.

Since 1907 the problem of distinguishing military from civilian targets has been magnified by the involvement of the civilian population in the logistics of war, so that observance of the principle that only military targets may be attacked is in practice much more difficult than it has ever been. This is particularly the case in such a situation as Vietnam, where the distinguishing indices of military and civilian targets are almost non-existent. There remain, however, certain considerations which should be kept in mind, and which, indeed, have dominated the draftsmanship of operational orders in Vietnam. The first of these is the fact that technological development has intensified the degree of accuracy of naval gunfire to the point where damage to non-military features can theoretically be virtually eliminated except by accident.

This follows the computerisation of gunfire. Whereas in 1907 targets were selected by rangefinder and line director, with only primitive methods for verifying speed, current and ballistic considerations, advanced methods are now available. The ship's position is fixed by visual and radar methods. The course, speed and tidal stream factors are fed into the computer in the gunnery control centre (TS/gunplot) by gyro and log. Radar fixing constantly updates the ship's position and provides a means of compensating accurately for unpredictable changes in the direction and speed of the tidal stream and the effect of wind on the ship's track. It is thus possible to keep the gun target line constantly updated. As corrections are made from a ground or aircraft spotter these are applied as a north–south or east–west variation. The ballistic factors are updated at regular intervals. Visual and radar fixing always has a margin of error, and both the gyro and magnetic log may be marginally inaccurate. The compounded errors mean that normally the initial rounds will fall off target, and several corrections may be necessary before the target is bracketed. However, in good conditions it is reasonable to expect that the first fall of shot will be within several hundred metres, and the corrected fall less than 100 metres, of the target co-ordinates.

It should be borne in mind that this level of accuracy is achievable only in conditions where the ship's gunnery team is well trained, the gunnery system is properly tuned and correctly aligned, and radar conditions and visibility enable the navigator to fix the ship accurately. These are the factors which a ship's captain must evaluate, and where conditions are marginal, or worse, then the captain would have to accept some blame for rounds which fell well away from the target.

In good conditions, however, this accuracy means that the ship's gunnery officer has the competence to minimise damage to civilian personnel and facilities, so that observance of the principle in the Hague Convention becomes basically a question of target selection. This is done mainly by ground-based or aerial observations, and even though naval officers may be instructed on the need for the evaluation of targets to avoid unnecessary civilian loss, such loss may occur through the inexperience, negligence or indifference of spotters. The development of communications to the point where the spotter in the air speaks directly to the gunnery officer in the ship, involving as it does rapid changes of target, has magnified the risk of indiscreet evaluation. It should be a primary concern of defence forces to instruct shore or aerial observers, more closely than has been the practice, of the need to respect the principle in the Hague Convention and to take care in evaluation.

MINE WARFARE

The modern 'influence mine' is a menace to shipping the extent of which has not been fully recognised. Advances in electronics have made it possible to incorporate complex circuits which are robust and very economical in electrical power, so that the mine is highly sensitive, able to distinguish between ship and sweep, and likely to function at the optimal moment for destruction. The present generation of mines is still static, sown *in situ* and dependent for its effectiveness upon the accidental passage of a ship within its radius of influence, but it is likely to be succeeded by a dormant homing mine with a greatly enhanced radius of danger. Mine counter-measures (MCM) involve the use of mine-hunting sonars as well as minesweeping. In the event of opposed amphibious landings it is likely that MCM will be employed close inshore, so intensifying the back-up support of amphibious operations.

The fact that today's mines are not of the anchored, contact type raises the question whether the rules of international law governing mining are obsolescent, and whether the only standards now available are derivatives of the principles of self-defence. The answers to the question will govern naval policy respecting when and how minefields will be laid.

Hague Convention No. VIII of 1907 forbids the laying of 'unmoored automatic contact mines' unless they are constructed in such a manner as to be rendered inactive at least one hour after the minelayer has ceased to have control over them, and of 'moored contact mines' which do not become inactive when they have broken their moorings. In any event, it forbids the laying of automatic contact mines before the coasts and ports of the enemy for the sole purpose of interrupting commercial traffic. When automatic contact mines are used, all possible precautions must be taken for the security of peaceful navigation, and the area of the minefield must be notified, 'as soon as military exigencies permit', by means of notices to mariners in those cases where the belligerent who lays them is not able to supervise the minefield. These rules represented a compromise between the policies of Great Britain, which favoured the outlawing altogether of unanchored mines and mines used for the purpose of establishing a commercial blockade, and those of Germany and other States which argued in favour of the defensive character of the mine, and the loopholes left by the deliberately ambiguous draftsmanship were adroitly exploited in both World Wars to the detriment of neutrals and the dubious achievement of strategic goals, which tended to cancel each other out. The laying of magnetic mines by Germany appears to have constituted the first disregard of the law in the Second World War, and the fact that reaction to it was subdued indicated a low level of international disposition to insist upon observance of the law. Indeed, the Admiralty was unclear whether the Hague Convention covered the magnetic mine or not, for on 2 December 1939 M Branch, detailing U-boat illegalities, queried whether 'unnotified mines were unanchored automatic mines laid within an hour before the explosion (which mines are not prohibited)'.[5]

The indiscriminate effects of mining make this mode of warfare inappropriate in the conditions of limited war, when there appear to be legal pressures towards containing operations within the areas of land and territorial sea of the parties invoking the right of self-defence against each other, and a premium is put upon the immunity of neutral shipping from self-defensive operations. The only occasion since 1945 when mining has occurred was in the Vietnam War, when

[5] Adm. 1 10244.

a minefield was laid in May 1972 to block Haiphong and other North Vietnamese ports. The role that law played in influencing the judgement to resort to mining may not have been decisive one way or the other, but it was a conspicuous element both in the strategy of the matter and in the tactics of the operation.

So far as the strategy of the matter is concerned, the possibilities of mining Haiphong were considered closely during 1968, and mine-laying aircraft were in fact deployed for training in anticipation that mining would be authorised. Technical studies revealed that the risk to minelaying aircraft, on the experience of the Second World War, was considerable, and this in itself put restraints upon the proposals. But the decision not to mine at that stage was taken on the basis of the risk to international shipping, notably Russian and Polish, and the hazards of moving to a new and more uncertain mode of warfare which might lead to a breakdown in the balance of attack and defence by the deployment of missiles. The way in which the decision was presented was by reference to international law, perhaps by way of reassuring the Soviet Union that the scale of mutually acceptable belligerency would not in fact be exceeded. The Director of the International Law Division of the U.S. Navy wrote at the time that, in the absence of declared war, the blockade of Haiphong by means of methods which included mining would be of doubtful legality.[6]

Naturally the logical point at which self-defence becomes attack is difficult to decide even in a contingent situation, and it is impossible to propose it in the abstract. If naval gunfire directed at bridges and railways is a legitimate exercise of the right of self-defence directed at destroying the logistical support for an 'armed attack', so might be the blockade of a port. A blockade of North Vietnamese ports was excluded on the principle of 'necessity and proportionality'. In the actual circumstances of the case in 1968 it was not militarily necessary to close Haiphong, nor would the interference with foreign shipping that would have resulted have been sufficiently proportional to the defence of South Vietnam against armed attack. Hence it was both logical and expedient at the time to limit Operation Sea Dragon to North Vietnam and its waters, and to North Vietnamese shipping, while merely maintaining surveillance for intelligence purposes of foreign shipping crossing the Gulf of Tonkin to and from Haiphong. When the decision to mine was taken three years later the circumstances had changed, with a major assault on South Vietnam in progress, supported by accelerated imports of military material

[6] Carlisle, in *The JAG Journal of the United States Navy*, vol. 22, 1967.

through Haiphong; a strong movement towards a cease-fire and release of prisoners of war to which the sustained momentum of logistical support to Vietnam was prejudicial; and a finer sense of the political possibilities of hampering Communist shipping that a closer dialogue with Russia and China had made possible. The argument for mining as a strategic device of self-defence had become stronger in the altered situation.

At the tactical level the mining operation had to be planned so that the objectives could be achieved while minimising the threat to international shipping, and the observance of international law was one of the methods of achieving this limited end with the fewest political complications. The rules of engagement for the operation were with the Seventh Fleet ten days before the President's announcement, although they had to be approved in the meantime at the highest levels. Consideration had to be given to the question whether Hague Convention No. VIII applied to unmoored acoustic mines as distinct from the contact mines to which it literally referred, and, if it did, whether the minefield had to be instantly notified. If instant notification was required, the tactical problem then would be the risk to the minelaying aircraft in subsequent waves of the operation. If it was not given, the risk to international shipping would be aggravated. As it worked out, the operation was highly successful. Of the seventy-two ships in Haiphong when the announcement was made that the minefield was being laid and would become active at a specified hour, over a quarter were under way to sea within three hours. No ship was lost, the traffic to and from Haiphong was effectively interrupted, and disengagement from Vietnam and release of the prisoners of war quickly followed. The self-defensive nature of the mining in the special circumstances was amply demonstrated.

The reaction of the Soviet Union and China to the mining of Haiphong is interesting in that no mention was made of the Hague Convention No. VIII, and reliance was placed only on the freedom of navigation under the Geneva Convention on the High Seas, 1958. It was bluntly denied that Article 51 of the United Nations Charter applied to the situation.[7] The failure of these two countries to make any special point about international law as it affects minelaying is puzzling, and may signify their view that the Hague Convention did not cover the matter.

Mine warfare is conceivable in circumstances of limited war only where, as in the case of Haiphong, full publicity is given to the lo-

[7] U.N. doc. s/10643, letters of 11 and 12 May 1972 to the Security Council.

cation of the minefield, a period of time is given for neutral shipping to escape, and the purpose is to close a port to shipping carrying war material against which self-defence measures are justified. In these circumstances the destruction of shipping as such is neither the purpose of minelaying nor its necessary effect.

General considerations tend towards extending the principles of the Hague Convention to cover all types of mine, whether or not they are moored. This is because the technology of mine warfare requires a tactical doctrine that is not easily accommodated to the notions of proportionality and necessity. Mine warfare depends for its effectiveness upon a theory of probability. A minefield laid with full publicity and consisting of mines that are sensitive to minor influences and activated to explode the first time they are influenced is easily and quickly eliminated by MCM. To be effective in the destruction of shipping, therefore, a minefield needs to be laid clandestinely (perhaps with homing mines that travel like torpedoes some miles from the dropping point to the sea lanes in which they will remain) and to consist of mines that are of varying sensibility to influence and are activated only after being influenced a variable number of times. They are, therefore, highly capricious in the targets they select, and have an effect in a time scale that can only with difficulty be reconciled with the requirements of immediate self-defence.

Furthermore, notification of a minefield is not a matter only of the applicability of the Hague Convention. The captain of any neutral merchant ship is entitled, as a matter of international practice, if not of international law, to obtain a safe course from the Naval Control of Shipping authorities of a belligerent. The belligerent is not obliged to disclose to him the fact that mines have been laid (except where the Hague Convention applies), but in practice a direction to avoid an area is a general indication of the location of a hazard.

CHAPTER VIII

THE ACCESS ROUTES OF SEA POWER

THE RIGHT OF TRANSIT

A central question in the history of the law of the sea since the Middle Ages has been that of freedom of transit through straits, which, in the earlier period, were the key to the situation of 'closed seas', and in more recent times to the commercial and strategic freedom of the maritime Powers. Much has been made of the point that if a twelve-mile territorial sea becomes standard, over 130 straits will cease to be high seas as, on the basis of a three-mile rule, they are presently thought to be. The statistics are a little misleading, because many of these straits are dubiously 'international' in the sense of being habitually used by shipping as required by the principles laid down by the International Court of Justice in the Corfu Channel case,[1] and indeed find themselves in the list only because of assiduous cartographical scrutiny on the part of those who seek to produce arresting figures.

Furthermore the statistical statement is a little tendentious, because it aims to propagate the assumption that if the waters of straits become territorial waters, passage through them would only be the 'innocent passage' which is more restricted than the freedom of the high seas, and overflight would be altogether excluded. But the assumption itself may well be incorrect, and it may be that the rules of international law relating to international straits allow for a right of transit (which includes overflight) that is greater than mere innocent passage, and is therefore irrelevant to the status of the waters as high seas, territorial waters or inland waters. If one accepts the Spanish six-mile claim, the Straits of Gibraltar at the narrowest point have been territorial waters for two centuries, except for a brief interval when the three-mile rule was experimented with after the Napoleonic Wars, yet it has never been suggested that passage there (and overflight) is less free than if the waters were high seas, and naval exercises are still conducted there which involve the use of

[1] See below, p. 103.

dunking sonar from helicopters and the dropping of sonarbuoys from maritime reconnaissance aircraft.

But even if the law of straits does not depend upon the fortuitous characterisation of their waters as high seas, territorial seas or inland waters, this does not alter the fact that the use of international straits for the deployment of sea power has emerged as the major issue of the law of the sea, and its intractability is evident when it is recognised that without the right of overflight through the Straits of Gibraltar the United States could not have replenished Israel during the War of the Day of Atonement of October 1973 without a political confrontation with her European allies respecting overflying. Spain is reported to have made it clear that military overflights to Israel would not be accepted, while Germany objected to the use of her airfields. If a route to Israel had not been readily available the defeat of that country was a distinct possibility. The Phantom aircraft were flown from the Azores, replenishing from carrier-borne air tankers, via the Straits of Gibraltar. If this route should cease to be available for overflight without authorisation, on the ground that the straits are territorial waters, the result would be portentous of grave strategic difficulties in the maintenance of peace or the assertion of national interests.

The legal status of the principal avenues of access between the world's seas is thus an intrinsic element in the global balance of deterrence, in the maintenance of equilibrium in the Middle East and in the retention of the ability to intervene decisively when national interests dictate the deployment of sea power. At least this is how the matter is viewed from the position of the major naval Powers. The so-called 'coastal States' bloc, on the other hand, mainly but not exclusively non-naval in character, see their claims to control of the straits that intersect their territories as an alternative to the balance of nuclear deterrence. For, the argument goes, if obstacles are put in the way of the deployment of the vehicles essential to deterrence, the resulting uncertainty as to equilibrium will psychologically lead to abandonment altogether of the idea of nuclear defence. This is a naive and dangerous element in what in other respects is an understandable coastal States' position, because in fact the threat to close straits would hardly alter the situation of the SSBN, which is largely independent of them in its actual mode of operations, and, while the use of straits for the purpose of surface transits might be made difficult, it cannot be supposed that the objections of coastal States will have much influence if vital issues are at stake.

But if for purposes of the balance of nuclear deterrence the threat of closure of straits can be regarded as an ineffective gesture, it is none the less real and significant in connection with sea power used for lesser purposes. And even if it is not a question of closing straits to naval deployment altogether, concessions to local jurisdiction would make their use for naval purposes in times of high tension operationally impracticable. The major naval Powers can therefore be expected to seek the perpetuation of the present ambiguities respecting straits, since this enables them to manipulate the law as exigencies demand, either by way of insistence upon the right of transit under acceptable operational conditions or by encouraging the invention of unacceptable conditions when they wish to block the use of straits to others. They prefer a rule of law that does not close the options.

These ambiguities are the product of several factors of legal history; of the way in which the provision respecting straits is embodied in the Geneva Convention on the Territorial Sea, 1958; and of technological innovations which have destroyed the traditional categories of conduct respecting innocence of passage. As for the first factor, the variegated history of straits has always made it difficult to achieve doctrinal coherence. On the one hand there was the special case of the Bosphorus, on the other the apparently standard cases of Gibraltar and Magellan, where transit rights have never been conditional. In between are the Danish Sounds, where during the first world war transits and overflights were not denied but were channelled along narrow routes defined by minefields. This was a device that satisfied the strategic exigencies of both naval belligerents, since it left sufficient tactical freedom of manoeuvre in them, particularly to British submarines which penetrated the Baltic, and minimised a surface strategic threat to the Kiel naval base.

As for the Geneva Convention, the one item on straits that is found in its text was introduced as a proviso, and is perhaps the most unsatisfactory aspect of what is in many respects a not very satisfactory instrument. It brings the question of straits into the context of 'innocent passage' in the territorial sea, and so conveys the implication that transit through straits is no different in quality and scope from any transit through territorial waters, with the one qualification that it may not be suspended in emergency in the way that passage through territorial waters may be suspended. This imports into the text on straits the issue of whether warships have a right of innocent passage through the territorial sea without authorisation (or at least notification). The range of uncertainties which the Geneva text has thus enlarged may not have bothered naval planning staffs unduly in the past, but, as in the analogous case of the extent of the territorial sea, the progressive intensification of coastal State control of shipping in straits which is now observable is likely to lead to the widespread adoption of patterns of regulation which the naval Powers cannot challenge without leading to a level of dispute which they are reluctant to contemplate so long as transit rights are only ancillary to their principal objectives and are not themselves the primary objects of political controversy.

The south-east Asian straits are complicated from a legal point of view by the archipelagic claims of Indonesia and of the Philippines, according to which these straits do not link portions of the high seas but communicate with inland waters wherein no shipping has a right of transit without authorisation. This has emphasised the need for a legal concept of sea lanes to augment that of straits (in the narrow technical sense of channels linking two parts of the high seas), wherein transit rights would be independent of the fortuitous characterisation of the waters as inland or territorial and would derive from the interdependence of nations whose communications pass through confined seas, as in south-east Asia. If the law were to make transits through the Malacca, Sunda, Lombok, Balabac, Sibutu and San Bernadino straits and the lesser channels operationally impracticable the strategic consequences would be incalculable. The Soviet navy is dependent upon these avenues for the deployment from European waters of its forces into the China Sea in the event of a crisis with China which would dictate a naval policy of containment or intimidation. The Arctic route is not a realistic alternative, because it is closed for most of the year, and memories are presumably still strong in the Soviet navy of the imagined threat posed to Admiral Rojestvensky's fleet by the Japanese in the Sunda Straits in 1905. The afloat support situation of the present Russian navy is such that the alternative route around southern Australia and through the Tasman Sea (Torres Strait being a difficult and confined passage for large warships) would greatly magnify the problems of deployment, and particularly that of submarine endurance. It is also worth recalling that the access route to Vladivostock through the Straits of Tsushima would be affected by a twelve-mile territorial sea.

A flexible policy of sea power in the Indian Ocean and China Sea therefore turns the question of the freedom of straits into a naval requirement of a high order of priority for the Soviet Union, but this is equally the case with the United States. The Panama Canal being inadequate, the passage of strike carriers and helicopter carriers from the Atlantic to the Pacific may be through the Straits of Magellan, where no question of the right of passage has arisen. The importance of an unobstructed route for deployment was demonstrated during the final bombing policy of the Vietnam War, at Christmas 1972, when three carriers moved to the Gulf of Tonkin from the Atlantic. During the Indo–Pakistan war of December 1971 the carrier *Enterprise* and escorts passed through the Malacca Straits —not unaccompanied by a manifestation of local emotion—to the Gulf of Bengal, and although the purpose of this movement is unclear, and may even have been unclear to its initiators, it did constitute an exercise of sea power which could have influenced India's conduct of operations by requiring her to divert naval and air forces in order to counter a possible American intervention. The availability of this level of superior force in the area, whatever importance is attachable to it, was possible only because of freedom of straits.

BELLIGERENT BLOCKADE OF STRAITS

To the world's two major navies maintenance of the law in a form that will not make operational deployment between the Indian Ocean and the Pacific Ocean unacceptably difficult is essential both to the maintenance of equilibrium between themselves and in order to permit intervention locally when national interests demand it, including the protection of national ships. The point was brought home during the Middle East war of October 1973, when some sort of blockade was maintained in the Straits of Bab el Mandeb. Whether this was conducted by units of the Egyptian navy or not was apparently deliberately obscured, perhaps because the Egyptian government had not made up its mind whether the appropriate concept was that of distant blockade of Israel as an enemy with whom Egypt was at war; or the exercise of belligerent rights in the territorial seas of an allied State engaged in a collective self-defence operation; or the right of a coastal State (in this case Southern Yemen) to close its territorial seas to enemy-destined traffic, even though the territorial seas lie within straits. Egypt's only official announcement on the subject referred to the 'legitimate right of the Republic of South Yemen', which also by decree unilaterally asserted sovereignty over the seaway. South Yemen, with only two ex-Russian submarine chasers, two minesweepers and a total naval complement of 200 men, was in no position to prevent the passage of ships in the face of any resistance, and it seems that units of the Egyptian navy did, in fact, fire warning shells, visit and search foreign ships and warn off those bound for Israel.

While the Bab el Mandeb operation was being conducted, a United States merchant ship, the *La Salle*, outward bound from the Red Sea, radioed that she was being fired on in the Bab el Mandeb Strait by a blockading Egyptian destroyer. The message was intercepted by the U.S.N. guided missile destroyer *Charles Adams*, then in the port of Djibouti, but her sailing was delayed by the French authorities until such time as the *La Salle* had turned back, it is believed to the port of Massawa. This possibly avoided a confrontation in which neutral rights would have been opposed to belligerent rights. At all events, a task force from the Seventh Fleet, consisting of the aircraft carrier *Hancock* and five destroyers with afloat support, entered the Indian Ocean from the Pacific, and was believed to have orders to protect American neutral traffic in the Straits of Bab el Mandeb.

The situation on this occasion was not allowed to become grave but it could easily have done so. Had the basis for the blockade been a general denial of the right of passage through territorial waters, then it might have had to be resisted. On the other hand, if the basis were belligerent rights in time of war the questions that would have arisen would have been: first, whether, in the light of the United Nations Charter a state of war can legally exist today in which neutral shipping can be denied passage into a belligerent port; secondly, whether a long-distance blockade unaccompanied by the procedures adopted in the two World Wars would have been legal; and, thirdly, whether any action could be taken at all in the absence of a properly declared blockade with its accompanying administrative apparatus for control of shipping.

It is clear that the United States Navy would have had to take into account these legal options and their concomitant difficulties before plunging into the Straits of Bab el Mandeb in defence of American shipping. The staff legal officer to the C.-in-C., Seventh Fleet, may have had time to reflect upon these matters while the U.S.S. *Hancock* was passing through the straits of south-east Asia, and the Pentagon was no doubt doing its studies of the problem, but it is questionable whether the issues in all their complexity were obvious to the captain of the U.S.S. *Charles Adams* on the spot and faced with immediate decisions. The lesson is that unless naval staffs have exercised themselves in the legal aspects of operational planning to the same extent as in other aspects, decisive action is likely to be either inhibited for uncertainty or rash for want of premeditation. It is probable that the *Hancock* and *Charles Adams* were intended only to embody expressive force, but it is easy to see how in the situation at Bab el Mandeb the line between expressive force and catalytic force could wear pretty thin, and escalation to definitive force result from an inability to maintain that line.

The tentative character of the blockade of Bab el Mandeb, which seems to have been based on no legal text, bears comparison with the Indian blockade during the Indo–Pakistan war of December 1971, when the threat was mounted but given no formal legal basis and was implemented at a low level of practical expediency. The despatch into the Indian Ocean of the U.S.S. *Hancock* appears to have been sufficient to secure the abandonment of the blockade of Bab el Mandeb as part of the cease-fire moves that eventuated. Had Egypt been confident in its legal position at Bab el Mandeb it is conceivable that it could have maintained a totally effective blockade, even during the cease-fire, and successfully defied its raising by the Seventh Fleet. Neither side could be sure of the law because of the entanglement of the question of straits and belligerency, and so the situation was not allowed to go beyond the level of sparring.

It must not be imagined, however, that all disputes over straits will dissolve in this fashion into futilities, or that they will not be allowed to rise above the level of polemics. The question of straits remains the most vital legal issue of sea power, because it is in confined waters that naval coups can best be effected under the pretext of self-defence, and there that intolerable obstruction can be effectively raised to strategic and tactical deployment.

THE CONDUCT OF WARSHIPS IN TRANSIT IN STRAITS

Both the abstract right of warships to transit international straits and the manner in which they are required to conduct themselves while doing so were the subject of the decision of the International Court of Justice in the Corfu Channel case in 1949.[2] This case arose out of the mining of H.M. destroyers *Saumarez* and *Volage* in the Corfu Channel on 23 October 1946, while they were escorting two cruisers in a demonstration of the right of passage which the Royal Navy had decided to make following the shelling of other British

[2] 1949 I.C.J. Reports (Merits), p. 5.

warships by Albanian shore batteries. After the mining incident the channel was swept and mines were recovered which were examined for evidence of Albanian complicity in their laying. The court upheld the right of the warships to transit the channel while cleared for action, and awarded damages against Albania in respect of the losses. But it also held that the subsequent minesweeping operation was illegal because it was not in itself an act of transit. On that count it confined itself to a declaration that the United Kingdom was in the wrong.

In modern war games involving the use of forces through straits which are territorial waters it is curious that the first step of operational commanders is usually to move theoretical minesweepers to sweep straits in advance of a task force, although this is the one activity that the International Court has ruled out. In that case the minesweeping operation was a separate episode, intended to acquire evidence of the minelaying as much as to clear the channel. Would the passage of the warships have been less an exercise of rights if they had been using paravanes during their transit, for the purpose of cutting the mine cables and avoiding the mines?

The important feature of the court's judgement was that the right of passage of the two cruisers and the two destroyers was not affected by the fact that they were at action stations in view of an earlier attack from shore batteries, because their guns were in a stowage position (main armament fore and aft, anti-aircraft guns outboard and elevated), and the fact that the ships were closed up did not present an ostensible threat to the coastal State. This point was made by the court in the language of 'innocence' of passage, which suggests equivalence between transit of straits and transit of the territorial sea generally. Now it is certainly true that warships passing through straits must not threaten local security, and that some textual expression must be contrived to indicate this reasonable limitation upon the right of passage. But equivalence of the rights of passage through straits and the territorial sea would mean subjection to local regulations respecting navigation which might unduly prejudice the precautions which warships would find essential in confined waters. The expression 'innocent passage' thus contains, from the naval point of view, elements subversive of the freedom which it purports to adumbrate.

If readiness for instant retaliation in self-defence is a concomitant of the right of passage, as the court held it was, the question posed for naval staffs is what is meant by this in modern technological terms. Attention has already been drawn to what a task force commander would consider prudent when in transit through straits where ambush is possible during a condition of high tension. If the threat is likely to take the form of attack by aircraft or land-based or ship-based missile, the question is whether the right of passage would be prejudiced if the ship's missiles were on their launchers. Is this equivalent to normal stowage of guns? Some smaller missiles, like Seacat, are frequently carried on the launchers in any event, although larger ones like Talos, Seadart, Seawolf or Tartar are usually kept in the hangar, so that naval practice itself gives confusing indications as to what shore-based watchers could conceive to be threatening. But prudence is perhaps reducible to consideration of the additional time it would take to move a missile from its stowage position on to the launcher after the operations officer activates the system to meet a detected threat. With solid-state (transistorised) electronics and therefore no warming up, the time (perhaps between a quarter and half a minute) taken to move the missile would probably not significantly affect the chances of timely interception. But when the instant case arises this is the type of point to be kept in mind, supposing that political direction requires respect for the law relating to straits.

It is not so much the abstract question of the right of warships to pass through straits that is critical as the problem of the conduct of naval operations in the course of passage. The possibilities of outright closure of international straits to warships can be discounted, despite the huffing and puffing that sometimes accompanies the movement of the Seventh Fleet, but the practical obstacles to transit that might result from the intensification of local jurisdictional control can prove to be serious. Coastal States' demands for protection from the hazards of pollution of the coastline and coastal waters, or radioactive contamination resulting from damage to nuclear shipping, and from damage and interruption to the fairway resulting from collisions and strandings, immediately come to mind. The proposals of these States for traffic separation schemes, buoyed channels and regulated passage could lead to a situation comparable to transit of the Suez Canal, and the question then would be whether this would be tolerable to naval traffic.

Of course, under ordinary conditions it would be, but it would be a rash task force commander who would take naval forces through the Sunda Strait at a time of high political tension without taking certain tactical precautions against a submarine threat in those confined waters, where submarines were in fact very effectively employed in the Second World War. These precautions would ordinarily involve a random zigzag pattern, which might be incompatible with a regulated traffic flow; the use of search radar and active sonar, which, even if it would not render passage through the territorial sea non-innocent, might contradict local regulations forbidding electronic emissions; and the employment of dunking sonar and sonar buoys, which would require overflight that might be denied by local aviation laws. If these precautions could not be taken the task force commander might have only two options—not to make the passage at all or to defy the local regulations. The latter may not be a practicable alternative if friendly relations with the coastal State are accorded a higher level of political priority than the immediate objective of the use of sea power.

What impediments to transit are legally permissible in the case of the Sunda Strait must be equally allowable in the case of Gibraltar, but, as the events of October 1973 have demonstrated, what might be tolerable in the one case would be intolerable in the other. Hence the view in some naval circles that passage through straits must be equivalent to high seas passage, whether the waters are high seas or not. This certainly corresponds with customary international law but it consorts ill with the obvious need in the case of some straits, such as the Malacca Straits, for traffic control.

The strategic situation of Gibraltar is obvious, but it is important to recall that it also has a characteristic shared with few other major straits, namely depth sufficient for SSBN submerged transits. (For such transits the Malacca Straits are of no importance, since transits there will be surface transits anyway, although this is not the case with the Sunda and Lombok Straits, even if they are not ideal by any means for submerged operations.) But if passage through straits is innocent passage, the ordinary rules for surface transits of submarines apply. Hitherto, because the question is unresolved whether passage through international straits is the same as passage through the territorial sea, submerged transits through straits of sufficient depth have regularly occurred, and may even have been tolerated when detected because tracking for the purpose of global deterrence has been facilitated by encouraging the use of such straits. But the hardening of the position of the coastal States group which has occurred since 1970 portends pressures to force submarines to the surface when in transit through straits. This may not matter except when strategic deployment of submarines has to be done covertly, but the problem is that if there is a dispute over the law as it affects straits the possibilities of violence occurring during submerged transits cannot be discounted. This is because some navies are disposed to attack submarines submerged in their territorial waters. In these circumstances the flag State of the attacked submarine does not retaliate, because the law is clear and the submarine has manifestly breached it and must be disowned. But if the flag State of the submarine asserts the right of submerged passage, attack on the submarine might conceivably be met with retaliation, which in this case would mean a torpedo launched from the submarine at its persecutor.

If coastal State grip upon traffic through international straits tightens to the point where their use operationally by navies is seriously prejudiced, this could transform the question of straits from one ancillary to the objectives of sea power into a primary issue of sea power, and thereby an occasion of violent confrontation. To avoid this occurring is the aim of diplomacy, and the subordination of naval planning to this aim is the point to which we must now turn.

TRANSITS, DIPLOMACY AND NAVAL PLANNING

The Corfu Channel case[3] may have been a legal victory but it was a naval defeat, and the lessons drawn from it have influenced naval practices respecting straits in subsequent disputes. The first lesson is that local susceptibilities must be kept in mind in any assertion of rights: the seeds of dispute were laid in that case because the susceptibilities of Albania were altogether ignored in the early stages of the crisis. It is not always remembered that the whole of the Corfu Channel had not been cleared of mines by the Mediterranean Zone Mine Clearance Board, but only a swept channel, which took an eccentric line towards the Albanian coast for reasons of expediency that overlooked political considerations. The task force was obliged to follow this channel at one point so that the ships faced directly towards the Albanian port of Saranda, which made their conduct appear unnecessarily threatening and also confined their movements so that evasive action as distinct from response to attack was ruled out on purely naval grounds.

The second lesson is that, even if the purpose of transit is to make a demonstration of the right of passage, there are risks in undertaking it unless all requisite naval precautions are taken, including the use of superior force to restrain local adventurers. The Corfu Channel

[3] 1949 I.C.J. Reports (Merits), 5.

operation was, in fact, catalytic—that is, undertaken for the purpose of influencing events—and it was an instance of the use of sea power to underscore a right which for practical reasons did not require that degree of emphasis at that moment. The right would not have lapsed for want of exercise, whereas there were risks in its assertion at a moment of high political tension when the whole question was confused by the fact that Albania considered herself at war with Greece over a border dispute, the Communist movement in Greece had produced a threatening and emotional situation between the two countries, and Greece had been allocated in 1945 the responsibility for mine clearance in the waters of the Corfu Channel. The loss of ships and men was a product of the Royal Navy's incomprehension as much as of Balkan brigandage.

In all subsequent issues respecting straits the probes have been infrequent, and of low key, with no signs of the instant gestures of defiance and bullying of the Corfu Channel affair, as Albania represented it. During confrontation with Indonesia the resistance to the Indonesian archipelagic claim was muted, except when a demonstration of the right of passage was thought to be necessary in order to indicate the requisite firmness of intention to respond to further escalation of the dispute. It was recognised that Indonesian attacks on Malaysian shores and vessels were a category of situation separable from Indonesia's highly strung sensitivity about her own security, and that there was a dangerous degree of excitement and alarm in Indonesia at the prospect of British retaliation. In September 1964 the Indonesian chief of naval staff proclaimed that 'a British strike against any part of Indonesia would mean war'. In particular there was a great fear of carrier-borne air attack.

Account had to be taken of the fact that, whereas U.S. Destroyer Division 31 had asserted the right of innocent passage through the Lombok and Mahassai Straits in 1958, when the archipelagic claim was first made by Indonesia, without incident because Indonesia did not apparently regard this as a direct threat, the despatch to West Irian two years later of the Royal Netherlands aircraft carrier *Karel Doorman* had aroused great emotion in Indonesia. In these circumstances demonstrations of the right of passage could have led to the use of the Indonesian air force and the larger units of the Indonesian navy in defence of what was claimed to be national territory, and this would have raised the level of hostilities to a more general situation of local, even if of limited, war.

It was against this background that tactical decisions were taken when in 1964 Indonesia made public announcements that if the Royal Navy's task force from the Far East Fleet, including the strike carrier *Victorious*, then engaged in manoeuvres off western Australia, entered the Sunda Straits this would be a threat to the integrity of Indonesia. The question posed was whether to proceed with the passage and risk a Corfu Channel type of event in circumstances where world opinion would not be so generally sympathetic, or to yield to the implied refusal of passage through Indonesian waters and so make a significant contribution to the effectiveness that is an essential ingredient of the evolution of a legal regime. The decision taken was to do neither. The Sunda Strait passage was abandoned and *Victorious* and her escorts made the transit through the Lombok Straits instead, in a condition of defence but in waters where the movement would not appear threatening because of their greater expanse and remoteness. The movement was without incident, and was thus a valuable demonstration of firmness of purpose and use of superior force in the maintenance of the legal situation, without the overtones of insistence of the Corfu Channel affair. It is believed that had *Victorious* forced passage through the Sunda Strait she would have been attacked and a naval battle would have resulted.

Governments will naturally take the line of least resistance when firmness embodies the risk of accelerated tension, and this will usually take the form of avoiding the use of the right of passage where possible. This has been the expedient in the case of the Philippines' archipelagic claim. The reactions of the Powers to that claim illustrate the tendency for the diplomatic branches of government to seek by means of formulas and understandings to suppress controversy, even at the expense of allowing insecure legal positions to harden as a result of the procedures and modalities adopted by way of compromise. In the case of the Philippines initial protests against the Philippine claims that all waters within straight lines linking the outermost islands of the country are inland waters, wherein shipping may pass only with permission, were followed by understanding that notification would be given when a warship wished to transit those waters. When Philippine claims upon Sabah were made in 1968 the presence of British and Australian warships in the area was treated by Manila as a gesture of expressive force, and their transit through the Balabac Strait and Basilan Passage was refused. The Philippines now took the position that the procedure of notification had been a concession upon her part which was revocable, whereas the other parties regarded it as their concession.

The diplomatic alternatives were to press on with the transit of warships through the claimed areas in defiance of the Philippines but at the risk of arousing emotion and disturbing other aspects of friendly relations; or of seeking prior authorisation, which would have involved acceptance of the claim; or of not proceeding at all, so leaving the *status quo* unaffected on either side. The last alternative was the one adopted for several years.

From a naval point of view the political requirements of unobtrusiveness and docility in the face of claims to regulate passage can be a nuisance. During the Vietnam War Australian troops were transported in the helicopter carrier H.M.A.S. *Sydney* through Philippine-claimed waters. While the likelihood of a covert submarine coup in the waters of south-east Asia on the part of unidentified sponsors or accessories of North Vietnam was obviously unlikely, it could not be altogether discounted in the circumstances of 1968, and routine ASW precautions were taken. The level of anxiety rose when Philippine-claimed waters were reached because then helicopters had to be kept on deck for fear of arousing Philippine feelings, and so a normal operational device of self-defence ceased to be available even where Australia claimed the waters to be high seas. Later in 1968 transits to Vietnam were switched through the Indonesian straits because, following the overthrow of President Sukarno, Indonesia was in a placatory frame of mind, while the Sabah dispute had led to the difficulties respecting passage through Philippine waters to which reference has been made. But this involved longer routeing with consequent additional afloat support problems, so that the mere existence of the Philippine claim placed some, even if not a serious, impediment on the freedom of operational decisions of the Royal Australian Navy.

It is evident from experience that, in the matter of straits, flexibility of response to attempted closure is facilitated by flexibility of law, and that the use of force to resolve the question of passage is unavailing unless it is both resolute and sufficient. A good example for discussion is the attempt to break the blockade of the Straits of Tiran following the withdrawal of United Nations forces from Sharm el Shaikh, the speech of President Nasser of 23 May 1967 that 'under no circumstances will we allow the Israeli flag to pass through the Gulf of Aqaba', and the statement two days later by the Egyptian Foreign Minister that contraband carried in neutral ships could not be allowed to pass either, accompanied by reports of the mining of the strait. President Johnson said, 'The purported closing of the Gulf of Aqaba to Israeli shipping has brought a new and grave dimension to the crisis. The United States considers the Gulf to be an international waterway and feels that a blockade of Israeli shipping is illegal and potentially disastrous to the cause of peace.' But firm words were not matched by equally firm intentions, and temporisation, as usual, substituted for them. Israel was reluctantly persuaded to allow the Western Powers to seek a solution, but the latter could not be brought to focus on any specific course of action.

The Strait of Tiran is a bad one for the purposes of a naval test of a legal cause because of doubts as to the real issues. The Gulf of Aqaba is less than twenty-four miles wide, so that if a twelve-mile territorial sea is licit no part of it would be high seas. Hence the strait would not be a strait as defined in the Corfu Channel case, since it would not link two parts of the high seas but lead to waters under national sovereignty. Other doubts arose because of an element of historic rights; because of the confused state of the law of belligerency; and because the location of the Gulf of Aqaba does not lend itself readily to demonstrations of naval rights.

None the less, when Mr George Thompson, Minister of State at the Foreign Office, went to Washington to discuss the crisis, accompanied by Service advisers, his initially preferred option was a naval solution, which would take the form of running an Israeli ship through the strait under powerful escort of international naval forces covered by some sort of United Nations resolution. Although a Royal Navy strike carrier, five escorts and a commando ship were available at Aden, and a United States strike carrier was in the Red Sea, implementation of the plan would have involved the disposition of the Sixth Fleet carriers in the eastern Mediterranean as additional cover with a view to establishing superior force, but this would have extended the geography of the dispute and have raised the level of escalation to the point of Great Power involvement.

So the naval solution was abandoned in favour of a users' conference, for which the precedent of Suez in 1956 was poor encouragement, and eventually of a mere affirmation of the principle of the right of passage which gained precious few adherents and had no greater status than that attributed to it by the Foreign Secretary on 31 May 1967 when he said that 'it would give us the extra time to find the longer-term solution'. The law having failed, Israel took it into her own hands by seizing Sharm el Shaikh in the Six Days' War.

The Strait of Tiran affair was not, therefore, a straightforward case of rights of passage through straits, and the law afforded shaky ground for international intervention, just as geography imposed obstacles to naval pre-eminence. Not only was the legal characterisation of the situation immensely obscure and complex but the United Kingdom had compromised the position by agreeing on 29 July 1951 to an arrangement whereby British merchant ships bound for Eilat were searched for contraband at Adabiya or Suez instead of in the straits. This was the sort of concession to belligerency which in the Spanish Civil War had been adopted so as to prevent hostilities spilling over on to the high seas, but the British agreement carried with it the implication of a recognition that Egypt had belligerent rights, and it contained no reservation as to rights of passage through the straits. Egypt also claimed that Danish and American ships had acquiesced in visit and search when manifested to Eilat. The ambiguity was magnified in the Security Council resolution of 1 September 1951 calling upon Egypt to terminate restrictions on the passage of shipping through the Suez Canal 'and to cease all interference with such shipping beyond that essential to the safety of shipping in the canal itself'. Did this cover the Gulf of Aqaba?

The lesson of the Aqaba crisis is that the law inhibited sea power and contributed to the condition of political inertia that led to Israel's pre-emptive actions. Had the plan of escorting a blockade-runner been adopted, the Royal and United States Navies would have had to be prepared operationally for the highest level of self-defence, since, although it is unlikely that such a level of superior force would have been challenged, attack by Egyptian *Osa*-class patrol boats firing Styx missiles, and even by submarines, could not altogether be discounted. Had this occurred, Egypt could have been expected to rely on the argument that the Gulf of Aqaba is Egyptian territory to the median line, and that Egypt was defending her territory against illegal incursion. This would have been sufficiently confusing to make the political outcome much less predictable than in the Corfu Channel affair. The escalation that would have resulted meant that measures might also have been necessary to contain the Soviet Mediterranean fleet, which at the time consisted of one *Sverdlov*-class cruiser and twenty other ships—not a force to be reckoned with but one capable at least of the distractions that the United States Sixth Fleet indulged in at the time of the Anglo-French attack on Port Said in 1956. The legal imponderables compounded the strategic and tactical uncertainties and to this extent influenced the political decisions as to the relevance and use of sea power in the situation.

The case reveals the way in which the existence of potentiality of armed conflict alters the impact upon politics of the law relating to straits. For if belligerents are entitled to visit and search passing neutrals and to seize passing enemy ships in the territorial sea— which is the least that the Spanish Civil War precedent allows[4]— the question arises whether straits are exempted, even though their waters may be within national jurisdiction. It must not be forgotten that Great Britain exercised belligerent rights in the Straits of Gibraltar as elsewhere. The fact that the question is posed expands the areas of legal uncertainty and so intensifies the political problem by depriving it of another element of security and credibility. This extension of doubt is not necessarily disadvantageous, for it may lead to hesitation on both sides, and so to the avoidance of conflict.

[4] See bibliography.

CHAPTER IX

THE AREAS OF
SELF-DEFENCE OPERATIONS:
THE HIGH SEAS

LIMITED WARFARE RESTRAINTS

Until the prohibition of the use of force in the United Nations Charter the high seas were the arena of naval conflict wherein belligerents gained rights not only with respect to each other but also with respect to neutrals. The struggle for sea power in the eighteenth century took the form primarily of denial to the enemy of cargoes of basic raw materials for the conduct of war, and, as systematised in the prize courts during the Napoleonic Wars, afforded guidelines for the naval wars of the nineteenth and early twentieth centuries. The rules covered attack on enemy warships, seizure of enemy merchant ships and attack upon them if they attempted to escape, the visit and search of neutral ships and the seizure of what was declared to be contraband, and effective blockade of an enemy coast. The last two were dubiously separate categories, for until 1914 the right to interfere with neutrals upon the high seas was widely believed to depend upon the establishment of a blockade, and therefore upon its effectiveness. The impossibility of maintaining a close blockade during the two World Wars led to the loosening of any connection between the two categories, and visit and search of neutral ships on the high seas was made tolerable only because clearance of neutrals not engaged in contraband traffic was facilitated by the navicert system.

It is unlikely that circumstances will occur where these rules of the law of naval warfare on the high seas will be revived. The nearest we have come to it in the era of the United Nations has been the Indo–Pakistan war of December 1971, but that lasted for only a few days, so that the viability of the traditional systems was not subjected to the test that would come with sustained operations. The question is whether belligerent rights are available on the high seas at all in modern situations of limited hostilities, where the use of force except in self-defence is outlawed by the United Nations Charter and the freedom of the seas is proclaimed in rather absolute terms in the

1958 Geneva Convention on the High Seas. It is a question which hitherto has been unresolved at the higher political levels, and therefore it has proved increasingly bothersome to naval staffs required to envisage operational contingencies and to anticipate the orders that need to be given to local commanders.

The pressures of the international community to confine disputes to the territories with which they are connected, and hence to insulate the high seas from belligerent operations, are evident in the cases of limited war from the Spanish Civil War to Vietnam. But, of course, this cannot be true when the subject-matter of the dispute is the high seas itself, or the question whether the area is high seas or within national jurisdiction. Fishery disputes or continental shelf disputes have involved naval confrontations, such as the Icelandic cod wars or the Franco-Brazilian incident over the spiny lobster. Clashes at sea, notably harassment, which have been a feature of naval manoeuvres, have no territorial dimension, but neither are they limited wars.

The point of departure for the modern effort to confine limited war to national territory and keep it off the high seas was the Spanish Civil War, but the relative bankruptcy of the policy of non-recognition of belligerent rights then, and the escalation of violence that the Royal Navy believed resulted from that decision, makes it questionable whether sustained hostilities can be so contained, and whether the law should attempt to contain them in this way.

A CASE STUDY: THE SPANISH CIVIL WAR

The involvement of the Powers in the naval operations of the Spanish Civil War began when on 10 August 1936 the Republicans declared a war zone around Cadiz and other Nationalist-held ports.[1] Ten days later the Republican cruiser *Libertad* stopped the German merchant ship *Kamerun* outside territorial waters and forbade her from proceeding to any Nationalist port. This provoked the presence of German warships off the Spanish coast, and led to the setting up of a multi-naval Non-intervention patrol, which began as a simple fleet operation but led eventually to the deployment of eighty British and French destroyers. The British government did not express any formal opinion about the *Kamerun* incident, but it was assumed in Whitehall that the Republicans had exceeded their powers.

The Spanish Civil War was anomalous in legal history in as much

[1] For authorities see bibliography.

as Great Britain and France denied to the combatants belligerent rights on the high seas which had been accorded in the previous century to the parties to a civil war who were qualified for it by virtue of their administrative and military equivalence with each other. The policy of seeking to confine hostilities to the territorial sea which made this refusal expedient may have been justified, but it undoubtedly distorted the legal situation by depriving both parties of facilities for conducting the war to which they believed themselves entitled; and it probably failed in its objective because it led to the very thing it was designed to prevent, namely covert and disorderly attacks on shipping in distant waters in lieu of a properly managed blockade. It put the Royal Navy in a difficult position wherein the scale of action and reaction was often hard to formulate because of the altogether ambiguous legal framework for the operations and the Foreign Secretary's indifference to the legal niceties.

The inevitability that the contradiction between Nationalist claims to the right of blockade and the British denial of belligerency would lead to a naval confrontation on the high seas was revealed when the S.S. *Thorpehill* was fired upon by the Nationalist armed trawler *Galerna* ten miles offshore near Bilbao on 6 April 1937. H.M. destroyer *Brazen* was summoned to the aid of the *Thorpehill*, and she ordered the *Galerna* to cease interference with a British ship on the high seas and sent a boat to the *Thorpehill* to investigate. At this point the cruiser *Almirante Cervera* approached, and when *Brazen* signalled to her that *Thorpehill* carried food only, the *Almirante Cervera* replied that her orders were to stop food going into Bilbao, and took station nearer the coast. Both sides gathered reinforcements, H.M.S. *Blanche* joining *Brazen* and the pocket battleship *Graf Spee* hovering within range so as to add an additional element of uncertainty and hence of indecision to the situation. The *Thorpehill* was in fact escorted by the two British destroyers up to the three-mile limit, whereupon the *Almirante Cervera* withdrew.

The incident provoked deeper consideration of the scope of naval policy than had previously been given. The local British commander reported that, so long as a close blockade was maintained by the Nationalists, British ships attempting to run it should either be more firmly supported or prevented from trading with Bilbao. The British ambassador supported these recommendations, and the Commander-in-chief, Home Fleet, instructed the local commander to inform British merchant ships that if they entered Spanish territorial waters off Bilbao this would be contrary to his instructions and they would not be protected. What he had in mind was the fact that legally the Spanish authorities had the right to jurisdiction in territorial waters, and if the right was denied to the insurgent government this would be intervention, which it was the very function of the Non-intervention patrol to avoid.

Mr Eden, however, did not agree that the law required so rigid a policy respecting the territorial sea, and thought that the commander-in-chief's instruction went 'too far'. The Cabinet met to consider the implications of the *Thorpehill* affair, and it is clear from the discussion that most Ministers had no doubt that the Nationalists lacked any rights on the high seas, but were badly briefed upon the rights of the Nationalists in territorial waters. Questions were raised as to whether a blockade could be resisted, and whether H.M. ships could recover prizes when in transit to another Spanish port through the high seas following arrest in territorial waters.

It must be said that this legal confusion at Cabinet level, which left the navy in the position of improvising the rules to suit the events, was not a unique or uncharacteristic situation, nor was the solution, which was to set up a Cabinet Committee on the Protection of British Shipping, unusual. When this committee met (with Beckett, a Foreign Office Legal Adviser, present) the navy's policy of protection on the high seas but not in the territorial sea was endorsed. It was then left to the commander-in-chief to prepare orders for the protection of British ships on the high seas. His orders were that it was unlikely that Nationalist warships would resort to force outside the territorial sea, and that H.M. destroyers were not required while extending protection to engage superior strength or act beyond what might be expected of them in war, but should confine themselves in the face of superior force to strong protests at interference with merchant shipping.

However, when the local British commander began assembling British shipping at St Jean de Luz with a view to escorting it on the high seas, the Nationalist government, anticipating that a convoy would be run into Bilbao, informed the British government that this would be resisted with force. On 11 April 1937 the Cabinet discussed the implications of the threat. The Foreign Secretary wanted to run the blockade and meet force with force, but the First Lord of the Admiralty, Sir Samuel Hoare, thought that food should be recognised as contraband, and wanted to prevent the convoy from proceeding. The Cabinet decision was the usual compromise, but came closer to the requirements of international law than either of these views of what should be done. The ships were to be warned that they would not be protected, but General Franco was to be told that Great Britain would not tolerate interference 'at sea'.

This decision involved a deliberate increase in the level of demonstrable sea power, and the battle-cruiser *Hood* took station in the Bay of Biscay. The Senior Naval Officer reported that his impression was that the Nationalists could make their blockade effective only by threats, and he recommended that British shipping should be convoyed into Bilbao. This was not accepted, but the Admiralty instructed him that H.M. ships were to intervene if the Nationalists opened fire on British merchant ships in territorial waters. On 14 April 1937 the Cabinet decided to protect British ships on the high seas, even if running the blockade.

The legal situation was allowed to become progressively more ambiguous, and the situation at sea proportionately more confused and dangerous. The Chamber of Shipping argued that the blockade of Bilbao was not effective, and was therefore illegal: for this reason British ships should be protected by the Royal Navy. This argument confounded the law of blockade in time of war, which is a law concerned with the legality of the interception of shipping on the high seas, with the right of a *de facto* government to prohibit entry into the territorial sea. The continued warnings to British ships against running the blockade were accompanied by inconsistent action to escort them if they insisted on doing so.

Matters came to a head on 21 April 1937 when several ships attempted to run the blockade and were halted inside Spanish territorial waters. H.M.S. *Firedrake* went to the limits of the territorial sea to protest, and when the Nationalist trawler *Galerna* fired a shot across the bows of a merchant ship *Firedrake* trained hers on the *Galerna*, whereupon the *Almirante Cervera* made to *Firedrake* 'Please tell steamers not to enter Bilbao' and *Firedrake* replied imperatively, 'Stop interfering'. The *Hood* appeared to afford cover and the Senior Naval Officer and *Almirante Cervera* exchanged protests. In his report of the situation to the commander-in-chief the S.N.O. quite correctly said that 'effective blockade' was a misnomer and should not have been used.

It was becoming obvious that the effort to manipulate the situation by extra-legal means was failing, and the Admiralty concluded that a grant of belligerent rights would be the proper course. This was discussed in Cabinet on 28 April 1937, but Mr Eden remained opposed to it. Following this meeting, the Admiralty signalled the

Senior Naval Officer that in the territorial sea ships were not to be protected unless unnecessary force was used, but that they were to be protected if they regained the high seas in an attempt to escape, even after an arrest had been effected—a corollary of the refusal of belligerent rights. On 10 July 1937 the Nationalist navy was told by the S.N.O. that if a Nationalist warship signalled a British merchant ship in territorial waters to stop, and then fired a shot across its bows, British warships would not interfere; nor would they seek release of ships on the high seas which had been arrested in the territorial sea and were under the escort of Nationalist warships. This was an indication that the legal situation was hardening in favour of the rights of the *de facto* government, which could be challenged only by resort to a level of force which the Royal Navy was reluctant to contemplate.

The Royal Navy's judgement that it would be difficult to reduce the level of violence at sea by the expedient of refusing to grant belligerent rights was to be quickly vindicated by events. On 3 August 1937 General Franco informed Italy that he had intelligence that large quantities of armaments were to be sent from Russia to the Republicans, and he urged Italian action to stop the transports in the Sicilian Narrows, either by the loan of Italian warships to his navy or by direct action of the Italian fleet. He was driven to this recommendation by the restrictions placed upon his forces by the British and French navies which made his blockade of the Republican Mediterranean ports ineffective.

Mussolini's reaction was to say that he believed the extent of the shipments to be exaggerated, but he was prepared to take some action by means of Italian submarines. On 10 August 1937 the Republican tanker *Campeador* was sunk off Tunis by destroyers, one of which was named in the press as the Italian *Saeta*, and three days later the *Conde de Absolo* was sunk off Pantelleria in similar circumstances. Although these actions were restricted to ships of the belligerents, the fact that they occurred on the high seas represented a defiance of the British- and French-imposed limitation on belligerent rights, and if in fact Italy was the assailant the matter was no longer one of civil war. A totally new situation now confronted the Royal Navy which required the improvisation of tactical solutions to comply with the assumed legal standards. There followed a rapid escalation, with a submarine attack on H.M.S. *Havock*, following which Rear Admiral Somerville proposed reprisals in the form of bombardment and action against aircraft. But the Admiralty would not go beyond protests to the Nationalist government at illegal attacks and visits and searches on the high seas, stating that, even if belligerent rights had been accorded, the attacks would still be illegal. The Nationalists replied on 7 September 1937 that their ships had orders to comply with international law when dealing with neutral ships.

The root of the evil, as the Royal Navy had early recognised, was the denial of belligerent rights on the high seas. Late in August the Admiralty discussed the whole problem from that point of view. 'On the one hand we tell Franco that unless he has verified the non-British nationality of a ship flying the British flag, he must not attack her, and that on the other hand, since we have not granted Belligerent Rights, he must not take steps to secure such verification.' This involved a much clearer perception on the Royal Navy's part of the practical reasons for the rules of law governing belligerency than is to be discerned elsewhere in Whitehall, and of the problems that are likely to result from failure to let the law govern the situation.

When the Admiralty proposed to the Foreign Office that the Nationalists should be told that they could stop British ships if they had grave reasons to suspect a misuse of the British flag, they pointed out that this concession had been made to the Japanese in Chinese waters. The Foreign Secretary was reluctant to accept the proposal because he said it would mean granting the same rights to the Italians. The Admiralty thought that this would be all to the good because it would remove the last vestige of excuse for covert attack on merchant ships. Mr Eden did not believe that the attacks would cease, and he would consider a verification policy only if reprisals were agreed upon in the event of future attacks. The First Sea Lord was consulted, and he expressed the view that the Spanish and Japanese should be treated identically, and that limited belligerent rights should be accorded to General Franco upon satisfactory assurances. He believed that the attacks would continue if belligerent rights were not granted. He did not like reprisals, and the redisposition of the fleet that would be necessary to execute a policy of reprisals would negate the whole naval position hitherto adopted.

A position paper prepared by the Director of Plans recommended as the best practical course intensive operations in the area of attack on British ships, with a view to sinking the attacker. Coincidentally the Non-intervention Board recommended that the naval patrol system should be wound up as ineffective in the new circumstances. Out of this position paper came the germ of the Nyon conference, which had been in Mr Eden's mind since early August.

On 4 September 1937, after difficulties with France over the list of participants, invitations were sent out to Italy, Yugoslavia, Albania, Greece, Turkey, Egypt, Germany, Russia, Roumania and Bulgaria by Great Britain and France. Italy declined to attend on the ground that the question of the Russian protest at the sinking of their ships was unresolved. Germany declined on similar grounds, referring to the Republican air attacks on German warships. The Nyon conference produced a treaty which is still listed as in force by the governments which became parties to it.

The Nyon treaty embodied a code of behaviour expected of submarines which was inspired by the London Naval Treaty of 1930, but it went further and designated unwarned submarine attacks as 'piracy', punishable by any party to the treaty. This was of dubious legality so far as submarines of non-parties were concerned, but it had important psychological consequences, both for the Spanish Nationalist submarines and for the Royal Navy escorts, who were now able to treat any attacking submarine as an enemy, and were to that extent freed from the shackles of the concept of self-defence. Naturally the problems of positive identification and hostile intent remained, but they diminished once Italy and Germany recognised the risks to their submarines and became more discreet in their deployment of them.

The treaty set up an international naval patrol with authority to hunt down any submarines believed to be attacking or encountered in the vicinity of any non-Spanish merchant ship which had been attacked in circumstances contrary to the London Naval Treaty provisions. Areas were designated for submarine exercises, and main routes were established for merchant ships of signatories. This enhanced the likelihood of a submarine contact in the shipping lanes being hostile, and, in effect, it amounted to a system of neutrality zones.

The Nyon patrol was instantaneously successful in bringing to an end clandestine Italian submarine operations, and for six months there was no attack on merchant shipping. In 1938, however, there was a recurrence of these attacks made by Spanish Nationalist submarines, usually acting contrary to orders. Following these outbreaks, Italy, recognising that her own position was prejudiced, agreed with Great Britain and France that any submarine detected submerged on the high seas in the areas subject to the operations of the Nyon patrol would be regarded as 'contemplating an attack on merchant shipping' and would be attacked accordingly.

The study of the naval side of the Spanish Civil War has useful lessons respecting the role of law in maintaining order at sea. Admittedly the matter was complicated by the more or less direct involvement of Germany and Italy, but this was less the source of the difficulties that arose than was the refusal of Great Britain and France to grant belligerent rights while involved in an effort to restrict the Nationalists beyond what traditional international law required. The blockade-running was the type of act which belligerents were legally entitled to defeat, and when they were deprived of the means of doing what the law allowed them to do the safety valve was removed.

This was clearly recognised by the Royal Navy, which throughout the whole episode exhibited an instinct for the exigencies of the law and a prudence and discretion that were not always evident in the higher levels of policy-making. On the spot correct decisions were taken to limit the process of escalation, and the judgement of naval officers respecting proportional response in the exercise of the right of self-defence was on the whole right.

THE UNITED NATIONS ERA

Admittedly the Spanish Civil War was the only occasion in modern history when the local hostilities did erupt on to the high seas, at least in a sustained and drastic form, so that the restraint which has become a pattern in the contemporary conduct of limited naval warfare at least places no impossible burden upon the operations. But this only poses the further question whether the confining of hostilities to the territorial sea is a matter of exigency or whether it reflects *per medium* of State practice a modern rule of international law derived from the prohibition of the use of force in the United Nations Charter—a rule that the high seas are free from belligerency, which would render obsolete the doctrines that accorded belligerents the right of visit and search on the high seas and the seizure of contraband.

In the evaluation of State practice circumstances obviously play an important part. In the circumstances of the Spanish Civil War it was difficult to establish the policy of restricting belligerency to the territorial sea, and if this was intended to constitute a new departure for the law (and there is no evidence that the British government had any clear ideas about the rights of *de facto* governments on the high seas) it was a manifest failure. In the Nigerian civil war of

1967–69 the Federal naval blockade of Biafra was confined to the coast and was close and effective. The problem of blockade-running did not develop on a scale large enough to threaten the limitations placed on the boundary of the operations. In the Formosa Straits in the 1950s the Chinese Nationalist navy, with the cover of the Seventh Fleet, maintained a surveillance patrol outside the territorial sea but did not visit and search foreign ships for contraband.

THE ALGERIAN EMERGENCY. The only extended and sustained operation on the high seas against neutral shipping since World War II has been that of the French navy at the time of the Algerian emergency, when visit and search of foreign ships pursuant to measures of control over infiltration of arms and munitions occurred as far away as the English Channel. In the first year of operations alone 4,775 ships were visited, 1,300 searched, 182 re-routed and one captured.[2] The ships of thirteen European countries were interfered with on the high seas, and with some of these countries France became involved in more or less serious diplomatic difficulties— particularly Germany, seventeen of whose ships were visited.

The Algerian operations did not attract the degree of self-criticism from French international lawyers that the Pentagon accepts as customary among its American colleagues when the United States Navy engages in anything abnormal, but Professor Rousseau got to the heart of the matter when he suggested that the recognition of the Algerian insurgents as belligerents would have provided a better legal basis for police measures on the high seas than the vague notions of national security upon which the French government, although it remained mute itself, was thought to have based its case.[3]

The justifications at various times advanced for the French operations were, in fact, mutually inconsistent, which could hardly have led to clarity of mind on the part of the French naval planning staffs. The decree of 17 March 1956 proclaiming a state of emergency in Algeria extended the existing customs zone to varying distances on to the high seas, and the legal basis for operations within those areas might therefore have been the doctrine of the contiguous zone. But in fact the supervision of foreign shipping occurred far beyond these established customs limits, and another theory to justify it was the existence of a French law of 1825 relating to the protection of maritime commerce. When the validity of the seizure of cargoes came to

[2] Significantly, no ships from Russia were visited.
[3] In *Revue générale de droit international public*, vol. 70, 1966, p. 1062.

be tested in the French courts the argument was put forward that no exercise of jurisdiction over foreign shipping is legitimate except under the conditions of Article 22 of the Geneva Convention relating to verification of flag, and it was met by a memorial submitted to the Tribunal Administratif de Paris by the Minister of Defence in which an attempt was made to locate a legal basis for the orders given by the French navy in the concept of national defence. Reference was made to the executive power of the French government to take police measures for the external security of the State, and the justification for these was said to be the residual right of self-defence which was said to be additional to the specific right of Article 51 of the United Nations Charter. As it happened, the courts treated the French actions as non-justiciable for reasons of Act of State, and so these legal aspects remained clouded.

The fact that France made no effort to justify her operations on the doctrines of belligerency deprived her of the one possible argument for them, since the notions of national security upon which she appears to have rested her case were in the context unconvincing, and, viewed in retrospect after the independence of Algeria, justified Rousseau's castigation of them as due to 'ignorance and misunderstanding of the clearest principles of international law'. If France had claimed the status of belligerency, which for political reasons she found it impossible to do, that would not have been the end of the matter, for then the question would have arisen of the need for recognition of that status by the flag States of the ships searched. But France did not even permit the first steps to be taken to justify her operations, and if these were illegal for that reason the facts are no contribution to State practice upon the question whether belligerency in limited war situations is now confined to the territorial sea. The Algerian case must, therefore, be set on one side as aberrant.

THE VIETNAM WAR. All the situations so far discussed have been civil war ones, where the question is confused by the controversy whether the governments parties thereto have inherent rights to proclaim a status of belligerency and proceed to the exercise of its concomitant rights, or whether recognition of that status is constitutive of those rights. The Vietnam War lies in the area where civil war shades into international war and collective self-defence because of the legally confused question whether there is one Vietnam or two Vietnams resulting from the Geneva accords of 1954 and subsequent political evolution. What is remarkable about the naval operations in Vietnam is the scrupulous regard paid to the territorial sea or contiguous zone limits as the boundaries of military action. This line of demarcation rigidified the whole operational concept. The only occasions when force might be used outside the territorial sea were in exercise of the right of hot pursuit strictly in accordance with the conditions of the Geneva Convention, or in immediate self-defence of the fleet against armed attack, as when Talos missiles were launched from the high seas at North Vietnamese aircraft believed to be about to attack a cruiser in the gun line off South Vietnam.

Admittedly the philosophy of the Vietnam War required that these operations be strictly confined according to the rules of the Geneva Convention, but operational advantages were also derived from it. The whole involvement in the Vietnam War was based upon the principle of self-defence following the alleged attack on the U.S.S. *Maddox* on 2 August 1964 in the Gulf of Tonkin, where, as the United States told North Vietnam the next day, her 'ships have traditionally operated freely on the high seas, in accordance with the rights guaranteed by international law to vessels of all nations'.[4] It would be difficult to sustain the right of self-defence if the United States herself was less than scrupulous in her observance of the freedom of the seas.

At the same time the maximising of that freedom assisted the overall naval operation because it left the whole area of the high seas as a conveniently proximate and reasonably secure operational and base area, within which the strike carriers could launch and recover aircraft, confident that submarine attack was unlikely (not only because Russian or Chinese adventures on the Spanish Civil War model could be politically discounted, but also because the sonar and other conditions in the Gulf of Tonkin are unsuited to submarine warfare); and also within which the fleet and surveillance vessels could replenish from afloat support with virtually no diversion from their operational functions.

At the same time, international shipping constituted no problem by reason of the confining of visit and search to the territorial sea and contiguous zone, for there was little of it in lateral transit along the coast: shipping to and from Haiphong took a northern course under the shadow of China and kept out of harm's way, and shipping to and from South Vietnamese ports followed routes that made

[4] *Dept. of State Bulletin*, vol. 51, 1960, No. 1313. For the incident see above, p. 64.

supervision easy. No incidents involving international shipping occurred on the high seas, and upon the only occasion when hot pursuit occurred it was terminated on the high seas without further gunfire— a trivial concession to make to ensure the operational freedom of the high seas for the Seventh Fleet.

The law in this case facilitated the naval objectives of the United States and its allies, and its promotion and reinforcement thus became an aspect of naval policy. Had North Vietnam been armed with surface-to-surface missiles of the Shaddock type and been disposed to use them against the fleet, the tactical situation would have been very different. A self-denying ordinance on the part of each side stabilised the twelve-mile limit as the boundary of hostilities, although not of manoeuvre. The *quid pro quo* for the United States allowing free passage to Haiphong was that North Vietnam refrained from any assault upon the fleet, which could have marked the point of escalation to a dangerously high level, wherein foreign shipping, and notably Russian, would very likely have become involved. The essence of the matter was that until the final moves were made in the Vietnam War to bring it to a halt, the freedom of the seas facilitated North Vietnam and its supporters no less than the United States.

Until the mining of Haiphong towards the end of the war, then, a balance of interests sustained the twelve-mile limit as the extremity of the war zone, but inevitably the presentation of the matter was put upon the basis of law—that the right of self-defence restricts the areas of conflict to the territories of assailant and victim, that the international community is to be insulated from the exercise of that right since it is not a legitimate object of it, and that the principles of necessity and proportionality would not justify interference with shipping on the high seas, except to counter immediate threat. The law thus played a useful role in the evolution of the operational concept, but the question is whether the conduct of the parties testifies to the recognition of a rule of law confining limited war to the territorial sea, or to mere exigency.

THE MIDDLE EAST. When we turn to the Middle East wars the practices of the parties certainly reinforce the notion that limited war must not be allowed to spill over the boundaries of national territory, because this would compromise the security of the community of nations. For example, on the outbreak of the War of the Day of Atonement in October 1973 both sides were reported in the press as having proclaimed war zones confined to their territorial seas. But again, as in the case of Vietnam, the operational requirements of Israel, Egypt and Syria have been coastal only, and the need to extend them on to the high seas has not often arisen. A self-denying ordinance in this case, as in Vietnam, has been advantageous to both sides. There have, however, been exceptions. On 11 July 1967 a naval engagement occurred sixteen miles from the coast of Sinai in which two Egyptian torpedo boats were sunk. On 8 June 1967 Israeli torpedo boats and aircraft attacked the U.S.S. *Liberty*, an electronic surveillance ship which was monitoring Israeli transmissions from the high seas during the Six Days' War. (The identity of the ship appears to have been mistaken.) The fact that something is done does not make it legal, and Israel is reported to have paid over $3 million in compensation. The illegality may have lain in the attack on a neutral warship or it may have been compounded by the fact that the attack occurred on the high seas.

The resolution of a question of law does not reside in the conduct of navies but in the attitudes of States towards that conduct, and it is the Security Council debates at the time of the *Eilat* incident that are of significance and not the fact that Israel has engaged in belligerent operations on the high seas or that Egypt has interfered with shipping in the Straits of Bab el Mandeb. On 21 October 1967 the Israeli destroyer *Eilat* was sunk by Styx missiles fired from a patrol boat alongside at Alexandria. According to a letter addressed on the following day by the United Arab Republic to the President of the Security Council, the *Eilat* was seen 'speeding in the United Arab Republic territorial waters off Port Said shores. United Arab Republic naval units in Port Said were compelled to act in self-defence to stop the advance of the Israeli vessel. The subsequent exchange of fire which took place resulted in the sinking of the Israeli destroyer . . . by its latest act of aggression in the territorial waters of the United Arab Republic Mediterranean, Israel is further aggravating the tense situation in the area.'[5]

According to the Israeli account of the matter delivered to the Security Council on the same day, the *Eilat* was on a routine patrol on the high seas to the north of the Sinai peninsula and was attacked by surface-to-surface missiles launched from within the harbour of Port Said when she was about fourteen nautical miles (that is, two miles beyond the United Arab Republic territorial sea) distant. The destroyer was on a normal patrol, following a route which had been

[5] On the *Eilat* incident the following U.N. documents are relevant; S/7925; S/8205, S/7930, Add. 43; S/PV. 1369; S/PV 1371.

known to the United Arab Republic for several months. At 17.30 hours a green Verey light was fired in Port Said harbour. Immediately thereafter a missile was launched from within the harbour and the destroyer was hit near the boilers. A minute or two later a second missile penetrated the engine room, where fire broke out. This was brought under control and rescue operations were initiated. The vessel was immobilised and dropped anchor. At approximately 19.30 hours in darkness two more missiles were launched from within Port Said harbour. One hit the ship aft and the other fell in the water and exploded. The destroyer started to sink and by 20.30 hours it was abandoned with casualties. Israel denied the Egyptian allegation that at 17.55 hours an Israeli ship had opened fire against Port Said. At 18.25 United Nations observers informed the Israeli defence forces that the United Arab Republic authorities had announced that the Israeli destroyer had been sunk. The event was described in the Israeli letter as 'an outrageous and menacing violation of the international law of the sea', and Israel stated that it regarded 'this deliberate act of aggression committed on the high seas with the gravest concern'.

Acording to the Chief of Staff of the United Nations Truce Supervisory Organisation, the officer in charge at Ismailia at 16.15 hours reported that at 15.50 hours GMT one Israeli ship had entered territorial waters, followed by a report five minutes later that the ship had opened fire and that the Egyptians had returned the fire. At 20.30 hours GMT a message was received from the United Arab Republic liaison officer to the fact that two Israeli armed boats 'were in vicinity local waters at about twelve miles from the shore carrying out rescue operations, the local commander had been forbidden to shoot'. On 25 October 1967 further information was received from the Chief of Staff of U.N.T.S.O. to the fact that that the *Eilat* had been 'shot by a guided missile from a United Arab Republic torpedo boat posted Port Said'. The *Eilat* was said to have been eleven nautical miles north-east of Port Said and that this distance had been measured by radar and other instruments from more than one place. The *Eilat* had tried to hit the missile by gunfire but had not succeeded.

On that day a debate took place on the matter in the Security Council, where the representative of the United Arab Republic took as his main point the assertion that the *Eilat* was in territorial waters and was heading towards Port Said approximately ten miles offshore. Israel took as its main point the assertion that the *Eilat* was on the high seas and that the attack was premeditated: after the first missile strike there had been an interval of one and a half hours until the second strike, which was the time necessary to obtain the higher permission to finish the ship off. Israel concluded: 'The United Arab Republic action was the gravest extension of the Egyptian maritime lawlessness and belligerence on the high seas after having instituted naval blockades in international waters in the area.'

The debate on the matter then turned on the question whether the *Eilat* was in fact in the territorial sea of the United Arab Republic or not. The Egyptian argument was that action had been taken against the *Eilat* because it was engaged in an aggressive operation in the territorial sea; the position of Israel was that Egypt had now escalated the hostilities to the threat of the international community by waging war on the high seas. In the debate the delegate of India referred to this as the main issue. He called on the Secretary General to order an investigation in respect to the facts. The Bulgarian delegate accepted the Egyptian statement that the *Eilat* was ten miles off the coast and on this ground supported the Egyptian action. The Soviet Union also supported the Egyptian position on the same ground.

Even if these debates were somewhat inconclusive they did reveal a consciousness of the notion that the right of territorial self-defence does not extend into the high seas. The Egyptian prize court has claimed as a virtue the fact that 'the United Arab Republic does not exercise her rights of belligerency on the high seas, but limits herself to exercising them within the confines of her territory, ports and territorial waters'. Admittedly this was said in 1960, and the law lacks focus and definition in the shifting sands of operational behaviour, but it is not altogether irrelevant to the question of legal conscience, without which focus and definition are altogether impossible to realise.

THE INDO–PAKISTAN WAR OF 1971. The Indo–Pakistan war of December 1971 involved a flurry of naval activity on the high seas, and ostensibly no more account was taken of the difference in legal status between high seas and territorial seas for belligerent purposes than in any of the classical instances of war at sea. The naval war was inevitably carried into the oceans by every means, and naval engagements occurred in which warships were sunk and submarines performed their traditional roles. In the course of one of these a Liberian-registered ship, the *Venus Challenger*, was sunk 26·5 miles offshore.

These are the facts, but what is perhaps more significant is the tentative, hesitating and inconclusive character of the attempts on the part of India to employ the classical laws of naval warfare in order to isolate Pakistan forces in East Pakistan. The newspapers carried reports at the time that India had proclaimed a blockade of Pakistan and that all ships would be visited and searched and could be liable to attack. It appears that there were one or two instances of the boarding and some machine-gunning of neutral ships in the Gulf of Bengal, but no blockade was formally gazetted, and belligerent operations were generally conducted close inshore, where the majority of shipping casualties occurred. The utilisation of the law of blockade seems to have been more of the order of suggestion than of actuality, but this may have been due to the fact that the war was over before a serious problem for international shipping could arise, and the Indian authorities were no doubt relieved that they were not obliged to make firmer decisions about the legal scope of their naval operations, which, had they gone on for some weeks or months, accompanied by a proper blockade, might have led to other nations escorting their tanker traffic to and from the Persian Gulf.

EVALUATION

Whether there is or is not a rule of law confining limited wars to national territory wherein the right of self-defence is logically linked to the exercise of sovereignty is less important to the present study than is the existence of the question, for the mere fact that the question is posed bears upon naval planning, whether it be planning against an assailant or planning to protect neutral shipping from an assailant.

Where it suits naval planning to preserve the high seas as an area immune from hostilities wherein forces may assemble, replenish and mount operations, the promotion of such a rule of law becomes an objective of naval policy, and this will be reflected in the type and scope of operational orders—as in Vietnam. Where restriction of belligerency to the territorial sea would be operationally inconvenient, naval staffs will wish to take a different view of the law, but they would be rash to overlook the questionable state of the law on the point, which accordingly will introduce an element of doubt and hence of hesitation and indecision into the planning process. Either the question of law will advance naval purposes or it will hinder them. Certainly it will influence them. But the danger of reliance upon precedent, to which governments and naval staffs are just as prone as lawyers, should not be overlooked. All the naval operations discussed in this chapter are peculiar, none more so than Vietnam, where favourable operational conditions existed that are unlikely to be repeated. The examination of the matter is valuable only if the special circumstances are recognised, for only then can the consistent links between the episodes be evaluated for the purpose of formulating behavioural rules.

CHAPTER X

THE AREAS OF SELF-DEFENCE OPERATIONS: THE TERRITORIAL SEA

TERRITORIALLY CONNECTED OPERATIONS

THE VIETNAM WAR. When it comes to the question of legal infusion in operational planning, the decision to confine hostilities to a territorial boundary dictates every aspect of the operation. In the Vietnam War a distinction was drawn between South Vietnam and North Vietnam. In the case of South Vietnam the functions and powers of the United States Navy derived from the national jurisdiction of the Republic of Vietnam, which enacted legislation on 27 April 1965 on sea surveillance, proclaiming a sea defensive area for the territorial sea of three miles, in which passage of vessels prejudicial to the peace, order or security of the republic would not be considered as innocent. Ships not in innocent passage would be subject to visit and search, and cargoes containing listed items would be considered to be suspicious. In the contiguous zone of an additional nine miles the rules of the Geneva Convention on the Territorial Sea and Contiguous Zone, 1958, Article 24, respecting such zones would apply. The entry of cargoes or persons through routes other than recognised ports of entry was forbidden by customs and immigration regulations.

The decree then specified that the Republic of Vietnam would act beyond the contiguous zone to prevent or punish any infringement of the laws of the Republic of Vietnam by vessels flying the flag of the Republic of Vietnam or reasonably believed to be South Vietnamese, though flying a foreign flag or refusing to show a flag. The action to be taken against such ships might include stopping, visiting and searching. If the reasonable suspicions as to Vietnamese nationality should prove unfounded and the vessel had not committed any act justifying those suspicions, the vessel would be permitted to continue, with prompt and reasonable compensation paid by the government of Vietnam for any loss or damage which might have been sustained. Vessels which might be within the territory, territorial sea or the contiguous zone of the Republic of Vietnam were to be subject to hot pursuit on the high seas 'as provided by international law'. The decree concluded by reciting the request of the government of South Vietnam for the assistance of the United States Navy to enforce these measures.

It is clear that the draftsman of this decree aimed at giving precise effect to the Geneva Conventions; but it is also clear that issues arise respecting the interpretation of the Conventions, and the situation in customary international law, which might occasion difficulty to naval staffs concerned with the preparation of operational orders so detailed as to minimise the possibility of diplomatic controversy. For example, the decree appears to envisage the interception and if necessary the arrest of foreign ships passing through the contiguous zone from the high seas, though it is arguable that no breach of local law can occur except in the territorial sea or inland waters, and that hot pursuit is hence permissible commencing in the contiguous zone only when the breach has occurred in the territorial sea or inland waters, that is, in the case only of outgoing and not ingoing ships. The decree does not render easier the task of the naval staff officer confronted with this question in as much as it does not explicitly legislate for a duty on the part of foreign ships to stop and submit to visit and search in the contiguous zone. It is merely facultative respecting the surveillance forces. Accordingly it is difficult to see what offence may have been committed by an incoming ship which flees into the high seas after being intercepted in the contiguous zone that would justify hot pursuit. And then the question arises what constitutes hot pursuit and what degree of force may be employed to terminate pursuit. In actual fact the naval surveillance forces have acted with circumspection, and on the one occasion to which publicity has been given, when a group of vessels was contacted and fled, action was taken only against those actually engaged in the contiguous zone, and others which escaped into the high seas were not subjected to hot pursuit.

So much for the operational twelve-mile zone of South Vietnam. As for North Vietnam, this country claims a twelve-mile territorial sea and no contiguous zone, so that it was possible to regard this limit as of the same legal status as the land, and affected by the harassment and interdiction policy applied there. This resulted in the setting up of the naval operation known as Sea Dragon at the time when the bombing of North Vietnam was instituted, with a view to interdicting North Vietnamese logistical support for the Viet Cong in South Vietnam. Because the operation was conceived in terms of self-defence, and not in terms of engagement of North Vietnam as a belligerent, it was inherently limited in scope. Within the twelve-mile territorial sea surveillance of vessels was undertaken, destruction of waterborne logistic craft (WIBLICKS) was authorised upon identification as such, and naval gunfire was directed at truck parks, assembly points, missile sites, coastal batteries, bridges and other military equipment and installations which supported the movement of supplies and personnel into South Vietnam.

In other words, Operation Sea Dragon was restricted to the 'territory' of North Vietnam, and only immediately defensible measures were authorised against direct attack when United States vessels were on the high seas. Because of the limited territorial scope of the operation, and the scrupulous regard that the United States Navy was obliged by higher authority to pay to the requirements of the Geneva Conventions as the governing system of rules, the infusion of legal concepts in the drafting of operational orders to cover positive identification, verification, visit and search, selection of targets, retaliation and hot pursuit was the most significant aspect of the matter, and will be considered later in connection with rules of engagement.

CONFRONTATION BETWEEN INDONESIA AND MALAYSIA. The pattern of surveillance operations in Vietnam derived to some extent from the experience in the confrontation between Indonesia and Malaysia of 1963–64. In that case the first act of hostility which raised the level of tension to a high classification occurred on 29 September 1963, where a Malaysian ship was reported to have been intercepted by an Indonesian patrol unit as it 'entered Indonesian territory' in the Celebes. From that date frequent attacks were made on Malaysian vessels, with use of gunfire against fishing boats. The legal issues were complicated by the dispute over the Indonesian archipelagic waters claim, which had the effect of treating as internal or territorial waters large areas of ocean which Malaysian craft had traditionally treated as high seas; by confusion between incidents of transit and fishing; by doubts whether the assailants were government vessels or mere pirates; and by the problem of security against smuggling and infiltration. Into these issues it is unnecessary to go, beyond drawing attention to the complexity of the legal situation, with its emphasis on the burden of proof and presumptions of innocence and governmental respect for international law which inhibited response to the raising of the levels of escalation.

Although the Royal Malaysian Navy arrested Indonesian boats on 9 October, its resources were inadequate for a sufficiently extended police operation, and other Commonwealth forces began to play an unofficial role in what developed into a naval war. When Indonesian infiltrators were found on 16 October to be crossing into Malaysia a patrol system was set up in the Malacca Strait, and it had to deal with Indonesian attacks on Malaysian fishing boats, normally by night, which increased in intensity, some boats being confiscated and money extorted and gear seized from the fishermen.

In August 1964 Indonesian guerillas made their first landing in Johore, where they were captured, and this further increase in the level of tension led to further development of the patrol system in order to deter any more such raids as well as to protect Malaysian vessels. Three lines of defence were established, namely coast watches, inshore police launches and offshore patrol boats, minesweepers and frigates. The whole operation was conducted on police lines, with intelligence playing a prominent part in detection and positive identification. In December 1964 H.M. frigate *Ajax* broke up a guerilla attack by force. When the land operations made North Borneo and Sarawak the primary scene of hostilities a similar patrol system was instituted, located mainly in inland waters, to control infiltration by sampan.

At no point were the legal issues in confrontation allowed to harden to the point where one or the other side was left with no room for manoeuvre. A draft Security Council resolution which mildly called upon the parties to refrain from the threat or use of force and to respect the territorial integrity and political independence of each other was designed not to assign causes and blame, for fear of promoting Indonesian intractability, although this reticence did not prevent Indonesia from withdrawing from the United Nations on 20 January 1965. Nor, for similar reasons, did Malaysia and her Commonwealth supporters meet the Indonesian archipelagic claim head-on. Reaction was confined to reliance upon protests already made, and the continued exercise of rights of passage. British, and even Malaysian, commercial shipping was not interfered with, and the Indonesian decree authorising the Indonesian navy to close portions of the archipelago for security reasons was treated by Malaysia and her supporters as the tentative and exploratory thing it really was. The subdued level of action and reaction confined the dispute to what it was called, a confrontation, and prevented it from moving to higher levels of escalation in which surface and even submarine forces, which had been plentifully supplied to Indonesia by the Soviet Union, might have been used in a threatening role.

The Commonwealth forces' objective being one of strict self-defence sustained at the lowest feasible level of response and as unobtrusively as possible, the role of law in the operation was more prominent than perhaps in any other deployment of naval power since 1945, and it imposed strains upon the procedures of drafting operational orders to which the Royal Navy was unaccustomed. While Indonesian territorial waters were excluded from the defensive patrols, the full demands of Indonesia for respect for its archipelagic claims obviously could not be met. At the same time, deployment of the Royal Navy in these claimed waters for purposes other than a demonstration of the right of passage had to be restrained to avoid any further degree of escalation. The solution adopted, which was to keep outside a line drawn twelve miles from the coast of Sumatra in the Malacca Strait, and from the neighbouring islands, and altogether away from the Indonesian baseline system elsewhere, except for a foray to demonstrate the right of passage through the straits, was a successful compromise, since it minimised provocation to Indonesia while ignoring the straight baselines in the areas where these mattered least and where the confrontation was actually occurring. But it cannot be denied that this observance of the twelve-mile limit served to consolidate that aspect of the Indonesian claim and made its contribution to the promotion of the limit as a standard rule for territorial waters. To this extent the exigencies of sea power facilitated legal evolution.

The confrontation episode was a striking instance of how a navy can be dragged by political exigencies into limited war without legal planning, and how this in practice confuses naval planning. Response to confrontation was a political and naval success, but this was a matter of luck more than of design. The operation was supervised by a committee consisting of Malaysian Ministers and the High Commissioners of the other three Commonwealth countries involved. Answerable to this committee was a service committee concerned with operational planning. For about three months a Foreign Office lawyer sat upon this committee, but no clear legal policy was at any time formulated. The implications were brought home when a Royal Naval vessel under fire from an Indonesian warship in Malaysian territorial waters signalled for permission to return the fire, and the supervising committee exhibited a state of nerves when it was reported to it that the navy, acting on the principle of self-defence, had authorised the return of fire. Confrontation made many naval officers aware that proper legal planning is an essential concomitant of effective naval planning.

THE BEIRA PATROL. A similar restraint upon naval operations in the case of the Beira patrol involved concessions to local territorial sea claims. Portugal claims a six-mile territorial sea drawn from a bay-closing line at Beira, and while it seems that the British government was not prepared to acknowledge this in the early stages of the Beira patrol, it may be assumed that H.M. ships were told to keep to seaward of the limits claimed. Operationally speaking, this increased the difficulties involved in the patrol, for the approaches to Beira are through an arc of 130 degrees, and the radar horizon of a Type 12 or *Leander*-class frigate is about seventeen miles. To detect and then intercept a tanker would require—on the supposition that the Royal Navy was to keep to the outer limits of the arc—the deployment of two frigates, which, it has been calculated, would in fact involve the detachment from other fleet operations of six frigates and two afloat support ships.

As it happened, the operational obstacles imposed by respect for the Portuguese territorial sea were not of a serious order because of the limitations upon heavy-draught ships imposed by the port approaches to Beira, where the landfall buoy is in fact on the high seas; and also because after the two or three initial efforts at 'running the blockade' there proved to be alternatives available to Rhodesia and her suppliers. What remains significant is the fact that there were serious doubts whether the Royal Navy's use of Portuguese territorial waters for purposes other than innocent passage could be justified on the basis of the United Nations resolutions. Serious consideration of the question was unnecessary because, although shipping could have reached Beira by keeping within the territorial sea for much of the lateral transit of the coast of Mozambique, it did not in fact attempt to do so, and the frigates had no occasion to enter the territorial sea either. But the existence of the question—which was not resolved by the authorisation to use force when the United Kingdom took the matter back to the Security Council after the *Joanna V* incident[1]—dictated an operational pattern that could have aided evasive action on the part of a resolute blockade-runner.

Throughout the Security Council debate the assumption was that the United Kingdom was seeking powers to be exercised on the 'high

[1] See chapter XIII, p. 174, below, for facts.

seas'. No doubt powers would have been granted if sought for in the territorial sea, and Portugal would presumably have been as bound thereby as other States were in respect of their ships, but the fact is that they were not granted, and operational planning had to proceed accordingly.

Except in the cases of fishery disputes, where the question of the extent of national jurisdiction is the very issue in dispute, the pattern of events since 1950 has been to regard controversies over the extent of the territorial sea as not a legitimate component of escalation policy. In the cases which have been discussed it is evident that a contest over territorial sea limits would have been a serious aggravation of the problem which sea power was employed to resolve, involving a progression up the scale of tension which in turn would have required a more intensive and extensive resort to sea power. Accordingly, opposition has been confined to protest and to carefully planned assertions of the right of passage which leave ambiguous the status of the waters in question. But this very ambiguity has been an element in the effectiveness of the claims made, contributing psychologically if in no other way to their embodiment in international law, and, by virtue of apparently successful example, to their proliferation. This factual observation is not necessarily a critical one, for it is manifest that naval opposition to disputed jurisdictional claims in the case of fishery disputes has generally proved in the long run to be unsuccessful, and in the short run to be productive of much political tension and a bothersome diversion of warships from their proper functions to a task for which they are not designed or particularly well equipped.

WARSHIPS IN THE TERRITORIAL SEA

The question of the transit rights of warships in international straits is an aspect of the more general question of the rights of passage of warships in the territorial sea. If warships have such rights generally they have them specifically in straits whose waters are territorial. But it has been inexpedient to present the case in this way because of the ambiguous history of the topic of warships in the territorial sea, and also because 'innocent passage' in the context of the territorial sea is an insufficient guarantee of freedom of naval deployment through straits. So the tendency has been to invest the problem of straits with a special character and to suppress the question of the territorial sea as likely only to compound the controversy.

In the nineteenth century, when the doctrine of innocent passage was becoming established, the particular case of warships was overlooked, partly because it was only after the Declaration of Paris of 1856 that the distinction between warships and other vessels became sharp, and partly because, until the technological revolution in naval construction of the 1880s, ironclad warships lacked the endurance to seek access to foreign waters. It is significant that it was in 1880 that the first academic challenge was issued to the inclusion of warships with merchant ships in respect of innocent passage. The subsequent history of the topic reveals in its most deplorable aspects the manner in which legal doctrine can be made the scapegoat of strategic policy. In 1910, for reasons that have never been discovered, Mr Elihu Root solemnly proclaimed in the course of the North Atlantic Coast Fisheries arbitration that 'warships may not pass without consent into this zone because they threaten. Merchant ships may pass because they do not threaten.' This aphorism came to dominate United States policy down to 1941. At the Hague codification conference in 1930 the United States led the field in resisting the right of innocent passage of warships, while the Soviet Union exhibited a withdrawn indifference to the question.

After 1945 there was a *volte-face*. The United States emerged as the leading advocate of the right of innocent passage for warships and the Soviet Union as the leading opponent. These respective attitudes were understandable when the United States sought to contain Russia by hemming her in and Russia sought to fend off her enemies. In the early 1950s the Royal Navy supplied patrol boats to the German Federal Republic which were used to land agents on the coasts of the Baltic Soviet republics, so that Russia's coast-defence phobia was not lacking in good reasons.[2]

The whole question of the strategic role of the territorial sea was lurking in the judgement of the International Court in the Corfu Channel case[3] but was never allowed to become explicit. The court was at pains to say that it was concerned with the question of the transit of warships through international straits and not with their transit through other parts of the territorial sea, but despite all the court's efforts to separate the questions it seems improbable that it would have upheld the right of passage in the actual case if it did not believe that there was a general right of transit through the territorial sea, and inevitably the decision has been used to reinforce

[2] Höhne and Zolling, *The General was a Spy* (Gehlen), 1972, p. 144.
[3] 1949 I.C.J. Reports (Merits), 5.

that general right. At the Geneva conference in 1958 the Western naval Powers failed at the committee stage to secure the right of innocent passage for warships, and at the plenary meeting they mounted a vigorous and successful campaign to prevent the Convention on the Territorial Sea from requiring more than 'notification of passage'. The Soviet Union's defensive tactic was to rally sufficient support to defeat altogether the adoption of the draft article on the subject of innocent passage of warships, which required a two-thirds vote.

The result was that the Geneva Convention's text was emasculated and left open to interpretation. On the one hand, the Western naval Powers could point to the fact that the Convention's articles on innocent passage referred to 'ships', meaning 'all ships', and that the rump provision left after the excision of the article on warships allowed for the regulation of their passage by the coastal State; on the other hand the Soviet Union could point out that there was no text expressly allowing for the passage of warships, and that the power to regulate necessarily includes the power to exclude. When ratifying the Convention the Soviet Union in fact reserved this interpretation of the text, so making for itself a legal straitjacket which is now found to be excessively constricting but cannot easily be broken.

The result of these tactics at the Geneva conference has been an impasse. The Western naval Powers have met demands for previous authorisation for passage in the coolest possible manner. Where it was unnecessary to transit the territorial sea they have not bothered to do so, therefore preventing the issue from arising. Where they have found it necessary, mainly in the sea lanes of Indonesia and the Philippines, they handled the matter by diplomatic modalities, which again have kept the problem confined to the theoretical. Whereas previous authorisation has been required in principle, the demand has in practice been satisfied by notification 'at a low level', which means the naval attaché telephoning a lieutenant-commander at the local Navy Office to say, 'Oh, by the way, H.M.S. So-and-so will be passing . . .' and giving details. On the whole, most coastal States have been cautious about striking attitudes on the question, and those that have, like Somalia or Bangladesh, which have solemnly proclaimed in legislation that warships shall not pass without permission, are imitating their mentors and have been loftily ignored by others. After all, even half a dozen swallows do not make a summer.

It is the mentors who are now having second thoughts, because, try as one may to distinguish the case of straits and the territorial sea, the one persists in remaining an analogue of the other, and in the sea lanes of south-east Asia they shade into each other so that they virtually overlap. The proliferation of broad claims to the sea portends the exclusion of warships from enormous operational areas. Admiral Gorshkov himself has calculated that if all countries declared a 200-mile territorial sea, then of the 360 million square kilometres of water on our planet about 140–150 million would be appropriated by the coastal States, and on the Soviet's own terms would be denied to the Red fleet. The Soviet Union has no intention of allowing this to happen, and so it resists claims beyond twelve miles. But if the fear remains that this resistance might prove ineffective, it is logical to suppose that the Soviet navy has gone cold on the notion that warships may not transit the territorial sea without previous permission. It may be significant that Admiral Gorshkov[4] avoids discussing the question altogether, although he does mention all the other relevant features of the law of the sea that affect naval operations.

These broad territorial sea claims portend disabilities for global sea power that even the concession of a right of transit cannot overcome. For example, there is no right of overflight in the territorial sea, and hence air cover is not legally available for transiting forces, which in the case of 200-mile claims could be gravely prejudicial, especially off places like West Africa which were favourite U-boat hunting grounds. Then, submarines must transit the territorial sea on the surface showing their flag. The great majority of submarines which have been detected in territorial waters in recent years are believed to have been Soviet, and they are rendered vulnerable by the Soviet view of the right of warships to traverse the territorial sea. Faced with extended territorial sea claims, the Soviet navy can complete oceanographical investigations, upon which its strategic doctrine is being erected, only by submarine invasion of the marginal waters of other nations. In this respect, too, the transition of the Soviet navy from a coastal defence force into an instrument of global sea power has distorted to the point of contradiction Soviet doctrine on the law of the sea.

The proposal to characterise only the first twelve miles of a 200-mile limit as territorial waters, leaving the balance as a 'natural resource zone' or 'patrimonial sea', salvages certain of these naval interests by permitting overflight and submerged passage. But it still

[4] See above, p. 13.

leaves the problem that the coastal States will increasingly resent intrusions into areas where they wish to claim exclusive economic rights, and where damage can be done to their interests. Inevitably they will want to regulate shipping in the area, and the lurking submarine is unlikely to escape their legal nets. The vastness of the areas in which global deployment of submarines can be affected has scarcely been realised. All the access routes to Cape Horn are covered by 200-mile claims, and the South American navies, with the latest detection equipment, the Ikara anti-submarine missile system and the predisposition to use force against unidentified submerged contacts, can only complicate the naval planning of the Great Powers who may use this route.

The law relating to submerged contacts is itself so malleable as to be a dangerous weapon to both sides. There is a belief in naval circles that the requirement that submarines transit on the surface is to be read with the requirement that the exercise of the right of innocent passage is to be read with the proviso that the right must be exercised in conformity with the Convention and other rules of international law, and with the authorisation to the coastal State to take the necessary steps in its territorial sea to prevent passage which is not innocent. The conclusion is drawn that submerged passage is not innocent passage and may be prevented by force. But it is dangerous to rely too much on this neat trick of exegesis because, for one thing, it is available only to the thirty-nine countries which are parties to the Geneva Convention on the Territorial Sea and, for another, it involves the supposition that breach of a duty to remain on the surface renders passage non-innocent, which is rather like saying that excessive speed on the road makes the journey illegal.

Since the Soviet Union seems to have been at the receiving end of most of the attacks which have been made on unidentified submerged submarines, it may have been hoist by its own petard. For if warships have no right of innocent passage the submarine should not have been in the territorial sea at all. It is an invader, to be dealt with like any other invader. Some countries of the Soviet bloc have declared that unidentified submarines will be attacked and destroyed. The victim can, therefore, hardly complain. But if a submarine is still in innocent passage although submerged, it would have the right of self-defence, and if attacked might well be justified in torpedoing its persecutor. Naval staffs have thus to anticipate the political impasse which contradictory legal arguments could lead to in the event of such an incident occurring. It is therefore desirable to see if the law can be tightened so as to produce a satisfactory result without escalation.

Certain considerations must be taken into account before an evaluation is possible of the right of a coastal State to attack a submerged submarine in its territorial sea. Where the territorial sea is narrow, and particularly where it is only three miles wide, the likelihood of a submerged submarine contact being there for other than purposes of innocent passage is greater than where it is extensive. The reason is that coastal waters may be hazardous for submarines in transit and such vessels would normally remain farther out to sea. This consideration, of course, is minimised when a territorial sea of 200 miles is claimed. In that case it would be reasonable to assume that a submarine in transit will pass through the territorial sea, and under certain weather conditions it may be more convenient, and even necessary in order to avoid damage, for it to do so submerged. The factors that are to be taken into account, therefore, in assessing the innocence or otherwise of a submarine's submerged passage through the territorial sea would appear to be the reasonableness of the use of the territorial sea for transit purposes, which may be in ratio with its extent, the weather conditions at the time, the political climate and, most important, the track taken by the submarine.

It would not be unreasonable for coastal States to require submarines in innocent passage to remain on the surface. Any submarine requiring to dive, for bad weather or other reasons connected with its safety or timely arrival at its destination, could inform the coastal State of its intention and of its planned 'dived' course—although it must be remembered that the possibility of its doing so depends upon radio propagation conditions, which can be very difficult, and on speed. While this may seem to weaken the argument of those nations claiming that no notification of warship passage is required, it still has grounds in its favour for the safety of life at sea.

It would be possible in bad weather, when sonar conditions are often poor, for two or more submarines to be dived in the same area at the same time. The risk of collision in this case is significant, but could be avoided by coastal States giving instructions to the submarines concerned to route them clear of each other. Submarines which do not conform could be a danger to themselves and others; and, as well, they may not be in innocent passage.

While the use of force against a submerged submarine in the territorial sea is not ruled out, on the argument that entry of a warship for purposes other than that of innocent passage is an intrusion upon national territory and may be repelled just as a military intrusion on land may be, every measure should be taken short of force to require the submarine to leave, as provided by Article 23 of the Geneva Convention. In the case of a conventional submarine it is possible for the destroyer escort to maintain close contact until the submarine is obliged to snort, whereupon tactics may be employed to make it surface. In the case of a nuclear-powered submarine—which, because of its size, would normally use only deeper territorial waters and is not, therefore, likely to be a problem for countries with restricted or shallow territorial seas—this tactic may not avail. It is possible to fire a mortar bomb to explode within half a mile of the submarine, which would be the equivalent of a shot across the bows, and warning may be given by dropping hand grenades, or the more modern warning charges now used by the Royal Navy. Only when these measures, protracted and exasperating though they may be, are exhausted should mortar bombs be resorted to by the surface vessel or aircraft.

It must be recognised, however, that the practice of navies, of both the NATO and Warsaw Pact countries, is to authorise immediate attack upon any submerged contacts which are identified as intruders. This is written into the legislation of some Eastern European countries, and into operational orders of some other countries. The United States Navy TACAID provides for what have become known as 'Uncle Joe procedures' for requiring submerged contacts in the territorial sea to surface immediately or face attack. These include the dropping of TNT charges or hand grenades to make five underwater sound signals at two-second intervals. United States and NATO submarines identify themselves pursuant to these procedures, but Soviet ones do not.

The consideration that human life is involved in the tactics to be employed against a submerged submarine in the territorial sea is proportional to the military threat prevailing at the time to the security of the coastal State. A navy engaged in limited warfare may have every justification based on self-defence in employing its ASW weapons against such a contact, and if the contact happens to be of a belligerent nation it must be regarded as responsible for its presence in a tactically threatening situation. It must also be remembered that self-defence operates both ways. A submarine which is attacked in the territorial sea may be justified in responding to the attack by torpedoing the surface vessel, so that a clearer appreciation of the delicate issues involved in the exercise of the right of innocent passage than has hitherto prevailed would seem to be incumbent.

It is evident, then, that the extent and condition of the territorial sea is itself a subject of the sort of conflict situation in which sea power will be used to resolve the issue, as well as an advantage or an encumbrance to its use for any other purpose. Admiral Gorshkov's comment is a warning: 'The key to the solution of this question is the strict establishment of limitations on the breadths of territorial seas, since a further extension could create the danger of an actual division of the high seas'.[5]

[5] See above, p. 13.

CHAPTER XI

THE AREAS OF
SELF-DEFENCE OPERATIONS:
THE SEA BED

Many of the possible naval uses of the sea bed fall at present within the realms of science fiction, and naval staffs are not as perturbed over proposals to internationalise the ocean floor for the purposes of mineral exploitation as some proponents of that notion have imagined. But the question has a sufficient practical interest for naval policy to warrant the scrutiny from a defence point of view of the various schemes for international control of the resources of the sea bed that have been put forward. Since the sea bed is an important medium of submarine detection by means of listening devices, legal obstacles to the choice of the location of this equipment obviously affect plans for submarine tracking and deployment, and ultimately affect the global balance of deterence, albeit in a marginal way. The sea bed is also the terrain upon which sundry devices can be placed, from explosive instruments to systems for the launching of projectiles; where locomotive vehicles can operate for whatever purposes navies may find them useful; and where manned stations can be set up.

The state of international law upon the availability of the sea bed for these purposes is one of obscurity, and naval staffs would prefer that it remained that way because this would maximise the options available. Within the territorial sea limits of a State the sea bed is subject to sovereignty and is as exclusive to the State as the dry land. The State is quite free to use its territorial sea bed for naval purposes, provided that it does not thereby incommode foreign shipping in their exercise of the right of innocent passage. Foreign navies may not use the territorial sea bed, even for the purpose of their submarines resting there. A navy which is preoccupied with coastal defence and is interested in using the sea bed may perceive benefits in the extension of territorial sea limits, while a navy which seeks to contain other navies to confined waters, or which aspires to global sea power or finds it convenient to track potentially hostile submarines off other coasts, will be concerned to shrink claims respecting territorial waters so far as convenience suggests and politics permit.

Beyond the territorial sea a coastal State enjoys 'sovereign rights' to the sea bed for the purpose of 'exploration and exploitation' of the natural resources thereof. The spatial projection of these rights under the Geneva Continental Shelf Convention, 1958, reaches at least as far as the 200-metre isobath, but that limit may be exceeded if 'the depth of the superjacent waters admits of the exploitation of the natural resources' of the sea bed. This formula was nonsensical when it was adopted and it has been the subject of a remarkable exegesis which has by no means been confined to lawyers, and which has not in fact shed a great deal of light on the ultimate limits to which the continental shelf in the legal sense can be extended.

From the naval point of view the indeterminate extent of the continental shelf, and the questionable departure from or approximation to 'sovereignty' of the concept of 'sovereign rights', raise questions for naval staffs as to the areas of sea bed in which activities are either permissible or prohibited, and as to the identification of those activities. A coastal defence navy which is concerned to restrain other navies from use of the neighbouring sea bed will be interested in a broad area of continental shelf, and so in a liberal interpretation of the 'exploitability criterion', as the formula above referred to is popularly described, in the Continental Shelf Convention; and in an equally liberal interpretation of 'sovereign rights' so as to acquire a legal monopoly of naval resort to the sea bed of the continental shelf. A navy whose interests are in distant waters will be concerned to limit the extent of the continental shelf by a strict interpretation of 'sovereign rights' so as to limit them to economic exploitation, leaving other uses of the sea bed to fall under the freedom of the seas.

Wherever the continental shelf as the area of the coastal State's sovereign rights in fact or in theory ends, there lie the ocean depths which used to be thought of as a naval no-man's-land wherein the same freedoms were exercisable as upon the surface of the high seas, but which are, in United Nations parlance, described as the 'common heritage of mankind'. This characterisation is prompted by the objective of inhibiting unilateral seizure of the mineral resources of the ocean floor thought to lie in precipitated form on the sea bed or to be encapsulated within its geological structure. This raises no questions as to the naval uses of the sea bed, but the parcelling out of the sea bed for exploration purposes by an international body which it is proposed should be set up obviously portends a similar problem of restricted access to the deep sea bed as has arisen in connection with the continental shelf. Navies, on the whole, would prefer that there be no restrictions on the use of the deep sea bed, but if there are to be restrictions they would prefer them to be minimal.

The major sea Powers, of course, have divided interests in these questions, since they are preoccupied at one and the same time with coastal defence and with the global exercise of influence and deterrence. For their naval staffs it becomes a question of judgement whether a broad territorial sea and a broad continental shelf, with coextensive monopoly of the sea bed for naval purposes, is overall to be preferred to a narrow territorial sea with a limited continental shelf and a shared naval use of the sea bed beyond the territorial sea, or vice versa. Although naval staffs are likely to prefer the minimal restrictions on uses of the sea bed beyond the continental shelf, this may depend upon their competitive technological position. Naval staffs also look at the question from the point of view of the extent of their commitment and their resources to meet it, as well as from the point of view of the strategic and tactical uses of the sea bed. As the coastal State's rights in the sea bed expand, either by prolongation of the continental shelf or by acquisition of exploitation blocks of the ocean floor, its navy's task of protection and surveillance spreads commensurately, with implications for fleet disposition, manning and procurement policies.

The degree of consideration which naval staffs are required to give to the law of the sea bed will obviously depend upon the importance of the naval uses of the sea bed, and appraisal must take into account the extent to which these uses are, or are likely to become, vital to the effective functioning of naval systems. If the sea bed is expendable for tactical reasons, naval Powers may not be disposed to make an issue out of it for predominantly defence ends.

UNDERWATER DETECTION SYSTEMS

The most practicable naval use of the sea bed is the location of devices for the detection of submarines in transit. If these devices are sufficiently dispersed to detect a submarine at many points in its course, and sufficiently extended to detect it in distant waters; if they can be located so as to detect it in such a way as provide a triangular fix so as to give range and bearing; if they are sufficiently sensitive to ascertain the signature of the submarine's nationality and classification, and located so as to detect a submarine's movement at considerable distances, then the tracking of a submarine is possible and its effective deployment operationally is to that extent prejudiced. The global balance of deterrence is served by means of tracking the SSBNs of the other side, so that the threat they pose can be neutralised; or, at least, it is served if the other side is obliged to suppose that their location may be known, whether or not it is known or could be known.

The systems presently employed, and known as acoustic arrays, are mainly of the passive sonar surveillance type. A submarine in transit is detected by the noise it emits or the cavitation of its propellors revolving at certain speeds and under certain conditions; the data derived from an array of hydrophones is computer-processed in a shore station to which several of the systems are connected. The utility of this means of surveillance depends upon the advantages offered by sonar conditions at specific depths in specific areas, because the performance of the devices varies greatly, owing to the natural accidents of bottom configuration, sound refraction from temperature barriers, salinity and presence of marine life. Legal boundaries based upon distance, and even in some cases depth, criteria can be quite eccentric when considered from the point of view of conditions of nature.

As it happens, some systems are primarily related to the continental shelf, as in the case of the Caesar system on the eastern seaboard of the United States, where the installations are said to be on the 200-metre line, but others, such as Bronco, go into the deeper sea bed, and it is reported that Project Artemis, which is an active sonar system, involves the location of transmitters on the ocean floor, and that Sea Spider off Hawaii will be powered by self-contained nuclear batteries at great depths. To navies which make use of these means of detection it is obvious that the less law there is to affect the choice of sites for their location the better, for even though some importance attaches to the securing of a monopoly of their own continental shelves for this purpose, it may be that there will be an equal interest in the location of systems such as the Barrier version of Caesar upon the continental shelves of other States, especially where straits or other narrow waters restrict the transit routes of submarines on deployment to their operational stations. Diplomatic difficulties have occurred in just this connection.

The effectiveness of acoustic systems depends upon the geography of their location, and in this respect the continental shelf is important.

This is because the axis of the sound channel varies in depth from the surface of the sea to 6,000 ft. The sea bed of the continental shelf and continental slope is generally of a depth within this sound channel. While deep ocean surveillance is feasible, implantation on the sea bed may not yield the desired range of detection of sound transmitted at great distance in the optimal focus of the channel, and hence suspended array systems may have to be resorted to, which could raise questions respecting freedom of navigation.

In the case of passive acoustic devices no reliance is placed on law to protect them from sabotage because they are not detectable. But active devices can be located and destroyed, and it may be that naval interest would favour the legal right of exclusion from the sea-bed areas where they are located so as to facilitate their insulation. At present the practicalities are such that no clear policy direction is perceptible. Interference with detection systems is more likely to be accidental than deliberate, but if underwater exploitation of mineral resources, especially by suction methods, develops to the point where the chances of destruction cannot be discounted, defensive measures may become necessary. The fear among the internationalists is that if this occurred the naval Powers could stake out sea-bed claims, not for economic but for military purposes; while the far-seeing among defence planners may be apprehensive that the internationalising of the sea bed could close that possible option. It follows that naval planning for the future must take into account the questions of the legality of the location of arrays upon foreign continental shelves and the legality of means of protecting arrays, especially upon one's own continental shelf, from foreign interference.

The mystery which necessarily encompasses the matter of sub-merged surveillance systems has promoted much ignorant speculation upon the subversive influences which defence policies are likely to have upon the law of the sea bed. The problem certainly exists, and as these systems coalesce into an ocean-wide barrier line where sub-marines can be detected in the act of penetration, attention is likely to concentrate on the question of the legal nature of the continental shelf because of the shallow character of many of the world's strategic access routes. But the implications of defence planning are not as sinister as some have supposed, because the problem of legal ob-stacles to the location of acoustic facilities is in fact one that naval staffs believe they can live with. If underwater detection were an absolute and infallible means for the location of all potentially hostile submarines, which accordingly could be eliminated in a first strike, they would be a vital naval interest, but this is far from being the case; and even if it were, it would transform the balance of deterrence—which is the ambition of no one.

Because there are limitations to the propagation of energy through water and to the refinement of the means of discrimination, it is unlikely that such detection and tracking systems will be more than incidental components of ASW. While the naval influence upon national sea-bed policies is thus likely to be in favour of maximum flexibility and resistance to any hardening of the law, freedom of the sea bed from all international authority is unlikely to be perceived as a non-negotiable national issue.

SEA-BED SUBMERSIBLES

The same questions arise in the matter of mobile vehicles or devices on the sea bed. While studies have been made in defence circles of the implications for their use that arise from proposals for internationalising the deep sea bed, the fact is that their role in naval warfare is so speculative as to preclude precise evaluation of the issues. In any event, the use of the sea bed beyond the continental shelf by such inventions is unlikely, even as major weapon delivery systems, and this development is now inhibited by the Treaty on the Emplacement of Nuclear Weapons and other Weapons of Mass Destruction on the Sea Bed and the Ocean Floor of 11 February 1971 (T.I.A.S. 7337). For other tactical purposes, such as manned or unmanned mobile mines, these projected sea-bed vehicles would logically be confined to continental shelf areas where they can be used for covert offence against coastal installations, oil pipelines and acoustic arrays, or for surveillance or the laying of sonar buoys or other devices or obstructions. But the legal problems here are not specific to these inventions, they are common to any submersibles.

WEAPONS ON THE SEA BED

In the 1972 Strategic Arms Limitation Agreement the United States accepted a ratio of inferiority in the absolute number of missile launchers for a period of five years because its possession of multiple independently targeted re-entry vehicles (MIRVs) in fact enabled it to threaten with instant retaliation twice as many targets as Soviet Russia could, and also because the American missiles were believed to be more accurate. The development of independently targetable multiple warheads by the Russians, together with the greatly enhanced destructive power of their SS-9 missiles, has deprived the United States of the requisite assurance of equilibrium which, despite the diminished ratio of its missiles in terms of quantity, gave it qualitative superiority. A counter-force first strike upon the missiles of the other side would place the victim in the position of submitting to nuclear blackmail or of retaliating with insufficient but none the less terrible power, which it might be reluctant to do, since the overall outcome might be unpredictable. The fear is that this alteration may deprive deterrence of some measure of its assurance of security because the risks involved in a first strike policy may be less than they formerly were.

Since land-based launchers can be targeted with some accuracy, these developments have enhanced the significance of the nuclear-powered ballistic missile submarine (SSBN), which is not easily detected from the surface and can achieve by covert means a degree of invulnerability that only submersible missile systems can possess. Hitherto the problem with the Polaris and Poseidon missiles carried by the SSBNs has been their limited range, which has required deployment in areas where consistent tracking by killer submarines has been possible, although not easy. Location of the longer-range land-launched missiles in submerged silos which might escape detection and accurate targeting is a theoretically possible way of achieving the requisite degree of concealment with the requisite range to permit convenient location. But this would be an expedient available to both sides, and it would disturb basic calculations of the balance of deterrence by unacceptably reducing the certainties. In fact the need for submerged fixed launching systems has been to some extent removed by the *Trident* programme, under which a new generation of SSBNs which are difficult to track could take station in inland waters within a 6,000-mile range of Soviet land-based launchers or other targets. This is envisaged as restoration of the balance which the development of multiple warheads has threatened, but it draws attention to the advantages of submerged weapon systems both mobile and immobile, and raises significant questions of the treaty rules prescribing the emplacement of the mobile varieties on the sea bed.

These rules were the first expression of United Nations concern with the deep sea bed, which, on the supposition that it was to be internationalised as the 'common heritage of mankind', ought logically to be dedicated to peaceful uses. On 18 December 1967 the General Assembly adopted a resolution to this effect and instituted

a study of the question. The outcome was the Treaty on the Prohibitions of the Emplacement of Nuclear Weapons and other
Weapons of Mass Destruction on the Sea Bed and the Ocean Floor
and in the Subsoil Thereof, which was 'commended' by the General
Assembly on 7 December 1970 as a revised version of a joint Soviet–
American draft which had been submitted to the conference of the
Committee on Disarmament in 1969. When the suggestion of outlawing weapons on the sea bed was first made in the United Nations
the initial reaction of the defence authorities of the major Powers
was that this was only a whimsical idea of people who were ignorant
of strategic matters, because in fact no serious consideration had
been given to the possibilities of locating delivery systems on the
sea bed. This was because of the great cost involved and the fact
that construction work on several fixed installations could not
altogether escape notice and hence detection. This would defeat the
purpose of sea-bed location, which is concealment only. If mobile
systems, called 'creepy-crawlies', were used they would be so huge
and cumbersome, and would involve such design problems to enable
them to be locomotive on a rugged sea bed, that they were seen as
only a dubious alternative to the SSBN.

But the second reaction to the proposal, at least in the Pentagon,
was to take the possibilities of sea-bed weapon systems more seriously
in case the law might come to close the option of their development
and use. Great research programmes, like Project Blue Water, were
undertaken with a view to focusing upon the issues raised by the
General Assembly's moves, and a great deal of friction, in retrospect
unnecessary, occurred between the Pentagon and the State Department before the treaty was finally resolved upon. The reasons for
lack of interest in the use of the sea bed, for purposes other than
detection devices, remain as valid as they were before excitement was
aroused, and, not surprisingly, lack of interest is again the mood of
defence planners. The likelihood of their seeking in the future to
revive interest in the concealment of fixed or mobile delivery systems
on the sea bed as an aid to restoration of equivalence in destructive
capability is thus low, but the possibility is not altogether discounted,
and at least some theoretical attention has been focused on the gap
in the existing treaty system which results from the definition of the
geographical scope of the sea-bed treaty.

Originally it was envisaged that the prohibition on the emplacement of weapons in that treaty would apply to the sea bed 'beyond
the limits of present national jurisdiction'. But this would have had

capricious results, considering the variations in claims by States to the territorial sea and continental shelf and in the pretensions to jurisdiction not derivable from either of these concepts; and in the light of the widespread assumption in the Committee on Disarmament (shared initially even by the Soviet Union) that the continental shelf is included in national jurisdiction for military purposes, this formula would have excluded from the prohibition unacceptably large areas of sea bed.

It is evident that between the date of the opening of this question and the date of the introduction of the joint Soviet–United States draft treaty, the Soviet Union made an examination of the question whether the Russian continental shelf was as significant to Soviet naval uses as the Soviet Union supposed their continental shelves were to the Western Powers, and concluded that it was not. This was probably because the vastness of the areas claimed by the Soviet Union to be inland waters, closed areas or historic bays—including the whole Arctic area—permitted the Soviet naval staff to conclude unabashed that most of the Russian continental shelf was not legally continental shelf at all but something else; and because the whole sea bed of the Baltic was to be proclaimed as a non-military area. Hence the Soviet delegation, after a time, came down firmly in support of the view that the continental shelf is not a militarily exclusive area of the coastal States which possess sovereign rights over it, because these rights exist only for the purposes of exploration and exploitation of natural resources. For purposes other than the location of delivery systems of mass destruction the sea bed of the continental shelf is, according to this view, as much an area of tactical manoeuvre as the sea bed of the high seas; for purposes of tactical concealment of delivery systems it should not escape the moratorium on the use of the floor of the high seas.

So the Soviet Union pressed for the territorial sea limit as the point of departure for the prohibition. This met with reservations on the part of the United Kingdom respecting the substance of the matter, and on the part of the proponents of broad areas and diffused concepts of national jurisdiction, including the Latin Americans, who feared that undue concentration upon the question of territorial sea limits might adversely affect the promotion of their ambitions respecting exclusive control of natural resources. The United States at first sought the best of all possible worlds by submitting that the prohibited area should be the area beyond national jurisdiction, 'whose boundaries would become clearer when the limits of national jurisdiction were more precisely defined'. This endeavour to blur the issue having met with the appropriate response, the United States abandoned the approach to the question by way of legal finagling and concluded that the continental shelf was expendable for the purpose of concealment of delivery systems because quantitatively and qualitatively the United States was thought to possess sufficient capability in its land-based systems to deter a first strike on the part of the Soviet Union, for the reasons outlined earlier in this chapter.

The interests of the Soviet Union and the United States thus having been brought into conjunction, their joint decision was to take a relatively short distance from the coast as the point of departure of the area of the prohibition. Although initially the Russians wanted twelve miles and the Americans three miles, it was eventually agreed to adopt the twelve-mile alternative, but the problem was one of legal expression, since this limit, while it represented the majority position on the extent of the territorial sea, did not represent the position of the United States on that subject. So the draft treaty proposal was that the prohibition would apply beyond the maximum contiguous zone provided for in the 1958 Geneva Convention on the Territorial Sea and the Contiguous Zone, which is twelve miles from the shore. The importation of the Geneva concepts into the discussions caused an eruption of controversy, and it may be questioned why the two Powers did not take from the beginning the straightforward course of proposing a distance of twelve miles from the coast without reference to legal definitions. The answer is that they wished to preserve from the scope of the prohibition their inland waters, such as bays and closed seas, which a distance-from-the-coast formula would not have done, and that the only apparent method of preserving their respective positions on this aspect of the matter was to import the baseline formulas for bays of the Geneva Convention.

Once disquiet had been removed by the introduction of a disclaimer clause to the effect that nothing in the draft Treaty on Emplacement of Weapons would prejudice a party's position on the territorial sea, contiguous zone or continental shelf, it became possible to agree that the area to be excluded from the prohibitions would be the twelve-mile outer limit of the contiguous zone as measured in accordance with the rules in the Geneva Convention, and this was the text finally adopted. The disclaimer clause benefits the Soviet Union as much as the Latin Americans, because it covers the great bays and closed seas which the Soviet Union claims as inland waters.

Since these claims are expressed in the terms of 'historic waters', the Soviet Union regards them as outside the scope of the Geneva Convention (which left historic waters for further consideration), and hence the importation of the Geneva rules for expressing the twelve-mile distance principle constitutes no inhibition on Soviet naval planning. At the same time, the elastic character of these rules makes it possible to expand the exempted areas as tactical requirements dictate by the use, in some localities, of the straight baseline method. The areas of concealment are therefore not insignificant.

It follows that, theoretically at least, the exclusion of inland waters plus twelve miles from the areas in which the emplacement of weapons of mass destruction is prohibited opens up the possibility of enhancing a second-strike capability by submerged location of launching vehicles, which would perhaps diminish the likelihood of detection and hence of first-strike destruction. But at the present time the possibility is a theoretical one only.

Apart from the question of areas covered, the Treaty on the Emplacement of Weapons offers some escape also respecting the systems prohibited. It prohibits the emplacement of nuclear weapons and other weapons of mass destruction, which is a very general notion. The problems of definition and evaluation were fully adverted to in the conference of the Committee on Disarmament, and it became clear then that the Powers had certain understandings about what was covered, including biological, chemical and radiation weapons, but speculation has extended even to lasers, weather modifiers and anti-satellite devices. At the more practical level, the question has been raised whether mine warfare is prohibited because of its mass-destructive potentialities. These exercises of imagination have been shrugged off on the basis that men of common sense know what is meant by mass destruction, and that if the science-fiction potentialities do become actual the treaty will be up for review anyhow.

What, from the point of view of naval staffs concerned with planning and procurement, cannot so easily be shrugged off is the question of what is meant by the prohibition of the emplacement of structures, launching installations or any other facilities specifically designed for storing, testing or using nuclear weapons and weapons of mass destruction. Is this directed at installations that are exclusively designed for the purpose, or does it encompass dual-purpose systems, such as bottom-based torpedo launchers or anti-missile missiles which can have conventional or nuclear warheads? The treaty's apparent emphasis upon design leaves open possible options respecting capacity.

Also the treaty refers to emplantation or emplacement on the sea bed, and this gives rise to questions about vehicles or devices that are mobile or in suspension in the water. While the United States has gone on record as saying that nuclear mines moored to the sea bed would fall within the prohibition just as much as those lying on the sea bed, the point has been debated and is obviously open to debate; for, if the mine were really a weapon of mass destruction, the interpretation might be pressed towards its inclusion in the treaty, but tactical nuclear mines of very low yield for ASW purposes might fall into a different category. The United States has also gone on record to the effect that mobile weapons of mass destruction, such as creeping mines or 'underwater fireships' would be caught by the treaty if they were locomotive only on the bottom. The drafting history makes it clear that submarines are obviously not affected by the treaty, but when does a submersible near-bottom vehicle cease to be a submarine? So naval 'creepy-crawlies' are theoretically entering the domain of legal ambiguities hitherto peopled by Alaskan king crabs and Brazilian spiny lobsters, even if at present they are phantoms and likely to remain so for some time.

The sea-bed treaty dovetails in parts of the western hemisphere with the Treaty of Tlatelolco (14 February 1967, 634 U.N.T.S. 364), prohibiting nuclear weapons in Latin America, but the two are very dissimilar. The Treaty of Tlatelolco covers only nuclear weapons and does not prohibit the emplacement of delivery systems as distinct from the weapons themselves. It extends to the superjacent waters, and thus applies to the SSBN as well as to bottom devices, although it does not exclude their transit to operational areas. It extends to the territorial sea and so to 200 miles in some cases and potentially in others, depending upon the vagaries of national legislation, and it provides for vast nuclear-free zones in the Atlantic and the Pacific, which are, however, unlikely to be activated because they depend upon participation of all of the nuclear Powers. And it is geographically confined to the areas south of the Bahamas.

So far as naval uses of the sea bed are concerned, the whole area of inland waters and territorial waters remains available to the coastal State. There is also no doubt that the sea bed of the continental shelf is also available to the coastal State, but the question is whether this availability is exclusive—whether, that is, it derives from the freedom of the seas and not from possession of the continental shelf. The argument that it is exclusive is stronger than has been thought. For it would be odd if naval uses of the sea bed were to prove inconsistent with the designation of the sea bed beyond the limit of the continental shelf as 'the common heritage of mankind', while the continental shelf remained the only area of mutual confrontation of sea-bed detection or weapon systems other than systems of mass destruction, yet this is an implication of some of the debates in the conference of the Committee on Disarmament.

The Soviet Union's view that any State may use the sea bed of the continental shelf for naval purposes is the product of strategic expediency, and in as much as it purports to derive from the concept of the freedom of the seas it leads to inconsistency. For the Soviet Union at the 1958 Geneva Conference on the Law of the Sea supported the Indian position that the building of installations for military ends on the continental shelf would be an appropriation of the sea bed which would contradict the freedom of the seas. Obviously, then, the freedom of the seas works both ways.

That States will use their own continental shelves for naval purposes is something that is unlikely to be effectively resisted, and there are arguments to which they might resort if they sought to make this use exclusive, such as the territorial character of the continental shelf (whatever restrictions are inherent in 'sovereign rights' as distinct from 'sovereignty'); the need to protect their own monopoly of the sea bed for economic uses which the presence of foreign devices and cables might prejudice; and even the requirements of self-defence, although the reluctance to use this argument to resist the placing of missiles in proximity to the United States during the Cuban crisis reveals the political restrictions to which it is likely to be subjected. So far no government has explicitly contended for exclusive naval rights to the continental shelf, but this is only because the interested Powers have hitherto benefited from the 'open-ended' character of the legal concepts. But this very ambiguity can become the occasion of dispute leading to resort to naval force to expel the intruder upon the continental shelf or to sustain the intrusion.

So far as the sea bed beyond the continental shelf is concerned, conflicts are possible here over the location of detection devices, but they are likely to be covert because if this is an area in which naval uses are legally prohibited the prohibition would apply equally to both sides, and if it is an area in which they are not legally prohibited neither side has the right to interfere with the other. This equality of legal position, however it may be thought to arise, is likely to be a restraint upon interference with sea-bed systems outside the continental shelf, not in deference to the law but because no ascendency can be gained politically by manipulating the law—and because any conflict which is not clandestine is likely to attract disapprobation based upon General Assembly Resolution 2749 of 17 December 1970 proclaiming that the sea bed beyond the continental shelf should be 'reserved exclusively for peaceful purposes'. The resolution in itself was incapable of affecting the legal position, but the reiteration of this formula in the Sea-bed Committee, and the persistent lip service which has been given to it, have created a political milieu in which no credit is likely to accrue to any assailant on the sea bed, however defensible his motives.

The United States has publicly taken the position that the reference to 'peaceful purposes' does not preclude naval activities on the sea bed which are not prohibited by a specific treaty negotiated within the framework of disarmament, but it has emphasised their 'passive defensive character', which indicates the extent to which the international sentiment embodied in Resolution 2749 needs to be accommodated. The pliable state of sea-bed law may be an advantage at present, but the 1974–75 Law of the Sea conference has implications that may make naval staffs wonder if the freedom of manoeuvre that the law at present allows them has not been bought at the price of stability and assurance in defence planning.

CHAPTER XII

THE AREAS OF SELF-DEFENCE OPERATIONS: THE RIGHTS OF NEUTRALS

The law of neutrality has not attracted legal attention since 1945, so that the requisite level of professional acquaintance with its rules is low, and this tends to deprive naval staffs of the proper infusion of ideas on the role of navies in the protection of neutrality. Some international lawyers even go so far as to say gaily that there is no such thing as a law of neutrality in the era of the United Nations, because there is no legal condition of war. It may well be that the prohibition of the use of force 'inconsistent with the purposes of the United Nations' has deprived belligerents of the rights which they previously possessed against neutrals, such as the right of visit and search on the high seas and seizure of contraband discussed in chapter IX, though even this must be regarded as doubtful, since naval blockades of a sort continue to be mounted; but to say that the converse is true—that neutrals have no rights—would be to leave them the unprotected victims of violence and would be retrogressive and hardly consonant with the aspirations of contemporary international law.

The extent to which neutral ships have been affected by naval operations in recent years makes it necessary to reassert the rights of neutrals to immunity from interference, attack and damage, and to compensation when these occur. The fact that the flag States of neutral ships sunk or damaged in the Indo–Pakistan and Middle East wars were often indifferent to the question of legal liability is not to be taken as indicating any attitude towards the State practice that contributes to international law. It is due to the system of insurance and reinsurance, whereby the loss is discounted. But in economic terms the extent to which prejudice is caused by interference with neutrals is likely to be underestimated, because it is ultimately reflected in consumer prices and does not fall on any one head.

War risk policies are covered either by insurance associations which have the right to require their members to deviate, or on the war risks market, where the premiums are considerably higher. Members of the associations pay minimal premiums to share the losses, and if extra money is required a 'back call' is made on the members to cover the deficit. Back calls have not been necessary.

Insurance claims cover total loss of a vessel from mines, shelling, air and missile attack, particular average or partial loss, deviation expenses arising from vessels deviating in accordance with the directions of the association that they should avoid a war area, loss of the vessel if detained for a fixed period of months, third-party liabilities to crew, passengers, pilots and others, and liabilities to public authorities for wreck removal or oil pollution and liabilities in respect of cargoes. In the Indo–Pakistan and Middle East wars vessels of the associations were instructed to avoid danger areas at an early stage in the conflict and, if they were already in the areas, to leave them at once.

The insurers are subrogated in international law in the rights of the neutral whose ship is lost or damaged, but claims against belligerents have not been made because of this distribution of losses and because, in the case of the *Venus Challenger*,[1] so it is said, for want of evidence that it was a missile fired by the Indian navy that sank the ship, although proof of the type of missile should not be difficult to establish. The point is that flag-of-convenience States have no interest, apparently, in protecting their ships, and this means that the traditional pressures on belligerents to avoid harm to neutrals, which was such a prominent feature of the war diplomacy of the past, are not so evident or persistent. Because of this, belligerents are less inclined to be restrained by the presence of neutral ships, and the possibilities of violence at sea are enhanced. The conditions for proliferation of disorder are thus created by the practices of the world community. The likelihood of the major naval Powers being themselves involved in war at sea is less than that they will be neutral in wars between lesser or even trifling Powers. The Indo–Pakistan war portended the problems of neutrality with which major naval Powers could be faced. For, if it is now a rule of international law that belligerent operations may not be conducted on the high seas, or neutrals subjected to measures of blockade conducted outside the territorial sea, the neutral naval Powers will have to enforce the rule by escorting their shipping. The lessons of the Spanish Civil War are quite likely to be repeated in this increasingly unstable world. For these reasons any navy with the capability may become involved

[1] See above, p. 87.

161

in self-defence operations to protect its neutrality in distant waters; while coastal defence navies may have to ensure that their neutral waters are not the scene of belligerent operations, which are likely to occur in bottlenecks like straits and hence in territorial waters. Naval preparation for exercises in neutrality is not only inadequate, it is non-existent; and legal analysis of the changes wrought in the law of neutrality since 1945 is so slight that the lawyer is more likely to confuse than to clarify the problem.

NEUTRALITY ZONES

One possibility for neutrals would be to seek to insulate themselves from belligerency by the drawing of a regional cordon of neutral waters. This could be conceived as an analogue of the various extra-territorial zones which some States are advocating to cope with pollution or the protection of natural resources. The fact that belligerency at sea could interfere with anti-pollution measures or with exclusive exploitation of the sea and its bed adds plausibility to the idea. As it stands, international law would not directly countenance such measures, but the history of the South American neutrality zone of 1939 does underscore the fact that such a zone can be made effective up to a point if the diplomatic situation is such as to require that the neutrals be placated.

The South American neutrality zone was initiated by the Declaration of Panama, issued on 3 October 1939 by all the American republics with the aim of having a zone around the whole of the hemisphere, excluding Canada, within which would be prohibited 'the commission of any hostile act by any non-American belligerent nation, whether such hostile act be attempted or made from land, sea or air'. Its legal justification, set forth in the preamble, was said to be the right of self-preservation from the dangers of war, which required that 'the waters to a reasonable distance from the coast remain free from the commission of the hostile acts or from the undertaking of belligerent activities'. The limits of the zone were defined by straight lines linking co-ordinates, and were roughly 300 miles offshore. The United States described the declaration as

an event of unusual importance. If we are able through our joint representation to persuade the belligerents to comply with its provision, the Declaration will have made a far-reaching contribution towards the attainment of that goal . . . that our twenty-one American Republics shall remain free from the horrors of war.

An Inter-American Neutrality Committee was set up, and, following the battle of the River Plate, when both belligerents were confronted by the obstacle of the zone's existence, this body issued detailed regulations in April 1940 which included the prohibition of 'any hostile act, detention, capture or pursuit, the discharge of projectiles, the placing of mines of any kind, or any operation of war' in the zone. Otherwise warships and merchant ships were free to pass there. The fact is that Churchill's recognition of the usefulness of the zone to the British cause added strength to the efforts of the hemisphere countries, and their intensified grip on the zone reflected the way in which Great Britain had reacted to the *Graf Spee*'s attack in the area. In fact the Admiralty neither accepted nor contested the zone. It said that the creation of the zone was 'the wisest way of proceeding', and that the only strictly legal limitation of hostilities related to cases where the belligerents engaged each other within the territorial waters of one of the States. It treated the declaration as an invitation, not an injunction, to be implemented by acceptance.

The German attitude towards the declaration was that it was best to leave the British and French, as the superior naval Powers, to earn opprobrium by contesting the zone's validity, and hence no attitude was immediately struck towards it. After the battle of the Plate an official statement on the subject was issued by the German government, which said that 'the recognised rules of international law were not to be regarded as a rigid and for ever immutable order, but are capable of and require adaptation to progressive development and newly arising conditions'. Taking their cue from the British, the Germans said that the declaration needed to be accepted to become binding, and they exculpated the action of the *Graf Spee* on the ground that this was covered by the old law, before Germany had agreed to the change. While hinting at agreement to validate the zone, Germany protested at the inequality of treatment of Allied and German warships there. No satisfaction being received on this point by negotiation, the pocket battleship *Admiral Scheer* was given strict instructions in November 1940 not to cruise in the zone. However, in April 1941 two U-boats were ordered to escort the German merchant ship *Leek* from Rio de Janeiro, but not to attack Allied shipping in the zone except to protect their charge. Otherwise the zone was respected until October 1941, when the American system of escorting Allied convoys as far as Iceland led to a rapidly deteriorating situation.

The fact is that for two years the zone was made effective, despite the want of any sound basis in traditional law. The argument of self-defence upon which it was based wore pretty thin as time passed, and it has been universally rejected by the analysts of the law of war. But although there were breaches of it apart from the battle of the River Plate, notably the scuttling of the Nord-Deutsche Lloyd liner *Columbus* when intercepted by a British auxiliary cruiser, and the chase of the *Arauca* by a British destroyer into Fort Lauderdale, politically the exercise was a moderate success, and self-defence made it plausible. Naval staffs should not be discouraged by legal scepticism from studying the case as a useful precedent.

OPERATIONAL ZONES

If the law concerned itself only with the position of belligerents it would not discriminate in respect of the areas of sea within which self-defence operations could be legitimated. It is because of the rights of neutrals that limitations on operations on the high seas can be envisaged. The question is whether areas of the high seas can be closed to international shipping on the pretext of naval operational uses. The absolute character of the freedom of the seas as it is expressed in the 1958 Geneva Convention on the High Seas makes it difficult to envisage the creation of operational zones beyond territorial waters within which special belligerent rights may be exercised or where limited war can be insulated, although naval speculation inevitably comes around sooner or later to the desirability or need of such zones.

There is a misconception running through the literature of international law that, in the past, battle fleets in time of peace could occupy great tracts of ocean while on manoeuvres, and that limitations on the freedom of the seas are thus inherent. Certainly the traditional battle line of the *Dreadnought* and Super-*Dreadnought* eras would extend beyond horizon range and would engage in gunnery practice at targets just within that range. But it is untrue that State practice has regarded this use of the seas as contradicting any other use of them, or as creating a monopoly of occupation of an area of ocean. On the contrary, the Clear Range Procedures of all major navies make it encumbent upon the commanding officer of a firing ship to ensure that the range is clear before opening fire. Notices to Mariners on Firing Practices and Exercise Areas are issued giving information on firing practices, and they are intended for warning only. It is understood that shipping cannot be ordered to leave the area. When shot fell near a Soviet merchant ship in a United States gunnery range in 1968 the United States contended only that clearance of the range had been established in accordance with normal safety procedures.

The buzzing of ships by aircraft is a mode of vexing without interfering with navigation. It was done by the Sixth Fleet during the 1956 Suez operations, and it can have the tactical effect of inhibiting the launching and recovery of aircraft from the carriers, the fouling of the range for naval gunfire support and the distraction of ships from station-keeping as well as surveillance and use of weapon systems. In 1960 the Soviet Union protested to the United States that this type of activity constituted a 'flagrant violation of generally accepted rules of international law'. In fact it is not much different from the Soviet's own form of harassment by ships.

The conduct of nuclear tests at sea has highlighted the problem of reconciling the use of the sea for practice purposes with this absolute concept of the freedom of the seas. At the Geneva conference in 1958 the United States delegation was instructed not to insist upon the right that one nation may unilaterally appropriate for its exclusive use a portion of the high seas for the purpose of nuclear testing. The fall of shot, missile splashdown and detonation of nuclear devices are all consistent with the freedom of the seas, if not prohibited by some other rule of international law, provided that shipping in the area is not incommoded.

Recently we have seen the deployment of naval power by New Zealand to create a situation where the exercise of the right of testing would contradict the exercise of the right of navigation. This attempt to oppose two emanations of the same right in order to produce an impasse where the testing party would have three options—namely not to test, to test and be damned, or to expel, with all the political hazards that either of the latter two courses would involve—is a classic example of the use of law in a coercive way. The United States Pacific tests of the 1950s were accompanied by notices to mariners prohibiting 'all vessels' from entering without specific clearance the territorial and inland waters of the test sites, and by warnings that a much greater area of adjacent high seas was 'dangerous to all ships'. The situation of foreign ships insisting upon the right to enter the zone did not arise at that time, and the United States is on record as saying that only American ships were to be excluded by force. But circumstances were different in the case of the French testing areas around Muroroa Atoll in the south Pacific.

When France was threatened by a plague of protesting yachts (which largely failed to materialise) the theoretical problem was deliberately made actual. Eventually, in 1973, France's notices to mariners went beyond declaring a *zone dangereuse* and for the first time in the history of nuclear testing amounted to a temporary appropriation of an area of the high seas from which all shipping could be excluded. One yacht was, in fact, boarded; but to hustle away H.M.N.Z.S. *Taranaki* or *Canterbury* was another matter. The outcome was a maritime pavane, executed with some grace and dignity, in which New Zealand made her point and France continued her testing.

Had the International Court of Justice[2] at the Hague found that the enclosure of the seas for the purpose of French nuclear testing was illegal, this might have ended speculation upon the legality of naval operational zones; if it had found that the enclosure was not illegal, it would have put a premium upon it. Either way, naval policy would certainly be affected by the development and elaboration of the law. Hitherto the sea has been fundamentally different from the land in the matter of combat uses. On land the population can be ordered to evacuate front-line areas, irrespective of nationality, while the combatants get on with the fight. But this is because the land is subject to sovereignty and everyone in it falls under the legal direction of the government or the military occupant. It is different at sea, and if operational zones are created they must be justified by reference to different concepts.

During the first world war Germany decreed all the waters around the British Isles to be a war zone, in which every enemy merchant ship would be sunk on sight and neutral ships put at risk, but this was justified on the ground of reprisals for Great Britain's failure to abide by the unratified Declaration of London of 1908 respecting the legal conditions for blockade.[3] Reprisals beget reprisals, and so the law circumvents the law. Great Britain's form of retaliation was prohibition altogether of neutral trade with Germany, and Germany's answer was an extension of submarine warfare to cut Great Britain off.

Although Japan had experimented with 'defence sea areas' during the Russo–Japanese war, the device was first systematised as a means of warfare in 1915. Eventually the German-declared war zones included waters around France, Italy, Greece, Asia Minor and North

[2] It declined to hear the dispute: I.C.J. Rep., 1974.
[3] See above, p. 20.

Africa as well as the British Isles, and these were treated as 'closed' (*Seesferre*). Submarines and minefields were the instruments of enclosure. The war zone proclaimed around the British Isles in 1940 was a resurrection of that of the first world war, but now another international-law justification was offered on 18 January 1940. It was argued that mining in the interests of blockade is legal; mines destroy belligerent and neutral shipping indiscriminately; the war zone was an area within which mining would be legal; what difference was there between destruction by torpedo and mine? The argument paid scant attention to Hague Convention No. VIII of 1907 relative to the laying of automatic contact mines, which may be hopelessly vague but does embody a general notion that minefields must be notified to neutrals and not intended only to interrupt commercial traffic.

At the Nuremberg trial of major German war criminals Admiral Doenitz was found guilty of war crimes respecting this creation of a war zone, for which no legal basis was acknowledged by the tribunal (although he was acquitted on the charge of waging unrestricted submarine warfare). One is obliged, therefore, to accept as a starting point for the purposes of strategic and tactical speculation that operational zones, if permitted on the high seas at all in cases of limited war, are permitted only for the purpose of belligerent operations among the protagonists and not for the purpose of molesting neutrals. The problem, of course, is one of positive identification, and the only purpose in declaring a war zone is to circumvent the difficulties of identification by supposing all contacts to be hostile, and to bridge the gap between hostile intent and hostile act, which is otherwise probably insurmountable, by supposing them to be assailants against whom the right of self-defence is exercisable. If operational zones are not an easy method of escape from that problem, speculation about their future availability may as well be abandoned.

But perhaps not without a little further reflection. In Korea a form of war zone operated because the rules of engagement authorised attack upon any submerged contact within certain areas. This was operationally successful because in the circumstances the law could be overlooked, owing to the supposition that the only likely submerged contacts would be Soviet, and if a Soviet submarine was sunk its government would be the last to admit it, and hence to make difficulties, for the Soviet Union was believed to prefer warfare by proxy to direct involvement. The question upon which ASW schools have concentrated is whether a solution to the problem of protecting a convoy under escort to a distant theatre of operations of limited war from submarine attack from a source that is a suspected but not a confirmed assailant would be a 'moving war zone'. Given the accelerated level of violence at sea in connection with territorial disputes, this possibility becomes ever more realistic, even if it is increasingly unlikely to be the Great Powers that will find themselves in the predicament.

The idea would be to allow for an operational zone of limited distance around a surface task force. One possibility would be that information on the extent and duration of such a zone would be widely disseminated in diplomatic and naval circles so that all mariners would be aware of its existence. The zone could be a moving circle centred on the task force and extending to the effective weapon range of likely submarine opposition. A submarine found submerged in the zone would be liable to immediate attack as being in a 'threatening posture'. A problem which would arise is that a predetermined and published position and speed of advance of a task force would often be necessary, and for obvious reasons nations are loathe to advise the movements of their forces. Without such notice, however, submarines submerged on innocent passage may find themselves inadvertently within such a zone and so liable to attack. The detection, attack, and destruction of a submarine in these circumstances would be regrettable. The creation of the type of zone under discussion would offer self-defence, and not blockade, as its justification. To this extent it would not have the characteristics of the war zones which were condemned at Nuremberg; and it would have the benefit of the precedent of the Spanish Civil War. This is not to eliminate legal doubts about the matter, but rather to indicate that the law appears to be sufficiently malleable to give naval staffs a certain freedom of manoeuvre in their planning.

CHAPTER XIII

RULES OF ENGAGEMENT

Naval operational commanders are supplied with rules of engagement, which specify in detail the circumstances under which fire may be opened, and it is in the drafting of these that international law today most directly impinges upon naval planning.[1] Rules of engagement may be general and comprehensive, so as to constitute part of the fighting instructions of a fleet, and in this case they must envisage a range of contingent situations; or they may be issued specifically for a particular operation. It is in the drafting of rules of engagement that the difficulties of legal appreciation lead to practical issues of expression, and there has in recent years been a developing awareness in naval circles of the role and importance of these instruments and a corresponding experimentation with their content. The problem of drafting general rules of engagement to encompass a variety of predicaments in which naval forces may find themselves in the discharge of their political tasks is manifest, yet the suddenness with which political situations erupt means that naval staffs may not have the luxury of time to formulate a reasoned set of rules of engagement, and, in the absence of these, naval operations are likely to be too hesitant for want of certainty or too uncontrolled to be politically acceptable.

Attempts to postpone the legal infusion into naval planning until the nature of a crisis is analysed have been made by the expedient of including in general rules of engagement references to signals to be received which will be to the effect that the rules of international law are either to be observed, ignored or observed to the extent consistent with the objective. This has been found to be no solution, because neither the authority issuing the signal nor the recipient is likely to have a clear idea of what these rules of international law are in the actual situation, especially since the lawyers themselves are unlikely to be clear about the matter. The tendency at present, therefore, is to aim at general rules of engagement with a view to their supplementation by specific ones as needed, and these general rules are necess-

---

[1] The expression 'rules of engagement' is a Malta coinage of the 1960s which gained currency in Vietnam and is now common among Western navies.

arily confined to tactical indications, with directions as to conduct to follow in the light of the actual legal situation. The assumption is widespread—perhaps too widespread—that the theory of graduated escalation will allow, as in the case of the Iceland cod wars, for the leisurely evolution of specific rules of engagement by the ordinary processes of governmental policy-making in committee. But even if there is this time scale available, the drafting operation is likely to be successful only if there has been the requisite thinking in advance about the questions that could arise, including the tactical factors that enter into the processes of legal appraisal. This is as legitimate a field of specialised defence study in preparation for hostilities as any other, yet it still forms an inadequate part of the defence curriculum.

In the absence of precise thinking and sufficient theoretical preparation, rules of engagement are unlikely to express sufficiently the detailed controls that contemporary political constraints on military conduct require. The history of limited war is one of political hesitation and reluctance. Short of declared war, governments have tended to despatch naval units or fleets for the purpose of catalytic force without any very clear objectives in mind, and in the hope that the navy will do something to resolve the situation and nothing to aggravate it. The 'Nelson touch' is expected by politicians yet feared, and naval officers correctly intuit this ambiguity and often oscillate between what is expected and what is apprehended. Vagueness and imprecision in the rules of engagement can only compound the dangers of uncontrolled escalation.

When Admiral Sinclair was despatched to the Baltic in 1918 with a squadron of light cruisers and a flotilla of destroyers his rules of engagement—though they were not then so called—were simply 'to show the British flag and support British policy as circumstances dictate'.[2] To this naval directive the Foreign Office contributed nothing, but the Admiralty added the following appreciation of the legal and political issue: 'A Bolshevik man-of-war operating off the coast of the Baltic Provinces must be assumed to be doing so with hostile intent and should be treated accordingly'.[3] When Admiral Cowan took command in the Baltic in 1919 these orders were amplified: 'British interests may be summed up as follows: to prevent the destruction of Estonia and Latvia by external aggression'. In the primitive legal environment of this operation the point of translation

[2] See Cable, *Gunboat Diplomacy*, pp. 50–51.
[3] *Ibid.*

of 'hostile intent' into 'hostile act' was not the conundrum it is today, but the Royal Navy's exasperation at the way in which it was increasingly drawn into hostilities by the vagueness of its mandate is evident from the Admiralty's minute to the Cabinet of March 1919: 'It is essential, if our naval force is required to undertake operations of war, that it should do so in pursuance of a definite and coherent policy'.

It was not that the Royal Navy was lacking in experience in rules of engagement for limited war, for the slave trade regulations under international treaties had been quite specific as to the occasions and manner of visit and search and the opening of fire; it was that precise rules are impossible when the government has not made its mind up, and this is likely to be the case in any catalytic use of sea power. The Spanish Civil War is a sufficient illustration, although in that case escalation occurred gradually, so that there was leisure to ponder upon the directions to be given.

Except in the case, perhaps, of definitive force, the philosophy of contemporary naval operation is that of self-defence, and this tends in the direction of prohibiting anticipatory attack and endorsing a policy of action and response. It follows that graduated rules of engagement are appropriate to the conduct of such operations. If the confrontation is with respect to disputed territorial or natural resource claims, as it is most likely to be, a series of rules are requisite, beginning with interrogation, requests to stop, the firing of warning shots and disabling shots when it is necessary to compel submission to visit to search, boarding (which may be courteous or forceful); and then progressing to deal with the situation where the opponent takes a determined stand in opposition and invokes its own view of the law. At this next stage the rules of engagement must choose between continuing the operation only in the absence of naval opposition or persisting in it despite such opposition; and, where a confrontation is to be persisted in, the rules of engagement must aim at catching the opponent at a disadvantage, which is something that can be done by manipulation of the rules of the road, harassment and interposition. If the threat of the use of weapons becomes imminent the rules must govern response in mode and degree. Since the law of self-defence requires that response must be only what is necessary and proportionate, the onus must, if possible, be put on the other side of deciding to progress to a higher level of force or a higher mode of weaponry.

In this theory of graduated rules of engagement it is evident that the initial question is that of directions to cover anticipatory self-defence or pre-emption. If it becomes accepted naval doctrine that there is no plausible index of the translation of 'hostile intent' into 'hostile act', a decision must be made whether to risk an initial casualty before authorising fire. If this is an unacceptable political or naval risk the rules of engagement may have to be drafted so as to avoid the occasion of it. At least they will have to envisage the requisite means of tactical evasion and defence so as to minimise the chances of an initial casualty if the other side opens fire. They will also have to provide for instant retaliation and direct the degree and mode of this response.

Rules of engagement have followed a pattern on the subject of 'hostile intent' since the Spanish Civil War, when the orders issued by the Admiralty on 17 September 1937 to implement the Nyon arrangements specified that a submarine was to be hunted and destroyed only after a merchant ship had been attacked in the presence of a destroyer, or was detected at such a distance from the place of attack and in such circumstances as would give valid grounds for the belief that the contact was the assailant. The difficulty was that the evaluation of these circumstances was left to the captain of the destroyer because no objective criteria could be isolated by which he could be precisely directed, and the rules broke down following a sinking in February 1938, and were then revised to allow the destruction of any submarine found submerged in a specified area of sea, which was in fact very large. In other words, a war zone was created.

The lessons of this have never been drawn, although escort commanders have long recognised that if a submarine threat became actual the tactical inability to determine hostile intent would require either an initial casualty—which the sinking in 1938 demonstrated was unacceptable to public opinion—or the hunting of any submerged submarine of the signature of a hostile State within a prescribed zone, such as a moving zone around a convoy. Hitherto the problem has been shelved because a submarine threat has not materialised, except in the Middle East and Indo–Pakistan wars, which were not really limited wars in the requisite sense; and the assumption is widespread that, because the submarine is an unsatisfactory vehicle for conflicts of self-defence, there is unlikely to be a submarine threat. The increasing resort to naval force and to the higher modes of weaponry has reduced the plausibility of this point of view, and future naval planning must envisage precise rules of engagement for ASW in limited war. These must take account of the importance of the target—a convoyed troopship is not an expendable initial casualty—as well as the tactical possibilities of fending off a submarine by methods of detection and prosecution; and, if the chances of avoiding loss cannot thus be discounted, they must envisage the insulation of the possible target by the hunting of any submerged submarine found within a certain range and designated hostile.

The problem is a most difficult one because if no submarine attack has yet occurred it cannot be supposed, in the absence of a war situation, that it will occur, yet the possible destruction of a potential target may be unacceptable. In the Spanish Civil War submarine attacks had occurred indiscriminately and frequently, so that there were grounds for predicting hostile attack when operational orders came to be drafted to deal with the threat. It is difficult to identify these grounds in advance, but they may recur, in which case legal analysis of the hypothetical problem will contribute to the choice of tactical options to be incorporated in the rules of engagement.

It is evident that the naval Power which seeks to protect its own waters is logically in a better posture of self-defence than the one which seeks to manifest sea power in distant waters, and this difference will clearly be reflected in the character of the respective rules of engagement. The Power despatching forces abroad must maintain a stricter posture of legality if its objectives are to be attained than one resisting pressure at home; and its rules of engagement must ensure tighter operational control and greater specification of the legal parameters of the operation. This covers also the modes of self-defence, particularly the translation of response from one mode to another. In the Corfu Channel case the mining was not followed by gunfire directed at the coastal batteries or by any other use of weapons, presumably because this was not authorised by the rules of engagement.

On the other hand, defence of national shipping abroad puts a navy in the same position as one concerned with coastal protection, and the rules of engagement may have to express a parity of self-defence, as in the Icelandic cod wars, where the Royal Navy's objective was to prevent the arrest of British trawlers in disputed waters or their harassment by Icelandic gunboats. The rules of engagement were strict. British ships had to wait till force had been used and then seek to fend it off by every means short of gunfire, which could be resorted to only when all other means were unavailing, and then at the lowest level of use. The only occasion when warning shots were fired was by H.M.S. *Contest* on 7 May 1959. In this situation, where the initiative is always with the other side, and self-defence can take two forms, harassment of the trawlers or attempts to seize them, the rules of engagement are inherently simple because they have to envisage only response to predictable and restricted actions.

The matter becomes more complex when the elements of predictability and self-restraint are absent, and especially in the multiple-threat situation and in a condition of high political tension. The Indonesian confrontation situation was characterised by a degree of uncertainty as to the assailant's intentions and a level of violence that opened up significantly a range of possibilities in self-defence that operational orders had to envisage. The emphasis in this case was territorial, with a prohibition on resort to Indonesian-claimed waters except in approved transits, interrogation on the high seas and immediate use of force in Malaysian territorial waters if a vessel acted suspiciously or fled when challenged. The authorisation to engage followed the opening of fire by the Indonesians anywhere and upon their failure to stop in Malaysian territorial waters. The operational orders thus had to take into account the legal nature of the terrain, the security limitations on the right of innocent passage, and the extent to which self-defence authorises visit upon the high seas. In this latter case challenge appears to have sufficed; and where vessels were boarded on the high seas the action was either vindicated in the event or was done in such a manner as not to excite objection. While this was the pattern that finally emerged, it was the product of a series of emergency decisions and not of logical planning, of expediency and not of policy. Improvisation of this sort has its obvious dangers, and it was largely because of the lessons of confrontation that the concept of rules of engagement, as instruments of carefully devised policy, entered naval doctrine with a view to controlling events rather than reacting to them.

The Beira patrol illustrates the delicacy of the problem of rules of engagement for visit and search on the high seas in the interest of law enforcement which is not tantamount to self-defence. It is evident from the events that the rules of engagement for this operation, as in confrontation, evolved progressively and were deficient at the outset. This may have been because the government was relying upon the existence of the Security Council resolution and the presence of the Royal Navy to deter any attempts to supply oil to Rhodesia via Beira, and hoped that the problem of the blockade-runner would not arise in the political circumstances. When the *Joanna V*, a Greek tanker, was visited by H.M.S. *Berwick* on 4 April 1966 but refused to divert from Beira, the government's bluff was called. It was decided that the existing mandate from the Security Council was insufficient for resort to force to prevent blockade-running, and so the question was taken back to the Security Council, which resolved to call upon the United Kingdom to prevent the arrival of blockade-runners in Beira by force if necessary, and to arrest the *Joanna V* upon her departure from Beira.[4] Greece was bound by the United Nations Charter and affected by this resolution, so that the legal circuit was complete and the rules of engagement could be modified accordingly to permit the use of firepower. The next blockade-runner, the *Manuela*, was boarded on 10 April and successfully diverted after verbal persuasion. In practice the Beira patrol eliminated most of the actual problems of visit and search by the issuing to the frigates on patrol of a list of innocent tankers manifested for Beira, the list being drawn up on the basis of intelligence gained from the oil companies and tanker owners. This left only the outsiders as possible blockade-runners, and these did not reappear.

The only incident subsequent to the last Security Council resolution was when H.M.S. *Minerva* intercepted the French tanker *Artois*, which was not on the innocent list. When the *Artois* failed to stop to receive a boarding party four shots were fired across her bows, but when she continued on course into the port no further action was taken. She was in fact innocent. It is reasonable to assume that the rules of engagement, which at that time forbade firing into a ship, were tightened to authorise this following the incident, because the Permanent Representative of the United Kingdom to the United Nations circulated a letter indicating the risk of damage run by any ship which failed to stop. Obviously the drafting of the rules of engagement was dominated by the concept of minimum force.

In this type of case the rules of engagement will need to lay down precisely every action which is to be taken consistently with the notion of minimum force and so to ensure the maximum control over escalation. Even the form of verbal warnings will need to be laid down, and boarding while under way may be prescribed (although the scantlings of a frigate make this an unacceptable manoeuvre today compared with the days when destroyers came alongside the illegal Palestine immigrants' ships).

All the Royal Navy's experience of limited operations has been of the low-level type, the only incident since 1945 involving the indis-

[4] Security Council Resolution 221 (xx).

criminate use of firepower being (apart from Korea) the affair of H.M.S. *Amethyst* in the Yangtse in 1949. Other navies, however, have been involved in extensive operations on the scale of war, but always limited in location and generally in purpose. In this situation the rules of engagement are more concerned with the rules of law that prescribe the operational zones and the concomitant naval control of shipping. The induction of concepts of international law into the rules of engagement for such operations is a significant feature of the drafting process.

In the Vietnam War two sets of rules of engagement covered the two operations, Market Time and Sea Dragon, off the coasts respectively of South and North Vietnam. Operation Market Time was concerned with surveillance and coast protection. The rules of engagement contained directions respecting positive identification, and they specified the instant when fire might be directed, as well as the occasions and degree of response respectively in the territorial sea, the contiguous zone or the high seas. Since North Vietnam deployed supersonic aircraft, surveillance forces as well as harassment and interdiction forces had to consider the possibility of attack in one of these three areas, and the immediacy of defence and retaliation. The rules of engagement thus had to make reference to the concepts of proportionality and necessity embodied in the concept of self-defence.

The rules of engagement for Operation Market Time also introduced into tactical doctrine problems of interception of incoming ships in the contiguous zone, for, while this was authorised by the relevant South Vietnamese legislation, it was the United States Navy that was answerable in international law, and a decision was necessary respecting non-South Vietnamese ships which threatened to breach the law but had not actually done so while still in the contiguous zone. This decision extended to specific directions respecting hot pursuit of a ship which had fled on to the high seas when interrogated, and the use of force in hot pursuit. The responsibility for taking this decision fell upon the Commander, Coastal Surveillance Forces (CCF 115), although approval of his rules of engagement had to come from higher authority. The rules of engagement also had to be supplemented by a stack of operational orders which superseded or amended each other as new situations developed or new insights into problems were gained, and these included: directions for drawing the territorial sea from basepoints; the method of delimiting the adjacent territorial seas of Vietnam and Cambodia; the situation of foreign warships in the territorial sea; the specific circumstances under which ships were deemed not to be 'clearly engaged in innocent passage'; the means of positive identification of hostile vessels or aircraft; the distinction between 'immediate pursuit', which is the pursuit of a vessel or aircraft which has initiated an attack, and 'hot pursuit', which is pursuit of a vessel which has breached the law; the use of mines for interdiction of entry into unrecognised ports of disembarkation; the procedures of visit and search; the need for specific instructions to visit and search certain classifications of foreign ships; and the degree of force to be employed.

In the case of Operation Sea Dragon the tactics to be employed were offensive, consisting in harassment and interdiction of the supply routes of North Vietnam, yet this had to be expressed in defensive terms. This made the concept unusually complicated, and between its acceptance and the issuing of the rules of engagement a drafting period of six months proved to be necessary. This was the task of the planning and operational staff of the Commander-in-chief, Seventh Fleet, which had to confront issues of international law and carry the principles of international law into the documents which it was required to draft. The concept was dominated by the twelve-mile territorial sea of North Vietnam, to which the use of force was confined, although outside that area a guided missile cruiser was located as Position Identification and Radar Advisory Zone monitor (PIRAZ) and there were two search and rescue destroyers (South SAR and North SAR), for the purpose of controlling the carrier-borne air strikes. PIRAZ also had the function of providing long-range surface-to-air missile defence for the ships on Sea Dragon, Yankee Station and the gunline off I Corps, north of Hué.

The rules of engagement covered all these activities, and were supplemented in detail by operational orders which amplified the application of the laws of war. For example, under Article 3 of Hague Convention No. XI of 1907, coastal fishing boats not engaged in any military activity are immune from seizure or attack. In the case of Vietnam, boats used for subsistence fishing were also used as waterborne logistic craft (WIBLICKS), and operational orders had to give directions respecting positive identification of WIBLICKS, based upon a study of fishing practices in the Gulf of Tonkin. The complexity of the system of control of limited war was indicated by the physical bulk of the rules that had to be introduced into the administration of every ship on mission.

All the rules of engagement which have been mentioned involved a territorial element wherein the law offers secure definitions as to the location of sea power. When confrontations occur on the high seas, however, both sides rely upon the freedom of the seas, and here the rules of engagement must import the rules of the road, since the primary step in the coercive use of sea power today is harassment or interposition, and a practised navy can gain its objectives by adroit footwork without the use of weapons at all. The cod wars have been the most striking demonstration of this tactic. The aim is to prevent the opponent from enforcing his asserted right of visit and search and seizure, or from executing tactical movements (such as the launch and recovery of aircraft by carriers) by manoeuvres to make him stop or alter course. The advantage of this expedient is that it is very difficult to classify it as illegal and hence as an initial resort to force, although this is what it well may be. It puts the onus of escalation on the opponent and gains for the assailant the benefits of self-defence if the opponent, in exasperation, resorts to gunfire or ramming. In this game the rules of the road become weapons, because even in the event of a collision it is often very difficult, short of a deliberate act of ramming, to attribute legal responsibility. This is because rule of the road No. 21 embodies a 'last opportunity' concept, which emerged as a complicating element in the enquiry into the running down of the U.S.S. *Evans* by H.M.A.S. *Melbourne* in 1969. Following that enquiry, charges were brought against the captain of the *Melbourne* (despite the fact that the *Evans* was found by the enquiry to have been negligently navigated) upon the question whether he had reacted early enough to the manoeuvres of the *Evans* by taking way off the carrier. As it happened he was acquitted, but after that event no navy will be content with the simple rule of thumb that, if you are to be hit, be hit on the port side, because then responsibility could well be distributed.

The ambiguities in the rules of the road as applied to carrier operations, where the necessity of turning into the wind limits the freedom of movement, have been exploited by the Soviet navy and have in fact led to collisions, notably between H.M.S. *Ark Royal* and the DDG *Kotlin*, and in the Sea of Japan between units of the Seventh Fleet and the Red fleet. At that time the C.-in-C., Seventh Fleet, issued instructions that his ships were to maintain course and speed even if collision resulted, and he recommended that the United States claim damages from the Soviet Union in the event of collision. After a period of negotiations following the general recognition of the dangers posed by this game, the Soviet Union and the United States concluded in 1972 the Treaty on the Prevention of Incidents on and over the High Seas, which prohibits harassment and enjoins observance of the rules of the road. The treaty is, in effect, a set of international rules of engagement.

It is evident that rules of engagement for limited war are specific to each case. The problem of testing them in the multi-threat, high-tension situation has not arisen since the Cuban crisis, and while discussion of their role and probable contents intensifies in naval circles, the element of international legal speculation in the debate remains slight, although this would appear from experience to be the heart of the matter of naval conduct in limited war.

Among naval officers there are two widely divergent points of view. The 'Nelson touch' school considers that tight rules of engagement will inhibit a commander on the spot from taking the requisite initiatives to achieve the objective of his orders. It is said that every commander knows that he can be politically disowned and his career affected if he has to be aggressive in executing his orders, but that is his traditional risk, and a navy which does not take initiatives consistent with political objectives is incapable of the effective use of sea power. It is pointed out that even in the cod wars the rules of engagement have been stretched and that policy was best served by doing so. This school views the rules of engagement with some suspicion.

The other school recognises the subservience of navies to political direction and the need for clear political responsibility for any breach of international law. In the situation where naval forces are despatched for purposes of catalytic sea power it is recognised that governments often do not wish to be committed. In these circumstances the 'Nelson touch' has no place. The history of the matter reveals that, as in the Spanish Civil War, the navy has to be circumspect—indeed, more so than the political branch of government, for the boldness which is appropriate in conditions of open warfare may only lead to escalation for which naval staffs have neither the resources nor the disposition. There is no public servant with such means of involving his government in international complications as the naval officer, and his responsibility is commensurate with the facilities at his disposal.

While detailed rules of engagement cannot easily be promulgated to cover every type of hypothetical situation, it is possible to envisage general rules which can be applied to any one of three broad situations, namely low tension, high tension and hostilities. The rules could provide that in the first situation ships might operate at slow speeds on steady courses, omitting torpedo counter-measures and mutual support, but in a higher than normal damage-control state and with full power available. Live weapons should not be loaded. In the second situation full torpedo counter-measures should be taken, war procedures implemented, and high degrees of action readiness and damage-control states reached. Live weapons might be loaded but should not be fired except in self-defence situations as these might be defined. In both situations practice weapons should be struck down, and in the case of maritime aircraft arming switches should be set to safe. In the third situation full war procedures would be executed.

In both the first and second situations care must be taken not to deprive a possibly hostile contact of the benefit of the rules of the road by too close a prosecution. A submarine denied seaway, or believing itself to be under attack, might be provoked into defending itself. To avoid this, the rules might provide that no contact is to be approached closer than, say, 500 yards. Also, the streaming of decoys should be done with circumspection, as submarine sensors have been known not to discriminate between the noise made by them and that made by anti-submarine torpedoes.

The conduct of operations in tension situations always involves a nice balance of threat and counter-threat on the part of both sides, and the main purpose of rules of engagement is to prevent that balance being disturbed by thrusting the apparent necessity of self-defence too obviously upon one player rather than upon the other.

CHAPTER XIV

THE SUITABILITY OF NAVAL UNITS FOR LAW-BASED SEA POWER

On the supposition that an instantaneous resort to global naval warfare is unlikely while the balance of deterrence remains intact, it is clear that a progression in the resort to sea power will be the continuing characteristic of naval operations, and that for this reason a discriminate use of types of vessels and armament is essential. It may be that some types are ruled out altogether; and, upon the supposition that political ambivalence will continue to require the justification of coercive force at sea by reference to the concept of self-defence, it may be that the unlikely use of some instruments may affect procurement policies. It may be recalled that since 1945 there has been remarkably little use of aircraft in a maritime role, and this may be because of a combination of politico-legal and tactical considerations. An aircraft is an unsuitable vehicle for a credible display of self-defensive force, since it has only a high strike capability and nothing short of it, save buzzing. It allows for no flexibility in the level of response. Because no clear role for land-based aircraft against maritime targets has been perceived and because of their lack of capability for low-intensity operations, crews have not been trained in the maritime role, and so the use of aircraft against warships with area and point defence capability has become largely impracticable.

The question has been much discussed recently whether the submarine is not equally excluded from most conceivable operations. The one weapon which has not been used since 1945, except in the Indo–Pakistan war of 1971 and perhaps in the Middle East, is the torpedo, and the reason is evident: except in conditions of open warfare, submarine attack is an excessively drastic means of attaining limited goals. In the theory of graduated escalation the submarine comes so high in the scale that its use can be envisaged only in the ultimate crisis. This is partly for psychological and partly for tactical reasons. A submarine represents hidden and unleashed menace. To station a frigate near a foreign coast is one thing. To station a submarine is another. To station a submarine there submerged is to conceal it and hence to negate its use in the exercise of coercion; to station it on the surface is to expose it in an environment for which it is not designed, where it is exceedingly vulnerable and even indefensible to air attack, and hence is to deprive it of all credibility as a coercive instrument. Where sea power involves visible presence and veiled threat the submarine is nearly valueless.

At the high levels of escalation the role of the submarine is also rendered doubtful if observance of the rules of necessity and proportionality is insisted upon. This is because a submarine is exposed to detection if it uses active sonar and hence will wish to rely upon its passive sensors to track a target. While it can detect classes of ships from their propeller noises or engine signatures, the intermittent and incomplete information acoustically acquired means that it cannot reach the level of positive identification requisite for self-defence operations, and which would presumably be prescribed by its rules of engagement, without using the periscope or its active sensors; but their use would place it at a serious disadvantage when confronted by escorts skilled in ASW. Even if the submarine obtains the requisite data for positive identification, its weapons are of such an extreme character that their use could be justified only in a self-defence role at the highest level of escalation.

The submarine, therefore, has only a reinforcement role, but even this is likely to be greatly circumscribed. Since most limited-force operations will be connected with territorial issues, they are likely to be inshore, where operating conditions for submarines are apt to be adverse. For example, sonar conditions in the Gulf of Tonkin made a submarine threat there impracticable. Moreover the reinforcement role in limited defence involves tight direction and hence close communications. Acoustic communication between submarine and surface vessels is possible only at close range, and for radio communication the submarine must be at periscope level. While the conventional submarine may remain useful for the clandestine landing of agents, its role in any capacity short of a roving commission to sink ships, which the nature of the operation is likely to exclude, is difficult to envisage. Even its use in surveillance is circumscribed, because in order to transmit the information it has acquired it has either to surface and be vulnerable to attack or withdraw while the information grows cold.

Other factors degrade the tactical capabilities of the submarine in conditions of tension short of war, and so limit its usefulness in the exercise of catalytic sea power. Among these are the enhanced detection capabilities of ASW escorts, which in conditions short of hostilities are not subject to sonar limitations imposed by considerations of self-protection. For example, escorts may not feel the need for torpedo counter-measures, such as towing noise-making decoys which interfere with sonar emissions, or to make frequent course and speed alterations, or to operate together in mutual support, or to stand off out of effective submarine torpedo range. In a tension situation an escort can stay close to a submarine and remain at slow speed on a steady course, making it difficult for the submarine to play a credibly coercive role or to use its intelligence-gathering sensors effectively.

The SSBN, of course, falls into a totally different category. It is the naval vehicle of the global balance of deterrence, and it relies upon the law for the purpose of its strategic deployment and not its operational use. It may be that the conventional submarine has so uncertain a role to play in the actualities of sea power as to have a questionable future. But this is no reason for terminating speculation as to the role of law in ASW, because sudden, clandestine submarine coups in limited war have been envisaged, notably during the Indonesian confrontation and in Vietnam, and because the submarine threat actually eventuated in the Indo–Pakistan war of 1971.

Turning to the question of the suitability of warships generally for law-based operations, one must again recall that in disputing over territory or resources both sides to a controversy can be expected to wish to avoid a slide into open warfare, and will seek to resolve the conflict by demonstrations and attempted exercise of disputed rights. It is clear that the first moves will be made by surface forces, and these must have the qualities of weapon flexibility, good communications and data acquisition capabilities, and weather lines and endurance necessary for the application of graduated force. In most of the sea-power contests of recent years the struggle has initially taken the form of interposition and harassment, and has often been confined to it. But the warships assigned to these roles have been the most ill adapted imaginable. In the 'cod war' and the Beira patrol ASW frigates have been used that are highly uneconomic for the purpose and have scantlings so thin that they are put to excessive risk by attempting to outmanoeuvre the opponent. Their only relevant quality has been their high level of communicability.

When the struggle goes beyond harassment and resort is made to weapons the notion of proportionality dictates the weapon mix. The only naval weapons that have been used since 1945 are the gun and the missile, and the latter only at the highest level of escalation. The gun is essential for warning, and then for minimal destruction in law enforcement; and it must be of sufficient range and calibre to constitute an effective use of force to restrain an opponent's naval vessels or clandestinely armed merchant ships from disputing a 'law and order' action. (Navies have forgotten what happened when H.M.A.S. *Sydney* closed the range, seeking positive identification.) The design of escorts with only missiles for point defence and no guns supposes that they will be available only in conditions of open warfare on the high seas or in the ultimate reinforcement role. The vessels suited to the initiation of sea power moves thus diminish in type and number.

Other weapons are appropriate and necessary to the concept of superior force without which the initiation of sea power is likely to be rendered abortive—a helicopter for air-to-surface attack, surveillance and transport, surface-to-air and surface-to-surface missiles and ECM to restrain the opponent from using aircraft or short-range defence missiles so as to dispute the 'law and order' vessel's presence and function, or counter it successfully if it tries to execute its task. If the initial response vessel is not so equipped it would need to be backed up by other units with this capability.

ASW is not a vital component for an initial response vessel, since a submarine threat would involve a dramatic move up the graduated scale, and hence is unlikely to be required in most peace-keeping operations. Where it is likely to be required, the reinforcement which would be necessary for high-tension operations would in any event be deployed, and the reinforcement units would embody the requisite ASW component.

It may be suggested, therefore, that if naval doctrine is to reflect the limitations which are embodied in legal concepts, a single-unit low-capability vessel is what is initially required, with principally a surface-to-surface and surface-to-air armament. The costly ASW frigates usually employed in this role are misused and uneconomical, and should be reserved for reinforcement so as to inhibit an opponent from persisting in escalation.

While the concept of the 'general-purpose vessel' is rightly criticised as seeking to achieve too universal a weapon mix, and hence too low a level of capability in any mode to be cost-effective, the initial response vessel must be versatile—able to deter an opponent by gunfire alone but also by missile if the opponent chooses to progress beyond gunfire to a higher mode of threat. The Soviet navy has demonstrated from its weapon mix the capability of trumping, if it chooses, every surface weapon that ships of other navies can deploy.

If it chose to intimidate with a *Sverdlov*-class cruiser or one of the new *Kara* class[1] it could place the onus of escalation to a higher mode upon the opponent, who could not match the cruiser in conventional firepower. If it chose to use a *Kresta*-class DDG it could equally intimidate with gunfire, and counter-escalation to the missile mode or submarine threat.

It follows that the Soviet navy could exercise sea power in areas such as the Indian Ocean by posing only the lowest and cheapest level of the use of force, namely gunfire, because it could not be challenged at that level, and it would be unlikely that any possible challenger would risk taking the initiative of a missile or submarine attack to counter a threat of gunfire. The lesson is that action and reaction can be an effective deterrent only so long as the likely threat can be met. It is not possible to envisage an engagement at sea today limited to an exchange of gunfire, but it is possible to suppose that a superior gun ship could successfully overawe opposition by shifting to the other side the burden of choosing a higher level of weapon for initial response purposes, and hence negating the initial response altogether.

The balance of deterrence thus resides not only in the SSBN and the strike carrier force but in every unit and task grouping appropriate to the graduated scale of the resort to power. The SSBN is the ultimate weapon because of its planned targeting. The aircraft carrier, whether in its traditional form or as the through-deck cruiser with NSTOL aircraft, is an essential component of the whole for two basic reasons: it affords air cover and maritime control for the exercise of sea power beyond the range of land-based aircraft; and, by posing a threat of simultaneous strike attack by large numbers of aircraft upon an enemy surface fleet whose capability of successful counter-measures is restricted to a maximum of two or three of the attacking planes each, constitutes checkmate in the move to use substantial sea power in order to disturb drastically the basic power equilibrium.

Since most exercises of sea power in recent years have been territorially connected, and supposing that the inhibition on warfare on the high seas consolidates, the characteristic operation is likely to be inshore. Hostile forces off a defended shore are vulnerable to land-based air power unless countered by equivalent sea-based air power or effective missile defence (hitherto all amphibious operations have occurred within range of land-based or sea-based air cover); to coastal

[1] The *Sverdlov* with 7·1 in. and the *Kara* with 76 mm.

surface forces of the guided missile-carrying type (e.g. the *Komar* or *Osa*); to gunnery; and to coastal surface-to-surface guided missile systems, which can be mobile.

Although the relative shallowness of coastal waters diminishes the operational possibilities of submarines, and tends to reduce the likelihood of escalation through this medium, the risk to forces operating in coastal waters is proportionately reduced by the distance they are operating offshore—in particular because, first, the acquisition and tracking of aircraft or missiles when low over the sea is less difficult than over the land, and secondly the response time available to detect a land-based threat is extended, with enhanced chances of interception. It follows that offshore operating forces may aim to keep at the limits of effective guidance range from surface-to-surface missile sites, namely twenty to forty miles, and hence will be compelled to operate on the high seas. The efforts of the law to confine self-defence operations to the territorial sea may thus be unavailing. The Vietnam War, where belligerent operations were confined to a twelve-mile limit, was exceptional in that the missile threat, if it existed there, could for special reasons be discounted.

Where amphibious landings on a defended coast are envisaged, the likelihood for the future would be the use of hydrofoils as landing craft for quick transits from transports held well offshore. This raises the question of naval support for such operations. The use of missiles from surface ships is possible at maximum effective range, so minimising the threat from land-based weapon systems, but the problem here is one of total effect, that is, the product in terms of damage of the total number of rounds available, which in turn is affected by the percentage of hits likely to be obtained. Theoretically the surface-to-surface missile is superior to the gun in maximum effective range and destructiveness, but its severely limiting factors are its size in proportion to that of a shell, with consequent restriction upon the ammunition supply, and its great cost. Hence the gun remains—as it did in Vietnam—an effective weapon of naval bombardment, since modern methods of fire control have increased its accuracy and it can be supplied with great quantities of cheap ammunition. When a weapon is needed to break up concrete the shell is superior to the missile. In the naval bombardment of the Viet Cong in the citadel of Hué during the Tet offensive of 1968 it was found that the 6 in. guns of the U.S.S. *Providence* were unavailing to breach the walls and nothing less than the 8 in. guns of the *St Paul* and *Newport News* were effective. The 4·5 in. gun in most modern ships is of limited value in naval gunfire support. The situation must thus be envisaged where naval forces will operate within gunnery range of the shore, particularly if surface-to-surface missiles are not included in the defence component of the coastal State.

Coastal waters are particularly susceptible to mine-warfare policies. The coastal defence forces may use mines for interdicting approaches to the shore; or mines may be laid by hostile forces in order to blockade ports and so influence the passage of strategic goods and accelerate political pressure—as in the mining of Haiphong in May 1972. The mine is a strategic weapon much underestimated, but its undiscriminating quality makes it politically and legally the most dubious one to use in limited war. It required a combination of exceptional political and military circumstances to warrant its use in Vietnam in 1972, so that not much in the way of lessons can be drawn, except the possibility of using mine warfare effectively without in fact sinking neutral shipping, provided the minefield is properly notified. So that, even if the Hague Convention rules have doubtful application to so-called influence mines, respect for them can in fact make the use of mines practicable.

If self-defence operations are to be mounted it is of the essence of the concept that they be tightly controlled. This puts a premium not only upon equipment but upon professionalism in its use. Law-enforcement vessels must have adequate data acquisition systems for detection, positive identification and accurate plotting of position course and speed, and a high capability of communicating, which is peculiar to surface forces. Since confrontations are likely to occur in connection with territorial boundaries, position-fixing and retention of the evidence become of the greatest importance. This became clear at the time of the battle of the River Plate, and it is obvious too in the case of fishery protection. But the problem of boundary location is acquiring ever novel ramifications.

Take the question of the 200-mile zone. This will extend far beyond the radar horizon, and unless Omega or at least Loran are available as ocean navigation aids there is likely to be an error in position-fixing. Even within the radar horizon, say at the twelve-mile limit, error is possible due to a combination of the standard of skill of the operator in strobing the echo; errors in radar indices; the accident of the radar beam painting elevated land at low water mark or inland, so affecting range; the thickness of the radar beam as affecting bearing; errors in the master gyro and misalignment of the repeater gyros—and the combination is unlikely to produce an observed position displaced from the true by less than half a mile in twelve. As the *Red Crusader*[2] enquiry pointed out, the burden of proof of position is always on the assailant.

To be on the safe side, a tolerance zone should be allowed for in territorially connected self-defence operations. Chile and Peru have agreed on a mutual tolerance zone of ten miles along the line of intersection of their 200-mile territorial sea. A ratio of 1:12 would not be inappropriate.

But on occasions much greater accuracy may be called for, particularly in the matter of location or policing of natural resources areas. If it is a matter of locating an oil rig, quite precise boundary-fixing is required. International law is silent on the question of whether this is to be done by reference to rhumb lines or great-circle lines, yet on an east–west axis in higher latitudes the difference can become significant. The divergence in the case of the territorial sea baseline between Cape Wrath and the Butt of Lewis is, in fact, 533 ft —nothing if the question is one of navigational fix but considerable if it is a question of legal use of territory.

An emerging area of controversy is the problem of maritime boundary-fixing as the struggle for natural resources accelerates. There are so many variables in geography that the application of the law can itself become the cause of dispute, and navies may find that the protection of national interests will take them ever further afield. In South America they are already predicting a massive predatory incursion of the northern-hemisphere fishing nations into the waters of the southern hemisphere, leading to their reservation for regional exploitation and their protection by the navies of the countries which are linked together by Antarctica.

The major naval Powers are unlikely to find the location of the initial threat to the balance of deterrence in European waters, and they would probably wish to avoid entanglement in that area until hostilities occurred elsewhere, whereupon attention will concentrate, as it always has in the past, upon the primary sea lanes of the Atlantic. The best chance of avoiding total warfare therefore resides in localising the areas of tension and avoiding, as far as circumstances permit, recourse to higher levels of threat which would have the effect of concentrating tension in vital theatres. From this it follows that the initial response and the reinforcement must be available globally, and notably in extra-European waters, where the causes of tension are likely to arise. The fallacy in the 'home defence' concept of sea

[2] See above, p. 66.

power thus derives from a contradiction of the basic premise upon which the theory of deterrence rests.

It is the law of the sea which dictates the practicalities of this deployment of sea power, related to areas of its exercise and the modes of its exercise. Changes in the law of the sea in these respects would alter the factors which give rise to or aggravate political tension, and so they bear upon the nature of deterrence itself.

In the past few years naval officers have become increasingly aware of the importance of international law to the conduct of naval operations. The accelerating speculation concerning the law-enforcement role of navies in the future is leading to reviews of the relevant aspects of public administration. It is no longer sufficient to leave the law to Foreign Ministries. Naval staffs must themselves be equipped to handle the legal aspects of naval planning, whether it be in the matter of drafting rules of engagement or in their interpretation. The machinery must be devised for rapid appreciation of the legal issues and equally rapid reaction if the theory of self-defence is to be effectively translated into terms of sea power. Above all, reflection must develop concerning the ways in which working technology influences the modes of self-defence and the ways in which the intensifying ambiguities of the law of the sea influence the decisions respecting self-defence. This calls for a continuing dialogue between lawyers who know enough of what goes on in the operations room of a warship and naval officers who have sufficient awareness of the advantages and inhibitions of the law to bring the necessary professional insight into the influence of law on sea power.

GLOSSARY

CODAR — See p. 75

AAM	Air-to-air missile
ASM	Air-to-surface missile
ASDIC	Anti-submarine direction indicator
ASW	Anti-submarine warfare
CODAR	See p. 75
DDG	Guided missile destroyer
ECM	Electronic counter-measures
ICBM	Intercontinental ballistic missile
IRLS	Infra-red line scan
LOFAR	Low-frequency analysation and recording
MAD	Magnetic anomaly detector
Mach	The Mach number is the ratio of vehicle speed to the speed of sound in the same air. Mach I is the speed of sound at sea level at ordinary temperatures.
MCM	Mine counter-measures
MIRV	Multiple independently targetable re-entry vehicle
MRV	Multiple re-entry vehicle
NSTOL	Naval short take-off and landing
PIRAZ	Position identification and radar advisory zone
SSBN	Nuclear-powered missile-firing submarine
SAM	Surface-to-air missile
SLSM	Submerged-launched SSM
SSM	Surface-to-surface missile
TACAID	*Tactical Aid*
VTOL	Vertical take-off and landing

BIBLIOGRAPHY

Allison, G. T., 'Explaining the Cuban missile crisis', in *Essence of Decision*, Little Brown, New York, 1971.

Andrassy, J., 'Present regime of the military uses of the sea bed', *Symposium on the International Regime of the Sea Bed*, Accademia Nazionale dei Lincei, Rome, 1970.

Barnes, Cmdr W. H., 'Submarine warfare and international law', *World Polity*, vol. 2, 1960.

Baxter, R. R., 'Legal aspects of arms control measures concerning the missile-carrying submarines and anti-submarine warfare', in K. Tsipis, A. H. Cahn and B. T. Feld, *The Future of the Sea-based Deterrent*, M.I.T. Press, Cambridge, Mass., 1973.

Beaton, L., and Maddox, J., 'The spread of nuclear weapons', Studies in International Security, *Survival*, vol. 5, No. 1, 1963, Institute of Strategic Studies, London.

Berber, F., *Lehrbuch des Völkerrechts*, vol. 4, *Kriegsrecht*, Beck Verlag, Munich, 1962.

Bowett, D. W., *Self-defence in International Law*, Manchester University Press, 1958.

Brennan, D. G., 'A note on bridging the differing Soviet and American objectives of sea-bed demilitarisation', *Symposium on the International Regime of the Sea Bed*, Accademia Nazionale dei Lincei, Rome, 1970.

Brock, Capt J. R., 'Hot pursuit and the right of pursuit', *JAG Journal of the U.S. Navy*, vol. 18, 1960.

Brown, E. D., *Arms Control in Hydrospace: Legal Aspects*, Ocean Series 301, Woodrow Wilson International Center for Scholars, Washington, D.C., 1971.

Brown, N., 'Deterrence from the sea', *Survival*, vol. 12, No. 6, June 1970.

— 'Strategic mobility', Studies in International Security, *Survival*, vol. 6, No. 2, March–April 1964.

Brownlie, I., *International Law and the Use of Force by States*, Oxford University Press, London, 1963.

Bull, H., 'The control of the arms race', Studies in International Security, *Survival*, vol. 3, No. 2, July–August 1961.

Butler, W. E., *The Law of Soviet Territorial Waters*, Praeger, New York, 1967.

Cable, J., *Gunboat Diplomacy*, Studies in International Security, No. 16, Chatto & Windus, London, for the Institute of Strategic Studies.

Calvocoressi, P., *World Politics since 1945*, Longman, London, 1968.

Carlisle, Capt G. E., 'The interrelationship of international law and U.S. naval operations in south-east Asia', *JAG Journal of the U.S. Navy*, vol. 22, 1967.

Cattell, D. T., *Soviet Diplomacy and the Spanish Civil War*, University of California Press, Berkeley and Los Angeles, 1967.

Clark, Admiral J. J. C., and Barnes, Capt D. H. B., *Sea Power and its Meaning,* Franklin Watts, London, 1966.

Colombos, C. J., *International Law of the Sea,* sixth edition, Longmans, London, 1967.

Colvin, R. D., 'The aftermath of the Elath', *Proceedings of the U.S. Naval Institute,* vol. 95, 1969.

Cox, Lt-Cmdr D. R., 'Sea power and Soviet foreign policy', *Proceedings of the United States Naval Institute,* June 1969.

Craven, J. P., *Ocean Technology and Submarine Warfare,* Adelphi Papers, No. 46, Institute of Strategic Studies, London, 1968.

— 'The challenge of ocean technology to the law of the sea', *JAG Journal of the U.S. Navy,* vol. 22, 1967.

— 'Sea power and the sea bed', *Proceedings of the United States Naval Institute,* Annapolis, Md., vol. 92, 1966.

— '*Res nullius de facto:* the limits of technology', *Symposium on the International Regime of the Sea Bed,* Accademia Nazionale dei Lincei, Rome, 1970.

de Chair, Admiral Sir Dudley, *The Sea is Strong,* Harrap, London, 1961.

Eichelberger, 'The law and the submarine', *Proceedings of the United States Naval Institute,* vol. 77, 1951.

Evensen, J., 'The military uses of the deep ocean floor and its subsoil', *Symposium on the International Regime of the Sea Bed,* Accademia Nazionale dei Lincei, Rome, 1970.

Fitzmaurice, Sir Gerald, 'The territorial sea and the contiguous zone', *International and Comparative Law Quarterly,* vol. 8, 1959.

Garner, J. W., *Prize Law during the World War,* London, 1927.

Gasteyger, C., *Conflict and Tension in the Mediterranean,* Adelphi Papers, No. 51, Institute of Strategic Studies, London, 1968.

Gibson, R. H., and Prendergast, M., *The German Submarine War, 1914–18,* Constable, London, 1931.

Gorshkov, Admiral G. S., 'Mezhdunarodnopravoy rezhim kontinentalnogo shelfa', *Morskoy sbornik,* No. 5, 1969.

Graham, C. S., *The Politics of Naval Supremacy,* Cambridge University Press, 1965.

Gretton, Vice-Admiral Sir Peter, *Maritime Strategy,* Cassell, London, 1965.

Harlow, B., Lt-Cdr, 'Legal use of force short of war', *Proceedings of the United States Naval Institute,* vol. 92, 1966.

Hartingh, F. de, *Les Conceptions soviétiques du droit de la mer,* Pinchon & Durand-Anzias, Paris, 1960.

Hayter, Sir William, *Russia and the World,* Secker & Warburg, London, 1970.

Hearn, Rear-Admiral W. A., 'The role of the United States Navy in the formulation of federal policy regarding the sea', *Natural Resources Lawyer,* vol. 1, 1968.

Herrick, R. W., *Soviet Naval Strategy,* U.S. Naval Institute, Annapolis, Md., 1968.

Hersch, S., 'An arms race on the sea bed', *War/Peace Report,* vol. 8, 1968.

Hezlet, Vice-Admiral Sir Arthur R., *Aircraft and Sea Power*, Stein & Day, London, 1970.

Hill, Capt J. R., 'Maritime forces in confrontation', *Brassey's Annual*, Clowes, London, 1972

— 'The role of navies', *Brassey's Annual*, Clowes, London, 1970.

Horelick, A. L., and Rush, M., *Strategic Power and Soviet Foreign Policy*, University of Chicago Press, 1966.

Kent, H. S. K., *War and Trade in Northern Seas*, Cambridge University Press, 1973.

Knapp, W., *A History of War and Peace, 1939–65*, Oxford University Press, London, 1967.

Kuenne, R. E., *The Attack Submarine*, Yale University Press, New Haven, Conn., 1965.

— *The Polaris Missile Strike*, Ohio State University Press, Columbus, O., 1967.

Lawrence, K. D., 'Military legal considerations in the extension of territorial seas', *Military Law Review*, vol. 29, 1965.

Lucey, Rear Admiral M. N., 'Resources of the sea', *Brassey's Annual*, Clowes, London, 1972.

Mahan, Rear Admiral A. T., *The Influence of Sea Power upon History*, Sampson Low & Marston, London, 1890.

Mallison, W. T., *Studies in the Law of Naval Warfare: Submarines in General and Limited Wars*, U.S. Naval War College, Newport, R.I., 1968.

Mangone, G. J., *The United Nations, International Law and the Bed of the Seas*, Ocean Series 303, Woodrow Wilson International Center, Washington, D.C., 1972.

Marder, A. J., *The Anatomy of British Sea Power*, Cass, London, 1964.

Marriott, J., 'Naval missiles', *International Defence Review*, 1969.

Martin, L. W., 'The sea in modern strategy', Studies in International Security, *Survival*, vol. 10, No. 1, January 1968.

Miller, Capt, 'New international law for the submarine', *Proceedings of the United States Naval Institute*, Annapolis, Md., vol. 92, 1966.

Ministère de la Marine, *Instructions sur l'application du droit international en cas de guerre*, Paris, 1966.

Ministry of Defence of the U.S.S.R., *Voenna-morskoy mezhdunarodno-pravoroy spravochnik*, Moscow, 1966.

Morris, J., *Pax Britannica*, Faber & Faber, London, 1968.

Moulton, J. L., *British Maritime Strategy in the 1970's*, Royal United Services' Institute, London, 1969.

Mulley, F. W., *The Politics of Western Defence*, Thames & Hudson, London, 1962.

McClintock, R., *The Meaning of Limited War*, Houghton Mifflin, Boston, Mass., 1967.

McDougal, M., and Bourke, W. T., *The Public Order of Oceans*, Yale University Press, New Haven, Conn., 1962.

McGuire, Cmdr M. K., 'The background to Russian naval policy', *Brassey's Annual*, Clowes, London, 1968.

— *Soviet Naval Developments: Context and Capability*, Dalhousie University Press, Halifax, Nova Scotia, 1972.

Nicholson, W. M., 'A Navy view of ocean resources', *Natural Resources Lawyer*, vol. 1, 1968.

Nierenberg, W. H., 'Militarized Oceans', in N. Calder, *Unless Peace Comes: a Scientific Forecast of New Weapons*, Allen Lane, London, 1968.

O'Connell, D. P., 'International law and contemporary naval operations', *British Year Book of International Law*, vol. 44, 1970.

— 'The legality of naval cruise missiles', *American Journal of International Law*, vol. 66, 1972.

Oppenheim, L. F. L., *International Law*, vol. 2, *Disputes, War and Neutrality*, seventh edition, ed. Lauterpacht, Longman, London, 1952.

Petrowski, L. C., 'Military use of the ocean space and the continental shelf', *Columbia Journal of Transnational Law*, vol. 7, 1968.

Polmar, N., *Aircraft Carriers*, Macdonald, London, and Doubleday, Garden City, N.Y., 1969.

Potter, E. B., *The United States and World Sea Power*, Prentice Hall, Englewood Cliffs, N.J., 1955.

Raeder, Grand Admiral E., *Struggle for the Sea*, Kimber, London, 1959.

Richardson, R. P., *An Analysis of Recent Conflicts, 1946–64*, Center for Naval Analyses, Arlington, Va., 1970.

Richmond, Admiral Sir Herbert, *National Policy and Naval Strategy*, Longman, London, 1928.

— *Statesmen and Sea Power*, Oxford University Press, London, 1946.

Robertson, Capt H. B., 'Submarine warfare', *JAG Journal of the United States Navy*, vol. 10, 1956.

Roskill, Capt S. W., *The Strategy of Sea Power*, Collins, London, 1962.

Rousseau, C., 'Chronique des faits', *Revue générale de droit international public*, vol. 70, 1966.

Sanguinetti, T., *Atome et batailles sur mer*, Hachette, Paris, 1965.

Schenk, R., *Seekrieg und Völkerrecht*, 1958.

Schofield, Vice Admiral B. B., *British Sea Power*, Batsford, London, 1967.

Schwarzenberger, G., *International Law*, vol. 2, *The Law of Armed Conflict*, Stevens, London, 1968.

Stefanova, S., 'On the problem of naval blockade', *Soviet Yearbook of International Law*, 1966–67.

Stone, J., *Legal Controls of International Conflict*, Maitland, Sydney, N.S.W., 1959.

Tucker, R. W., *The Law of War and Neutrality at Sea*, International Law Studies, U.S. Naval War College, Newport, R.I., 1957.

United Nations, Leg. Ser., *Laws and Regulations on the Regime of the Territorial Sea*, ST/LEG/SER B/6.

United States Naval War College, School of Naval Command and Staff, *Selected Readings in International Law*, U.S. Naval War College, Newport, R.I., 1965.

United States Navy Department, Office of Naval Intelligence, *Fuehrer Conferences on Matters Dealing with the German Navy*, vol. 1, 1947.

Vinogradov, A. P., 'The danger of militarizing the ocean and sea bed', paper presented to the nineteenth Pugwash conference, Sochi, U.S.S.R., 1969.

Windchy, E. G., *Tonkin Gulf*, Doubleday, New York, 1971.
Whitestone, Cdr N., *The Submarine: the Ultmate We apon*, Davis-Poynter, London, 1973.
Wood, D., *Conflict in the Twentieth Century*, Adelphi Papers, No. 48, Institute of Strategic Studies, London, 1968.

THE 'ALTMARK' INCIDENT

Altmark Saken, Instilling fra undersøkelsekommisjonen au 1945, Oslo, 1947.
Borchard, E., 'Was Norway delinquent in the *Altmark* case?', *American Journal of International Law*, vol. 34, 1940.
Brassey's Naval Annual, Clowes, London, 1940, p. 73.
Brookes, E., *Prologue to a War*, Jarrold's, London, 1966.
Castren, E., *The Present Law of War and Neutrality*, Annales Academiae Scientiarum Fennicae, Helsinki, 1954.
Derry, T. K., *The Campaign in Norway*, HMSO, London, 1952.
Documents on German Foreign Policy, 1918–45, Series D, vol. VIII, U.S. Government Publishing Office, Washington, D.C., 1954.
Correspondence respecting the German Steamer 'Altmark', Cmnd. 8015, HMSO, London, 1950.
McChesney, B., 'The *Altmark* incident and modern warfare', *Northwestern University Law Review*, vol. 52, 1957.
Moulton, J. L., *The Norwegian Campaign of 1940*, Eyre & Spottiswoode, London, 1966.
Omang, R., *Altmark Saken 1940*, Gyldendal Norsk Forlag, Oslo, 1953.
The Times, 19 February 1940, p. 6, col. 1; 20 February 1940, p. 8, col. 1.
Vian, Vice-Admiral Sir Peter, *Action this day*, Muller, London, 1960.
Waldock, Sir Humphrey, *British Year Book of International Law*, vol. 24, 1942.
Unpublished documents
Public Record Office, London:
  War Cabinet minutes, Cab. 65.
  Foreign Office political correspondence, F.O. 371.
  Foreign Office Green Papers, 1939, W17451/14744/49, W17504/14744/49 W17521/14744/49, N4607/490/42, N6919/64/63, N7522/64/63, N7523/ 64/63, N7567/64/63, N7696/64/73, N7567/64/63, N7523/64/63.

THE BATTLE OF THE RIVER PLATE

Millington-Drake, Sir Eugene, *The Drama of the Graf Spee—the Battle of the River Plate*, Peter Davies, London, 1964.
Roskill, Capt S. W., *The War at Sea*, HMSO, London, 1954.
McCall, Admiral Sir Henry, *The Second World War*, London, 1966.
Unpublished documents
Public Record Office, London:
  War Cabinet minutes, Cab. 114, 4; 116, 3; 117, 2; 118, 2.
  Admiralty and Secretariat papers, Adm. 1, 9759/39, NIDO 2356/39, 9945,

9465 (Preparation and despatch of operational orders to the fleet in the event of war).
Foreign Office general correspondence, political, F.O. 371/22848-9, Nos. A8755-7, A8776-8, A8780, A8794, A8797, A8802, A8804, A8812, A8814-16, A8818-22, A8843, A8865, A8867, A8883.
New Zealand Naval Board:
Reports concerning the action of 13 December 1939: letter from commanding officer, H.M.S. *Achilles*, No. 1698/0222; appendix II, Control officer's narrative; appendix III, Report on enemy tactics; appendix V, gunnery material.
Militärarchivs:
Kriegtagebuch des Panzerschiffes *Admiral Graf Spee*.
B.St.S. Seekrieg 1; Uruguay; 34097-152, 44225-63; Pol. I.M., 264, Politik 23 Ag., Bd. 2; Rechtsabteilung, Völkerrecht/Kriegsrecht, Nr. 8, Bd. 1.
Documents on German Foreign Policy, 1918-45, Series D, 1937-45, vol. VIII, HMSO, London, 1954.
Akten zur deutschen auswärtigen Politik, 1918-45, Serie D, Bd. VIII, Baden-Baden, 1961.

THE DECLARATION OF PANAMA, 1939

British and Foreign State Papers, vol. 1939.
Documents on German Foreign Policy, Series D, vols. VIII, IX, XII, HMSO, London, 1956.
Scott, J. D., *The International Conference of American States*, first supplement, 1933-40, Carnegie Endowment, Oxford, 1940.
Castren, E., *The Present Law of War and Neutrality*, Helsinki, 1954.
State Department Bulletin, vol. 1, 1939; vol. 2, 1940.
U.S. Naval War College, *International Law Situations*, Newport, R.I., 1939.
Whiteman, M., *Digest of International Law*, vols. 5, 11, U.S. State Department, Washington, D.C., 1968.
Unpublished documents
Public Record Office, London: Foreign Office Green Papers, A8146/5992/51, A6401/6061/45.

THE 'EILAT' INCIDENT

United Nations Documents S/7925, S/7930, S/8205, S/pv 1369.

THE SPANISH CIVIL WAR

Cervera Valderrama, Admiral J., *Memorias de guerra*, Editorial Nacional, Madrid, 1968.
Eden, A., *Facing the Dictators*, Cassell, London, 1962.
Edwards, K., *The Grey Diplomatists*, Rich & Cowan, London, 1938.
Moreno, Admiral D. F. F., *La guerra en el mar*, Editorial Ahr, Madrid, 1959.

Padelford, N. J., *International Law and Diplomacy in the Spanish Civil Strife*, Macmillan, London, 1939.

Puzzo, D. A., *Spain and the Great Powers, 1936–41*, Columbia University Press, New York, 1962.

Thomas, H., *The Spanish Civil War*, Eyre & Spottiswoode, London, 1961.

Unpublished documents

Public Record Office, London:

Cabinet minutes, Cab. 23/88

F.O. 0221/7/IV, 371/21353.

Adm. 1420/16/IV, 116/3679, 2130/28/IV.

INDEX